FEMINISM
AND THE
HONOR PLAYS
OF
LOPE DE VEGA

Purdue Studies in Romance Literatures

FEMINISM AND THE HONOR PLAYS OF LOPE DE VEGA

Yvonne Yarbro-Bejarano

Purdue University Press
West Lafayette, Indiana

98 97 96 95 94   5 4 3 2 1

The paper used in this book meets the minimum requirements of
American National Standard for Information Sciences—Permanence of
Paper for Printed Library Materials, ANSI Z39.48-1984.

Printed in the United States of America
Design by Anita Noble

Library of Congress Cataloging-in-Publication Data
Yarbro-Bejarano, Yvonne
        Feminism and the honor plays of Lope de Vega / Yvonne Yarbro-
Bejarano.
            p.   cm.   —(Purdue studies in Romance literatures ; v. 4)
        Includes bibliographical references and index.
        ISBN 1-55753-044-0 (alk. paper)
        1. Vega, Lope de, 1562–1635—Criticism and interpretation.
2. Honor in literature. 3. Women in literature. 4. Sex role in literature.
5. Feminism and literature. I. Title. II. Series.
PQ6490.H7Y37 1994
862'.3—dc20   93–33884
                                                          CIP

For my mother—
Esperanza Bejarano Yarbro

Contents

Contents

List of Plays and Abbreviations

The chronology is that suggested by Morley and Bruerton. Following the date for each play is an abbreviation indicating the edition from which the Spanish quotations in the text were taken and the number of the volume where the play may be found. O = *Obras*. Ed. Marcelino Menéndez y Pelayo. ON = *Obras* (nueva edición). Ed. Emilio Cotarelo y Mori et al. The English translations are mine.

Alfreda
    La hermosa Alfreda;   1596–1601   ON 6
    Alfreda the Beautiful
Animal
    El animal de Hungría;   1608–12   ON 3
    The Animal of Hungary   (probably 1611–12)
Batalla
    La batalla del honor;   1608   ON 3
    The Battle of Honor
Bella
    La bella malmaridada;   1596   ON 3
    The Badly Married Beauty
Caballero
    El caballero del milagro;   1593   ON 4
    The Miracle Gentleman
Carlos
    Carlos el perseguido;   1590–95   O 15
    Carlos the Pursued
Cardona
    Don Lope de Cardona;   1608–12   ON 4
    Don Lope de Cardona   (probably 1611)
Catalán
    El valeroso catalán;   1599–1603   O 8
    The Valiant Catalan
Celauro
    Los embustes de Celauro;   1600   ON 12
    Celauro's Tricks
Comendadores
    Los comendadores de Córdoba; 1596   O 11
    The Commanders of Córdoba

Contienda

La contienda de Diego de   1600   O 11
Paredes y el Capitán Juan de
Urbina; The Dispute between
Diego de Paredes and Captain
Juan de Urbina

Corona

La corona merecida;   1603   O 8
The Well-Deserved Crown

Cortesía

La cortesía de España;   1608–12   ON 4
The Courtesy of Spain   (probably 1608–10)

Cuerdo

El cuerdo en su casa; The Wise   1606–12   ON 11
Man in His Own Home

Desposorio

El desposorio encubierto;   1597–1603   ON 4
The Secret Betrothal

Dina

El robo de Dina;   1615–22   O 3
The Abduction of Dina

Discordia

La discordia en los casados;   1611   ON 2
Discord in Marriage

Discreto

El castigo del discreto;   1598–1601   ON 4
The Discreet Man's Punishment

Estefanía

La desdichada Estefanía;   1604   O 8
Estefanía the Unfortunate

Fabia

Los embustes de Fabia;   Before 1596   ON 5
Fabia's Tricks

Ferias

Las ferias de Madrid;   Before 1596   ON 5
The Fairs of Madrid   (probably 1585–89)

Firmeza

La firmeza en la desdicha;   1610–12   ON 5
Steadfastness in Misfortune

Fuenteovejuna

Fuenteovejuna; Sheepwell   1611–18   O 10
    (probably 1612–14)

Galán
  El galán escarmentado;   1595–98   ON 1
  The Chastened Suitor
Halcón
  El halcón de Federico;   1599–1605   O 14
  Federico's Falcon
Hungría
  La corona de Hungría;   1623   ON 2
  The Crown of Hungary
Indicios
  En los indicios, la culpa;   1596–1603   ON 5
  In the Evidence Lies the
  Guilt
Laura
  La inocente Laura;   1604–08   ON 12
  Laura the Innocent
Locura
  La locura por la honra;   1610–12   ON 7
  Mad for Honor
Mal
  Del mal lo menos;   1604–09   ON 4
  The Lesser of Two Evils   (probably 1608)
Nacimiento
  El nacimiento de Ursón y   1588–95   O 13
  Valentín; The Birth of Ursón
  and Valentín
Peligros
  Los peligros de la ausencia;   1613–20   ON 13
  The Dangers of Absence   (probably 1615–18)
Peribáñez
  Peribáñez y el Comendador de   1605–12   O 10
  Ocaña; Peribáñez and the   (probably 1605–08)
  Commander of Ocaña
Pleitos
  Los pleitos de Ingalaterra;   1598–1603   ON 8
  England's Disputes
Pobreza
  La pobreza estimada;   1597–1603   O 14
  Poverty Esteemed
Porfiar
  Porfiar hasta morir;   1624–28   O 10
  Persistence unto Death

Portugués
>El más galán portugués;   1608–13   O 10
>The Most Gallant Portuguese

Príncipe
>El príncipe despeñado;   1602   O 8
>The Fallen Prince

Resistencia
>La resistencia honrada y   1596–1603   ON 9
>condesa Matilde; Honorable   (probably 1599–1603)
>Resistance and Countess
>Matilde

Rosambuco
>El santo negro Rosambuco;   Before 1607   O 3
>The Saintly Black, Rosambuco

Rústico
>El rústico del cielo;   1605   O 5
>Heaven's Rustic

Testimonio
>El testimonio vengado;   1596–1603   O 7
>The Avenged Testimony

Toledano
>El toledano vengado;   1596–1604   ON 2
>The Avenged Toledan   (probably by Lope)

Veneciano
>El piadoso veneciano;   1599–1608   O 15
>The Compassionate Venetian

Venganza
>El castigo sin venganza;   1631   O 15
>Punishment without Revenge

Vitoria
>La vitoria de la honra;   1609–15   ON 10
>Honor's Victory   (probably 1609–12)

Acknowledgments

I would like to thank the University of Washington for grants and sabbatical leave which made the development and completion of this book possible. Part of Chapter Six appeared as "Masquerade, Male Masochism and the Female Outlaw: A Feminist Analysis of Lope's *Embustes de Fabia,*" in *Revista de Estudios Hispánicos* 24.3 (1990): 11–29. I am grateful to the editors of the journal for permission to reprint a condensed version of my article. Thanks also to research assistants Arline García and Jane Adam for their help at various stages of the project, to the editors at PSRL, and to the two anonymous readers for their many helpful suggestions for improvement. I am indebted to numerous colleagues and friends for their guidance and encouragement. In particular, the book has profited greatly from conversations with Cynthia Steele, George A. Shipley, Anthony L. Geist, Mitchell Greenberg, and members of the Feminist Colloquium at the University of Washington. Special thanks to David Román, who gave so generously of his time and expertise, and to Eleanor Soto, who provided ongoing motivation for the completion of the project.

Introduction

Lope de Vega, founder of Spain's national theater, wrote numerous plays between 1585 and 1631 dealing with the theme of conjugal honor.[1] In these texts, the husband suspects that his wife is guilty of adultery, or that she is being pursued by another man. Since a Spaniard's honor depended, in part, on the sexual conduct of his wife,[2] the husband must act to prevent dishonor. In the event that he has already been dishonored, he must "wash away the stain with blood," murdering rival and wife, if she is (perceived as) guilty. The ideal wife resists the advances of the rival through the cultivation of the feminine virtues of chastity, constancy, and *vergüenza,* or "shame." By and large, I define "honor play" as one in which the husband believes in the existence of a rival pursuing his wife, as opposed to Donald Larson's more restrictive criteria. However, like Larson, I include *Dina* and *Fuenteovejuna,* which Alix Zuckerman-Ingber excludes as not dealing with conjugal honor, and deviate from both their lists in considering *Toledano.*[3] Although in general I have excluded plays featuring single women whose honor conflicts can be resolved through marriage, I include *Dina* and *Fuenteovejuna* because this option is rejected in favor of bloody vengeance. *Fuenteovejuna* precludes marriage due to the difference in social status between the dishonored and the offender; in addition, Laurencia is married to Frondoso at the time of her abduction by the commander. My decision to work with such a large pool of texts responds in part to a desire to avoid the "masterpieces" approach to the *comedia,* which can obscure its character as mass cultural phenomenon. Besides raising questions of canonicity, intentionally focusing on lesser-known plays allows certain constants in the patterning of formulas and conventions to become visible, as well as the enormous variety and flexibility in Lope's honor plays. For the same reason, I usually avoid using characters' names in favor of the generic "agents" of the honor-play narrative ("wife," "husband," "rival"). The intent is not to suggest that they are unchanging archetypes, but rather to foreground their particularly gendered and mutable functions in the plot.

I have chosen to limit my study to the honor plays of Lope de Vega rather than undertake a comparative or genre-based analysis such as Matthew Stroud's recent examination of wife-murder *comedias*. There is merit in identifying characteristic treatments of a topic within the opus of a single dramatist before looking at the work of others in future studies, as the tradition of single-author books in *comedia* and honor-play studies suggests, especially when the dramatist under consideration influenced the further development of the *comedia* so profoundly, as in Lope's case. Within honor-play studies, I place my project in complementary dialogue with Donald Larson's and Alix Zuckerman-Ingber's monographs on Lope, contributing a new perspective by focusing on issues of gender and sexuality. Rather than examine the diachronic evolution of Lope's honor plays as Larson does, I have concentrated on a synchronic analysis of consistent patterns and variations in the gendering of honor. While the early date of *Fabia* seems to support Larson's division on the basis of Lope's shifting attitude towards vengeance into "early" (comic endings), "middle" (bloody vengeance), and "late" (tragic tonality), the result of my broader focus on conjugal honor, including texts that celebrate what Larson calls the "feminine value of *vergüenza*" (170–71), offers for consideration the possibility that Lope recycled "types" of honor plays through all phases of his career, for example, rewriting *Pleitos* (1598–1603) as *Hungría* as late as 1623.

Ideals of masculine and feminine behavior and representations of sexual desire play prominent roles in these texts,[4] yet most studies comprising the voluminous bibliography on the honor play do not foreground gender or sexuality as critical categories.[5] The major focus of honor-play criticism has been the relationship between honor conflicts in the theater and the function of honor in early modern Spanish culture, for example, Zuckerman-Ingber's exploration of Lope's implicit criticism of honor. The interpretations I propose by no means exhaust the meanings of the plays; in fact, they are decidedly partial, concentrating on the representation of sexuality and gender in relation to the unequal distribution of power in sixteenth- and seventeenth-century Spanish society. Hopefully this study may suggest possible paths for comparing and contrasting other dramatists' representation of sexuality and gender in the context of conjugal honor. One of my main objectives is to offer new ways of reading well-known texts through feminist theory, as well as to present lesser-known plays as objects worthy of such study. I hope to contribute to *comedia* critics' appreciation of the importance of gender and sexuality, in tandem with other hierarchical relations, as structuring principles of the honor play rather than as peripheral or secondary to the analysis of what is "really" going on in the plays. Feminist theory is a powerful tool in coaxing texts to give up some additional secrets about how they encode characters, action, and meaning through gender and sexuality.

While Lope's honor plays do produce discourses on femininity and masculinity that help reinforce dominant power relations, I have learned from recent cultural-studies theory to see them as sites of negotiation and struggle for meaning. In this I count myself among a group of critics of sixteenth- and seventeenth-century Spanish literature attempting to nuance José Antonio Maravall's excessively monolithic view of cultural apparatuses as vehicles of the dominant ideology (*Teatro, Culture*).[6] This project calls for a theoretical paradigm that accounts for multiplicity, as formulated by David Román: "in order to understand more completely the relationship between dramatic practice and social ideology in early modern Spain, studies of the *comedia* will need to consider the intersections of the theatre with the cultural constructions of gender, race, class, sexuality, and nation" ("Calderón's Open Secret").[7] Besides sexual difference, I consider differences of rank and ethnicity among women as well as among men, figured as differences of "blood" in seventeenth-century Spanish discourses (noble versus plebeian; "pure" or Old Christian versus "impure" or Jewish and Moorish).[8] Shifting the focus from sexual difference to multilayered differences within and among the various characters that people Lope's honor plays entails an understanding of seventeenth-century subjects as products of "the intersection of a variety of contradictory positions, . . . situated in a multiplicity of ways simultaneously" (Mariscal, *Contradictory Subjects* 37).[9]

In this study I attempt to identify the *comedia*'s possibility of both containment and resistance in what Stuart Hall calls the "double movement" of popular culture. In this sense I am less interested in condemning or praising Lope for his treatment of women or honor than in seeing his honor plays as participating in a complex of nonunitary cultural attitudes and signifying practices that exist to some extent outside of the author's control.[10] As Valerie Traub asserts in her study of homoeroticism in Shakespeare ("Desire"), polarizing the debate in terms of the author's denial or affirmation "employs a reductive account of cultural power" and provides an inadequate theoretical model to explain the complexity of such representations (94). I concur with Peter Evans's characterization of the *production* of the text, whose author is both "conscious creator" and "the unconscious, fragmented, dissolving mediator of the cultural and ideological assumptions of his day" (51), as well as George Mariscal's view of the *consumption* of the plays as cultural products in the public theater, "the potential for multiple and even contestatory responses within the performance text itself" ("History and the Subject" 27).

This approach not only decenters the playwright's authority, a move characteristic of feminist criticism, but also identifies the texts' "blind spots" and contradictions (Modleski), the moments when woman escapes triangular transaction or the rigidity of narrative's "bounded text" (Kristeva). These are clearly plays about masculinity and woman's relationship to male authority, but they do not represent male entitlement or the control of femininity *unproblematically*. They enact the ways in which woman eludes total domination as well as the difficulties for the male subject in living out this particular ideal of masculinity. Jean Howard's characterization of certain Shakespearean texts holds true for Lope's honor plays as well: "Collectively they play a role in producing and managing anxieties about women . . . who are not 'in their places' " and the "fragility of male authority" (429). I believe that the honor-play subgenre was so popular precisely because it represented the *contradictory* predicaments of the male and female subjects constrained by early modern constructs of gender and sexuality. I hope I succeed in communicating some of the excitement involved in discovering these lacunas in canonical and, especially, in noncanonical texts. My goal has been to facilitate the vision of Lope's honor plays as sites of *pleasure,* not only for early modern spectators, but for critics who share my sense of urgency in locating moments of rupture, contestation, and negotiation in early modern culture.

In addition to cultural-studies theory, I make use of the psychoanalytic model for concepts of the subject, desire and gender.[11] As a feminist, I acknowledge the "fit" between Freud's and Lacan's narrative of psychosexual development and the texts' construction of subjectivity, sexuality, and gender while critiquing its normative positioning of the male subject and its binary and ahistorical formulations. In this theoretical model, the subject is constructed *as* gendered subject through entry into language, or the symbolic order, characterized by the paternal prohibition (Law of the Father) triangulating the child-mother dyad and dominated by the paternal signifier (Name-of-the-Father). Language pre-exists the subject and already attaches phallocentric cultural *values* to the gendered subject positions that the subject will become aware of and eventually inhabit ("man," "woman," "he," "she," etc.).[12]

In this passage into the symbolic order, the male subject renounces the desire for the mother to avoid being "castrated" like her and identifies with the paternal position, the site of power and punishment. The female subject must renounce her active desire for the mother and identify with her as "castrated" (inferior, powerless) in order to assume the "normal" position of feminine passivity. Sexuality is assumed to flow directly from gender role and conflated with object choice, defining active masculine desire for man and passive feminine desire for woman.[13] Thus, heterosexuality is enshrined concomitantly with phallocentrism. The "power" and "lack" that seem to adhere in male and female anatomy should be seen as assigned retrospectively, through the cultural filter of language, which defines sexual difference in terms of hierarchical opposition.

However, neither the son nor the biological father can ever become the ideal paternal image (the symbolic father). Since male subjectivity is defined by this "lack,"[14] a sense of coherent unity is achieved through projecting it on woman as inferior

Other. But the representation of woman as either lacking or whole, other or same, incites anxiety in the male subject concerning his own fundamental unity. Sartre expresses the contradictory nature of masculine desire in the formula "let the Other become me without ceasing to be the other" (10). For Lacan, desire is the product of the multiple divisions that constitute the subject and initiate the sense of lack. Lacan characterizes this desire as "impossible," since the endless series of identifications with ideal images can only inspire a further sense of insufficiency, confirming both male and female subject's self-perception as "castrated" (Lacan 265). Kaja Silverman refers to the symbolic order as the "factory of desire" (*Subject* 178), since both the subject's desires and the ways "lack" is perceived are culturally mediated. As I will discuss below, the symbolic order is structured by family and kinship nominations (Lacan 66) that ensure woman's status as object of exchange.

Allowing for historical differences, I apply this theory to the representation of father/son relationships in the broader social context of the problems and privileges of the early modern male subject, defined largely through the exclusion of woman and the repression of the maternal. While Lope's honor plays seem to ultimately enforce the conflation of gender and (hetero)sexuality (masculine desire as active and feminine desire as passive), they simultaneously evoke the circulation of desire as it transits through sites of activity and passivity regardless of gender. To avoid the passive ramifications of *feminine desire,* I use the term *female desire,* which is constructed as both active and transgressive in Lope's honor plays except in those texts in which the female subject channels her activity in the service of masculine power. My employment of the terms *masculinization* for the active desire and behavior of female characters and *feminization* for the passive desire and behavior of male characters is not intended to affirm the binary dichotomies of the psychoanalytic model, but rather to signal the powerful constraints operative *within* seventeenth-century Spanish discourses conflating gender and sexuality in the production of subjectivity (the female and male subjects' "soy quien soy" ["I am who I am"]). Lope's honor plays represent ideal masculine and feminine images as well as the failure of female and male characters alike to fulfill them. In demonstrating this, I align myself with those critics who strive to show both men's power and women's marginalization as *culturally* produced. For Kaja Silverman, understanding the ideological naturalization of the technology whereby subjects are produced can reveal the "mechanisms that prevent cultural change" (*Subject* 149).

Central to the intersection of gender, sexuality, and power is the issue of control, and throughout the study I am concerned with its establishment as well as its subversion. Although the male subject reimposes his control at the end of most plays, text after text returns to the loss of control caused by the very codes that purport to secure it. I am particularly interested in arguing that in spite of pervasive discourses and practices designed to enclose them, the female characters, in many different ways, are "not where they appear to be" (Modleski 85).

On the level of reception, I propose that viewers of Lope's honor plays elude the control of textual positioning to manufacture alternative spectator positions and meanings. I hope to restore some sense of the rowdy participation of consumers of culture in the production of the meanings attached to important signs of early modern social life, such as woman, Spanish, Jew, or husband. One of my reasons for stressing the elusiveness of woman in the texts is the question of early modern women's *agency* within a culture that, while phallocentric, was not monolithic. The focus on "woman as representation" is intended to help delineate the field of discourses and constraints within which "real" early modern women continually negotiated for power. The constructions of femininity and sexuality in Lope's honor plays present interesting correspondences with other nonliterary discourses studied by historians such as Mary Elizabeth Perry, particularly the notion of "enclosure."

My analysis of the relation between gender and the plots of the plays draws on narrative theories developed by Julia Kristeva, Teresa de Lauretis, and Rachel Blau DuPlessis. Finally, I read Lope's honor plays through the anthropological/ psychoanalytic model of "male traffic in women," as elaborated by Gayle Rubin, Luce Irigaray, and Eve Kosofsky Sedgwick. In Lope's honor plays, male traffic in women is carried out first through marriage and then through the mechanism of cuckoldry in the erotic triangle. Despite the apparent symmetry of the erotic triangle, woman actually functions as the conduit of a relationship between men. These texts represent transactions of power between male subjects, who, through the body of a woman, either engage in a struggle for dominance or recognize their mutual entitlement. Sedgwick uses the term *male homosocial desire* to designate the entire continuum of men's relations with other men.[15] As a rule, male characters jockey among themselves for power—over each other, the narrative, and woman. Woman in all these cases is the object to be known and controlled, the medium of exchange of male power.

***

Chapter One examines the encoding of femininity and masculinity in Lope's honor plays. The "wife," the predominant sign for woman in these texts, has only two options open to her: to protect her husband's honor or to transgress the male homosocial bonds forged through marriage. Whether the "bad" wife is expelled or the "good" wife revalidated within marriage, both closures negate woman as subject. The historical circumstances of the Reconquest contributed to the equation of masculinity with aggressivity, honor, national identity, and "pure" or noble blood. In the early modern period, the social contract between absolute monarch and individual male householder further conflated Spanishness and masculinity, at the expense of woman.

In the texts studied in Chapter Two, woman as "sexual outlaw" reciprocates or initiates adulterous desire. These plays represent both the threatening and the consoling aspects of female sexuality: she first exceeds, then is brought within the limits of patriarchal control. The murder of the transgressive wife and the display of her corpse provide an "exercise in terror" (Foucault, *Discipline and Punish*), making women aware of the unlimited power of male authority. *Fabia* presents the only female outlaw who escapes the dynamics of male rivalry. At the end, the "bad" Fabia is supposedly negated by a "new," reformed Fabia. But Fabia's claim to moral rebirth is merely a performance in her skillful masquerade.

The representations of the ideal wife discussed in Chapter Three attempt to reconcile her use value (her beauty and her reproductive function) and her exchange value. In marriage, physical desirability is prized by the husband, but it also means that she can become the object of desire of other men. Wives who deploy passive strategies of "honorable resistance" are brought face to face with their own powerlessness, since only men can decide their fate. When her passive strategies of honorable resistance end in murder or rape, woman is punished for having a body identified with sexuality. Only the male subject can redeem her, since masculine desire and honor have constructed her body to begin with.

Chapter Four examines duplicity and disguise, including cross-dressing, as active strategies through which the female subject resists ideological or literal containment. Female cross-dressing challenges the notion of woman as male property, since she herself constructs the body most appropriate to accomplish her goals. Dressing in the other gender's clothes calls attention to the cultural construction of gender and undermines male superiority, as the female subject easily performs masculine behaviors. The energies of these wives, however, are channeled in the recovery of their husbands' honor and masculinity. These texts also evoke the possibility that the female cross-dresser might be desired by another woman, setting up situations between two female characters perceived by the husband as heteroerotic (since he thinks one is a man), and by the spectators as homoerotic.

The texts discussed in Chapter Five feature bonds of rivalry in which husband and rival share the same ethnic identity and social rank. The male subjects occupy opposing but complementary positions in the traffic in women: the rival affirms woman's value in circulation; the husband withdraws one woman from collective to private ownership. Both run the risk of losing their position of ascendancy in relationship to other men. Most texts focus on the husband's trajectory, though some highlight the rival's predatory ways leading to reward or punishment. Occasionally, the rival retains his dominance over the husband at the end, but more often the husband recuperates the active subject position. The proliferation of texts in which the husband misreads innocent circumstances or invents a nonexistent rival indicates the male subject's besieged sense of masculine identity as well as the danger this hypersensitivity presents for women.

When the bonds of mutuality examined in Chapter Six are formed through shopping for "women on the market," the male subject is in jeopardy of being "feminized" (forced to assume the dominated feminine position): the husband for neglecting his wife and the unmarried man for delaying his own passage into the world of the fathers through marriage. In other texts, the negative consequences of homoerotic male bonding without woman as medium are dissipated through the exchange of woman. Bonds of mutuality are volatile: when the husband suspects his wife of adultery, the wife's male relatives quickly become hostile, since their own masculinity is threatened. But if the wife is found guilty, her punishment fortifies their ties with the husband. The frequency with which men of different social ranks bond positively through the practice of masculine behaviors demonstrates how gender functions to smooth over inequalities among men. But other texts foreground power differences among men, demonstrating the value of (temporary) submission. In these texts, the husband is powerless to defend his honor because his rival is the prince or the king himself. The loss of honor may lead to madness or death, but in most cases the husband's domination by the king is a prelude to greater honor. The reward reaped by these husbands, besides affirming the social hierarchy, is symptomatic of the ways the sex-gender system works to reproduce dominant power relations.[16]

The articulation of discourses of "race," masculinity, and nation is taken up in Chapter Seven, analyzing how the Spanish male subject defines himself, not only against woman, but also against Jew and black. *Testimonio* presents a myth of national origins in which "Spanishness" signifies masculine domination of Jew and Moor through the medium of woman. Blacks denote comic inferiority and animality, yet the representation of the racial other can both affirm and deny otherness by appealing to a common value, for example, saintliness or military valor. In contrast, the Jew is always male and always determines a feminized position for the male subject, signifying cowardice and "impurity."

Chapter Eight focuses on the heterogeneity of the audience of the public *corral*. My perspective involves a critique of the limitations of psychoanalytic theories of spectatorship that posit a passive reception by "the" spectator (male or female) of the fixed meaning imposed by the text. Given the wide range of differences present in the extensive *comedia* audience, I find theories of spectatorship helpful that take into account the active participation of the viewers in the production of textual meanings that may resist or contradict hegemonic intention.

The book covers two areas not commonly joined; I hope to address both feminist scholars who may know little of sixteenth- and seventeenth-century Spanish theater and Golden Age colleagues intrigued by the possibilities of feminist analysis. With this in mind, I have provided English translations for the Spanish quotations. All translations are mine unless otherwise indicated. Longer translations are found in the Appendix, keyed by the number in brackets following the reference for the Spanish quotation. Lope's plays are referred to by short title and page number. The List of Plays and Abbreviations should be consulted for the full title, edition cited, and volume number, as well as approximate date of composition.

Chapter One

The Contradictory Constructs of Gender

Historians have recently documented the relative equality with men enjoyed by Spanish women[1] from early medieval times to the beginning of the modern age (Ortega Costa, Dillard). However, by the time Lope was writing for the theater, the situation of women had deteriorated. The growing restrictions placed on women in the sixteenth and seventeenth centuries were in part a result of new social structures accompanying the consolidation of the early modern state.[2] José Antonio Maravall and other historians have demonstrated that the early modern state is characterized by the alliance between ruler and "individual" (Maravall, *Estado moderno* 408).[3] Ruth El Saffar clarifies that this individual simultaneously needed and controlled by the state is not gender neutral, but specifically the male householder (176). One of the most important changes for women during this time was the strengthening of pre-existing patriarchal power relationships within the family. From the fifteenth and well into the seventeenth century, church and state "provided powerful new theoretical and practical support" for the "reinforcement of the despotic authority of the husband and father" (Stone 151). Patriarchy provided the pivotal structure to organize both the family and the state, establishing a "relation of subordinate correspondence . . . between the father who is as king in the family and the king who is as father in the state" (Barker 31). The arrangement that ensures the absolute power of the king and the autonomy of the male individual "encourages, as part of the agreement, the parallel power of every man over his wife" (El Saffar 177). In Catholic Spain, God as King and Father provides the metaphysical authorization of the sovereignty of the father/king in both state and family.[4]

In Spain, the great allure of the authoritarian state and the independent individual stemmed from the promise of relief from decades of chaos and anarchy and, on a psychological level, the promise of completion and totality.[5] However, as in the psychoanalytic narrative, this sense of autonomy and unity depended on separation from and repression of the feminine (El Saffar). The identification of the male individual with the Crown represented a "new definition of belonging" (165) that replaced social origins and "the bonds of home and family around which awareness of self was previously based" (166).[6] The break from home and mother led to discourses on gender constructing the male subject as reason, will, and order in opposition to woman, embodying the reverse.

In her study of women and the social changes of the sixteenth and seventeenth centuries, Mary Elizabeth Perry focuses on the role of gender in official attempts to preserve and restore order (*Gender and Disorder*).[7] Ecclesiastical and secular authorities collaborated to maintain a gendered moral order in the service of religious orthodoxy and the developing state (118). The key strategy in the control of women was enclosure, which extended from physical confinement of the body to the closure of its orifices. As male property, women must be controlled by codes that dictate a closed mouth, a closed body, and a locked house (Stallybrass). Enclosure was necessary because of women's supposed vulnerability to the devil and hence inclination to disorder. Religious and social ideologies further colluded in the association of enclosure with purity, linking the feminine virtue of chastity with theological purity of faith and the genetic purity required by *limpieza de sangre* ("blood purity") (6). The "partnership" of secular and ecclesiastical authorities underwrote the understanding that the social order reflected a divine order; in this schema, hierarchical gender roles are both "natural" and divinely ordained.[8]

Marriage was one of the most effective institutions of social stability through enclosure of women, and it provided one of the few options of respectability open to women.[9] As in other preindustrial European countries, marriages in Spain were arranged in order to cement alliances between the men of different families and to transmit family property. On the highest levels, marriage was a "crucial diplomatic as well as economic instrument of dynastic forms of government" (Perry, *Crime and Society* 128). Social, political, and economic interests played a role in the marriages of the nobility and the wealthy "bourgeoisie" as well. After marriage, "husbands insisted on female chastity to ensure that all heirs would be legitimate offspring of their respective families" (Vann 199). In Spain, as noted, an additional factor in the insistence on female chastity was the obsession with pure blood; a sexually uncontrolled daughter or wife could taint the families' lineage with "impure" blood (Donald Larson).

Marriage provided a context for channeling women's sexual energies into procreation and their labor power into domestic production. Printed guides for women spelled out the feminine ideal and the preservation of the husband's estate. Women were urged not to marry for love, so as to more easily limit the purpose of sex to procreation as opposed to sensuality or carnal desire. Yet the wife's principal responsibility was not procreative sex, but the management and multiplication of domestic wealth (Durán). In relation to production, women's lives varied greatly, from the aristocratic or wealthy woman who was basically an adornment in the home to the rural peasant housewife who, in addition to labor in the fields, gardening, and dairy and poultry work, managed what amounted to a "small multipurpose factory" in the home.[10] In Lope's honor plays the only women represented working (besides the occasional stitch of embroidery) are Old Christian peasant women; respectable women of the urban "bourgeoisie," like their male counterparts, are simply not represented at all.

While the various measures of enclosure were intended as "antidotes to disorderly women" (Perry 3), they were not necessarily effective. Perry is careful to distinguish between the actual behavior of women in this period and the beliefs that were intended to govern their behavior. In fact, it is her thesis that gender prescriptions became increasingly invoked as women participated more actively in society due to men's preoccupations with war and colonization (9). The growing alarm about unenclosed women, who escaped male authority, led to increased efforts to confine women in the home, the convent, and the legal brothel.[11] As Perry points out, widespread bigamy, abandonment, and adultery proved that marriage clearly did not provide an "antidote" to the social disorder arising from relationships between the sexes.[12] In spite of the multiple controls applied to women's lives, the number of women living outside the normative feminine ideal kept growing, increasing the pressure on respectable women to submit to stricter enclosure.

Symbolic discourses on femininity such as Lope's honor plays may have played a primary role in this project of social control described by Perry.[13] The growing diversity of women's practical roles was paralleled by more restrictive symbolic roles, especially after the mid-sixteenth century (Perry 33). Religious symbols such as the virgin martyrs and the Virgin Mary functioned as a "common language . . . setting expectations and interpreting reality in terms of these expectations" (41). Lope's texts both reproduce discourses enforcing order through gender and capture the dilemmas and multiplicities of women's position.

The Construction of "Woman"

The various discourses constructing gender and sexuality in seventeenth-century society invest the sign "woman" with particular cultural meanings, for as Mieke Bal points out, "rather than expressing a content, a sign models its content" (16). As opposed to the Spanish women whose situation has been studied by Perry, Melveena McKendrick, and others, woman is "a fictional construct, a distillate from diverse but congruent discourses dominant in Western cultures" (de Lauretis 5). Both the "good" and the "bad" woman are defined in relationship to an ideal that represents the abstraction of certain gender-specific characteristics. In the sixteenth and seventeenth centuries, woman's greatest virtues are chastity and silence. While men's honor stems from their noble or "pure" blood, and could be augmented by the performance of masculine attributes, in Lope's honor plays feminine honor is conflated with chastity: "in women honor was limited to her sexual behavior and the most she could do was to preserve her honor, never to increase it" (Rothe 129). Feminine honor, then, is reflective of male power in that it takes on meaning only in relation to masculine honor. A woman is "honrada" ("honorable") if she protects her husband's honor and rights of private sexual ownership through the practices of enclosure and self-effacement prescribed by the feminine virtues of chastity and silence. Texts such as *Príncipe* and *Dina,* in which a woman's rape dishonors her husband or her male relatives, illustrate the reflective nature of feminine honor.

According to Patricia Parker, "one of the oldest topoi of misogyny is the fabled inability of women to keep their mouth shut" (9). In her discussion of the brank or Scold's Bridle, Parker links "feminine speech potentially out of control" with anxiety surrounding the control of female sexuality: "quite clearly in what it encloses and restricts [it is] a kind of chastity belt for the tongue" (27). Perry notes that the prescriptive literature extolling enclosure as the natural state for women "warned against talkative and footloose females."[14] In Lope's honor plays, woman's loquacity is linked to indiscretion (*Alfreda* 229) and to insatiable curiosity (*Alfreda* 228; *Peligros* 13). Woman is defined as a "dangerous enemy" in *Halcón* for her ability to manipulate speech. In both this text (446) and in *Dina* (219), woman's uncontrollable talking is linked to the venomous power of the snake. Just as the virtue of chastity keeps the female body closed, the cultivation of *vergüenza,* or shame, closes woman's mouth. In *El passagero,* Suárez de Figueroa privileges shame among all feminine virtues (McKendrick 13). Several of Lope's honor plays underline the function of *vergüenza* as an antidote to excessive female talkativeness in contexts of uncontrolled sexuality.[15] In *Carlos,* the wife correctly perceives shame as an obstacle to the satisfaction of her illicit desire:[16]

> ¿Qué sirve tanto callar,
> Pues al bien de mi remedio
> No hay mayor peligro en medio
> Que es la vergüenza de hablar?
>
> (441 [1])

Lope's *Animal* displays an unusually complete clustering of the topoi that define woman in seventeenth-century Spanish culture. The "animal" of the title has been driven out by her husband, the king, to be devoured by beasts as punishment for her alleged adultery. She raids the countryside for food, terrifying the peasants, who surround her with an oral mythology that exaggerates her violent barbarism: she is referred to as monster, wild beast ("fiera"), sphinx, harpy, siren, giant, a ferocious animal with eyes of fire, and Hungary's horror ("espanto de toda Hungría" 430). The text enacts the binary opposition between nature and culture in terms of female and male, and affirms the foundation of culture through the exchange of women between men.[17] Since woman's value is defined in terms of her status in exchange, the loss of wifehood deprives her simultaneously of human status. Teodosia, the "animal" clothed in furs with a wild mass of hair covering her face, signifies woman as Nature, deprived of her role in the civilizing and culture-conferring mechanisms of kinship.

While the residue of proper gender behavior lingers in Teodosia's passive acceptance of her fate, Rosaura, the girl she has stolen at birth and raised in the wild, is completely ignorant of kinship structures and gender roles. She is given to violence, appropriating the active "masculine" role in her physical defense of Felipe, who has been abandoned by his grandfather the Count of Barcelona, and in her interaction with Felipe, the object of her desire. The restoration of Teodosia, Rosaura, and Felipe to their rightful places is dependent on the re-establishment of kinship structures, accomplished through Teodosia's instruction of Rosaura in proper gender roles and Rosaura's marriage to Felipe. By showing Rosaura's "natural" proclivities and subsequent transformation, the text also inadvertently reveals the cultural construction of femininity, supporting de Beavoir's assertion that "one is not born a woman, but rather, becomes one" (301).

Rosaura's lessons include the story of the creation of woman out of Adam's rib in Genesis (434), which has "for centuries authorized woman's place as second place" (Parker 179). The privileging of temporal priority in phallogocentric thought (first principles, first causes, or firstborn sons) concomitantly defines that which is later as "secondary in the sense of derivative or inferior" (Nyquist 158).[18] *Animal* exemplifies a particular discourse on femininity that fuses the narrative of female subordination from Genesis with the Aristotelian account of female imperfection. Teodosia teaches Rosaura to value her beauty and her reproductive function as the source of her value to men, as opposed to the male's moral superiority:[19]

> Ha dado Naturaleza
> al hombre más perfeción,

y, por la misma razón,
a la mujer más belleza,
y como proceden de ellas,
guárdanlas ese respeto.

(444 [2])

In such binary oppositions, "the former of the two is the standard or universal equivalent," and the second, or female term, the privation of the other and hence inferior of the male (Parker 180). These twin authorizing narratives influenced explanations of sexual difference and the definition of woman through the Middle Ages and well into the seventeenth century.[20] Teodosia seeks to control and channel Rosaura's sexuality by teaching her femininity as passivity and subordination to the superiority of the male. Rosaura must learn about feminine honor, which validates her sexuality only when channeled through kinship structures (443). She must also be instructed in the *vergüenza* she lacks as quintessential feminine attribute: ". . . en mujer de honor / es bajeza y deshonor / mostrar amor declarado" ("in an honorable woman, it is base and dishonorable to declare love openly") (443–44).

These lessons in the fundamental inequality between the two genders continue at court when Rosaura is captured. Here, Rosaura learns that a king is the one who rules and authors the law (mirroring an earlier mention of the divine "Autor"); he depends on no one and represents God (451). A queen, a role for which Rosaura is being groomed, is reduced to reproduction. To Rosaura's question "¿También da aquésta la ley / con que viven donde reina?" ("Does this one also make the law with which they live where she rules?") Teodosia answers that the queen's function is "[d]e dar reyes / para que den esas leyes" ("[t]o make kings so that they may make those laws") (452). This explicit exclusion of queens from ruling and their relegation to procreation contrasts sharply with the historical figure of Isabella of Castile, who together with Ferdinand of Aragon unified Spain and ruled as absolute monarch.[21]

Rosaura is now prepared to enter the world of culture and the fathers, leaving behind her existence as "natural woman" for her proper role as both use value (her beauty and her ability to produce heirs) and exchange value (her marriage with Felipe creates ties between Spain and Hungary). Her transformation from violent creature to submissive wife is signified through the replacement of the metal chain that subjugates her unchanneled female energy with Felipe's symbolic one: "Y yo, mi adorada fiera, / te quiero hacer de mis brazos / otra más fuerte cadena" ("And I, my beloved beast, wish to make of my arms another, stronger chain for you") (460). This substitution emphasizes the simultaneous creation of passive femininity and male dominance in the relation of exchange.[22]

Besides the construction of woman's passive subordination to man, as in *Animal,* Lope's honor plays define femininity through a proliferation of virtues and defects that at times contradict one another. Woman is both easily deceived (*Laura* 344) and deceitful.[23] The description of compassion ("piedad") as "the proper virtue of women" (*Locura* 92) coexists with the assertion that woman is a monster of cruelty. Linked to her innate compassion/cruelty is woman's inability/ability to avenge herself. In *Peligros,* Fortune behaves "like a woman," that is, jealous and vengeful (184), while the inherent incompatibility of vengeance and feminine nature forms the basic plot of *Animal.*

Some texts assign the two poles of these contradictions to different kinds of women. In a speech in *Cardona* denouncing women, the speaker insists that he is only talking about bad women (680).[24] Various texts make it clear that "good" means "chaste," a gender-specific collapsing of orders of virtue that would never be assumed in the case of a "good" man (*Nacimiento* 496). In some cases class position determines the presence of defects or virtues. *Desposorio* ascribes the defect of fickleness to plebeian women and the virtue of constancy to noble women (514), while in *Halcón* noble women who talk loudly run the risk of appearing common (462). Chastity and high rank are linked (*Discreto* 209), just as willing female adulterers are confined to the plebeian group.[25]

By distinguishing between "good" and "bad" women and then aligning feminine virtue with nobility, Lope's honor plays participate in the ideological project of upholding the binary hierarchies that determine the unequal distribution of power in seventeenth-century Spanish society. While these texts do represent some of the social differences among women, between respectable and nonrespectable and noble and plebeian women, for example, they do so selectively and in such a way as to reaffirm the values of an aristocratic ideology. This results in distortions of social life that express themselves in absences or silences as well as in what is concretely represented. Not only are respectable urban plebeian women *not* represented, Old Christian peasant women, besides signifying the usual attributes of the feminine ideal, are made to bear additional meanings that correspond to the general idealization of the countryside and the notion of peasant honor peculiar to seventeenth-century Spanish culture.

The most common mechanism for representing differences among women is the mistress/servant duo. In this binary set, the prejudicial distribution of attributes according to class standing operates hand-in-hand with the integration of the sometimes hostile, and numerically huge, group of servants studied by Maravall ("Relaciones"). In some texts, the female servant attempts unsuccessfully to lead the wife away from the path of feminine virtue, exhibiting the baser sexual nature of her social group; in others, solidarity is exemplified, either negatively in the case of transgressive pairs, or positively, in the case of the wife and maid who resist adulterous desire.

The superseding of class difference by feminine virtue or vice within the mistress/servant pair illustrates the overriding tendency in Lope's honor plays to subsume contradictory attributes under the general term *woman,* despite the coextensive representation of class and ethnic differences.[26] This generalizing move is accomplished through a kind of metaphoric shorthand that equates the particular behavior under inspection with the general term *mujer.* Some examples equate *woman* with characteristics of the "weaker" sex, such as fear in the face of danger as opposed to masculine bravery (*Hungría* 35), and the need of male protection.[27] Commenting on woman's fickleness, a rival declares: "Basta decir que lo eres" ("It is enough to say you are one") (*Celauro* 99). In other texts, the term that *woman* replaces is *talkativeness* (*Halcón* 455).[28] But the vast majority of these examples define *woman* in terms of sexual availability. In numerous texts male characters pronounce the formula "es mujer" ("she is a woman") when they perceive that the woman they believed chaste is in fact unfaithful (*Rústico* 254; *Cardona* 680; *Laura* 341 and 348; *Alfreda* 238).[29]

Contrary to some texts' compensation for gender devaluation through noble or royal blood, in this leveling discourse class privilege does not cancel certain traits that characterize woman in general. In *Mal,* the king says of his sister, "que casalla es mejor medio / . . . / que, aunque es mi sangre, es mujer" ("it is better to marry her off, for, although she is my blood, she is a woman") (475). When the king in *Hungría* answers a defense of the queen's virtue with the condemnation "es mujer," Liseno replies: "No es mujer quien ha heredado / sangre de tan alto ser" ("She who has inherited the blood of such a lofty being is not a woman") (29). To claim that a woman's high rank does annul the negative characteristics that construct woman means denying that she is one.

Alongside the dichotomization of women into good and bad perceived as necessary for social order, other discourses consistently betray the underlying belief in *all* women's marginal status. Perry reads the 1639 decree prohibiting the use of veils by all women, regardless of class or status, as revealing that "all women were seen as dangerous, not simply those required to identify themselves as prostitutes" (151). The placement of all women on the margins of respectability creates an "ambiguous area where rules can be played with, questioned or waived" (9).[30] Despite the division of women into good/bad, highborn/lowborn, ugly/beautiful, smart/stupid, and so on, the representation of woman in Lope's honor plays affirms Ruth Kelso's judgment:

> the theory of the favored class [did not] distinguish the lady from the inferior sort of womankind [because hierarchical social theories proclaimed] as the first law of woman . . . submission and obedience. Theory does not divide women into two groups, the rulers and the ruled, and prescribe to each a different set of laws. . . . Practice did just that, but not theory. Theory said that all women must be ruled. (Quoted in Ferguson et al. xx)

Lope's honor plays produce a discourse that levels differences in the generalization that woman means, above all, trouble (". . . siempre fué cuidado / Del hombre la mujer, ó fea ó hermosa" ["woman was always man's worry, whether ugly or beautiful"] *Dina* 229); hence the need for control.

Woman as "Wife"

The most conspicuous sign for woman in Lope's honor plays is that of "wife." In these texts, woman derives meaning, status, and value from her function as object and sign of exchange between men in the marriage contract. As such, she has only two responses available to her: to be a "good" or "bad" wife in relation to the same feminine ideal. She may protect her husband's rights of private sexual ownership or transgress the bonds between men forged through marriage, dishonoring her husband by putting herself back into circulation. Female sexuality becomes the signifier of male power relations, since the options of expressing or suppressing it are played out in the scene of a struggle between two men for dominance and ownership.

Raymond Bellour has commented on the doubling necessary when woman as "lawless sexuality" is represented in the classic film (Bergstrom 64). The female outlaw must give way to the heroine, "who reverses the image, through whom the masculine subject will find . . . the positivity of a regulated sexuality, . . . the woman who permits the fixation of his desire. . . ." Most honor plays that depict a female sexual transgressor split woman into two characters, balancing the bad with the good—for example, the new wife given to the husband in reward for his manly vengeance at the end of *Comendadores, Vitoria,* and *Toledano;* or the virginal Hipólita in *Discreto* and Aurora in *Venganza.* In other texts, this doubling occurs within the same character. Since all Lope's honor plays entail at least the suspicion that the wife is unfaithful, the falsely accused woman who initially represents "lawless sexuality" in the imagination of the male subject is "redeemed" by the end in such a way as to reassure the male subject of his power and control over her.

The doubling of the sign "woman" into good wife and bad wife in Lope's honor plays can be further illuminated by Rachel Blau DuPlessis's model of the "marriage/death closure" of romance plots. The "euphoric" plot, with its ending in marriage, signifies a successful integration of woman into society; the "dysphoric" plot, with its ending in death, signifies "her sexual and social failure" (1). In effect, both endings mean the same thing: a re-production of woman within the heterosexual marriage contract: "Marriage celebrates the ability to negotiate with

sexuality and kinship; death is caused by inabilities or impro-
prieties in this negotiation" (4). Whether the transgressive wife
is eliminated at the end or the good wife is reintegrated within
the marriage context, both closures signify the cancellation of
her as subject.

The exclusion of both sexual outlaw and secular saint from
the subject position is facilitated in the theater by the spectators, who co-produce meanings in their possession of certain
shared ideological codes. The cultural meanings for "femininity" encoded in blocking, costume, movement, and poses
sexualize women onstage, inviting all viewers, male and female, to see woman as the male protagonist and other male
characters see her, that is, as object of desire (Kaplan). The
objectification and sexualization of women onstage are foregrounded in Lope's honor plays, which are ostensibly plays
about sex.[31] In these texts, woman is not only the object of male
desire, she is also the object and sign of exchange between men.
For the plot to be set in motion, it is essential that the wife of
one male subject become or be perceived to be the object of
sexual desire of another. Her physical beauty and desirability
are insistently highlighted in these texts, as is the graphic description of the rival's sexual desire to possess her. In these plays,
heterosexual desire is the field in which men strive to establish
relations with each other. It is in this sense that Cowie states:

> To talk of "woman as sign" in exchange systems is no longer
> to talk of woman as the signified, but of a different signified,
> that of: establishment/re-establishment of kinship structures
> or culture. The form of the sign—the signifier in linguistic
> terms—may empirically be woman, but the signified is not
> "woman." (60)

The relegation of woman to the position of sexualized object
of desire and sign-object of exchange between men concur-
rently defines the subject position as male. Woman is represented as Other, as not-male, as that which delimits and defines
what it means to be male. Lope's honor plays constitute what
Julia Kristeva calls

> a centered system (Other, Woman) whose center is there only
> so as to permit those making up the Same to identify with it.

> It is therefore a pseudo-center . . . whose value is invested
> in the Same giving the Other to itself in order to live as one
> alone, and unique. (50)

For Kristeva this amounts to the refusal to recognize difference
in any relationship that is not hierarchical.

Containment and Resistance

The construction of woman in Lope's honor plays participates
in the ideological linkage between Crown and male subject,
who appropriates the identity "Spaniard" by assigning all those
who threaten this hegemony to the status of Other. The relative
absence of the mother in the *comedia* in general reveals the
matrophobia underlying the alliance between early modern
state and autonomous male individual. But in their analyses of
the parallels between historical, literary, and psychoanalytic
narratives, both El Saffar and Valerie Traub stress the insistent
return of what was repressed upon the male subject's entry into
the social order (El Saffar 176; Traub, "Prince Hal's" 470). In
Lope's honor plays the family paradigm that represents fathers
as "sole and sufficient parent" (Ferguson et al. xxiv) is constantly undermined by the wife, who bears the representational
weight of the (m)other. The signifier "wife" is capable of slip-
pages that suggest that woman is not always what or where she
is supposed to be. Just below the surface of the image of idealized feminine virtue are visible the features of the mother,
whose bodiliness threatens not only the corporeal and psychological integrity of the male subject, "but also the integrity of
the household as an arena for patriarchal control" (Ferguson et
al. xxv). Traub characterizes the maternal as a figure of profound ambivalence; the female reproductive body is represented both as Bakhtinian "grotesque" capturing fears of
engulfment and contamination and as idealized Virgin Mother
allaying anxieties about the male subject's state of physical
dependency ("Prince Hal's" 464). While some texts represent
the maternal as destructive or contaminating, the majority of
Lope's honor plays distance woman from the physical realities
of the female reproductive body through idealization.[32]
     As in the case of the return of the repressed maternal, strate-
gies for the enforced (en)closure of woman in Lope's honor

plays are coextensive with representations of woman's resistance to containment. Even though the hegemonic discourse on femininity requires of woman a closed mouth, the theater necessarily creates female characters who are speaking subjects, users of signs as well as sign-objects in male exchange.[33] These texts condemn woman for her loose tongue (a trope for sexual "looseness"), but nevertheless provide dialogic situations in which the female subject can use speech to construct her story in the interstices of masculine narrative. While enjoining enclosure in the home, Lope's honor plays recur again and again to a favored device in which the wife escapes the confines of feminine space through disguise.

Just as these texts are only partially successful in maintaining the literal and symbolic enclosure of woman, there were women in seventeenth-century society who challenged their culture's definition of woman's place. Milagros Ortega Costa speaks of a

> widespread dissatisfaction that manifested itself in role changing [passing as men] . . . or in the writings of despairing young women forced into marriages they did not want or forced into convents to satisfy their parents' desires. (110)

In spite of the high degree to which women internalized official expectations of them, Perry remarks that "neither the eloquence of preachers nor the numbers of books could bridge the gap between the order they idealized and the disorder of society" (179). Lope's honor plays capture this tension in their "double movement" (Hall), attesting to women's resistance even as they attempt to recuperate that resistance within the discourses of ideal femininity.

The Construction of "Man"

Masculine and national identity are deeply interpenetrated in Lope's honor plays. To belong to the category "Spaniard" requires the performance of certain masculine gender attributes. It also requires the possession of the "right" kind of blood, either noble or Old Christian. While the lack of noble blood in a male subject can determine a comic treatment of his lack of masculinity, the possibility also exists that cross-class male bonding may occur through the defense of masculine gender attributes such as honor.[34] On the other hand, the requirement of pure blood is so deeply embedded in the definition of masculine Spanishness that it functions as a given not worthy of comment: the noble (male) Spaniard is by definition Old Christian. When blood purity does become a topic, it signifies the lack of pure blood, masculinity, and therefore "Spanishness" in the *converso* male subject. When a non-noble male subject plays the role of protagonist in the honor conflict, his "belonging" to the conflated categories of Old Christian, masculinity, and Spaniard compensates for his lack of noble blood.

As in the case of femininity, these texts construct masculinity through a variety of contradictory discourses that are used in different dramatic situations by different speakers for different purposes. One of the most common topoi equates man with the sexual use of women. The first lesson Teodosia, the woman-animal, gives Rosaura about "man" underlines sexual predation: "es hombre, y que ha de obligarte / a perder la mejor parte / de una mujer principal" ("he is a man and will oblige you to lose the dearest possession of a noblewoman") (443). The pursued wife of *Corona* characterizes all men as capable of anything to fulfill their desire (586). When *Halcón*'s wife sends her servant to spy on her husband and report if he is seeing other women, the servant asks with surprise, "¿Mujeres había de haber?" ("Must there be women?"), to which the wife replies, "¿No es hombre?" ("Is he not a man?") (448).

Just as this shorthand formulation succinctly conveys woman's essential nature ("es mujer"), the phrase "es hombre" presents the heterosexual circulation of women among men as a "natural" inclination. When the husband suspects his wife of infidelity with the king in *Resistencia,* the king's gender ("es hombre") excuses his behavior, even though his actions contradict his obligations as sovereign: "que es hombre, al fin, aunque es Rey" ("for he is a man, finally, even though he is king") (215). In many texts, the words "es [muy] hombre" ("he is [very much] a man"), pronounced approvingly by either male or female speaker, evoke a masculine ideal combining manly attractiveness and the performance of masculine gender attributes; the statement "es mujer" is always an indictment or an indication of weakness or imperfection.

The rival spurned by the queen in *Nacimiento* believes that sexual difference levels class hierarchy, and that any man can have sexual access to any woman, simply because he is a man: "Pues si es por humana ley, / Ella es mujer, yo soy hombre, / Bien me debe estar sujeta" ("Since by human law, she is woman, I am man, she must be subject to me") (492). In a passage crossed out in the autograph text of *Príncipe,* the doorkeeper who lets the king in to rape Blanca expresses the idea that women not only accept but enjoy man's power over them: "No le pesará á mi ama / Que le calentéis la cama; / Que sois hombre á toda ley" ("My mistress will not be sorry that you warm her bed, for you are a real man") (144). *Corona*'s king and his men define "man's condition" as abandoning and even despising women after using them sexually (569).[35] The peasant wife of *Cuerdo* states that if she stopped wearing finery, her husband's desire would quickly wane (551). Not only is man's desire fickle, demanding, and quickly transformed into disgust when consummated, it is self-aggrandizing. The king's daughter in *Locura,* fearful of what her lover may tell his new bride, generalizes enhancing one's own importance through sexual talkativeness to all men: "no hay soldado fanfarrón / como un amante acostado" ("there is no boasting soldier like a man in bed") (297).

Many texts equate Spanish masculinity with military conquest and bravery, and the streets of Madrid provide ample opportunity for tests of manhood. Under attack, the male subject often employs the formula "I am a man" to signify valor (*Bella* 623). The sword stands in metonymically for masculinity, as in *Pleitos*: "Hombre soy, pues ciño espada" ("I am a man, since I wear a sword") (523).[36] *Indicios*'s female servant judges the manly fighting man the most attractive (264), and an aristocratic rival believes that women of all social classes desire martial men (*Cuerdo* 557). Man's warlike nature sets him in bipolar opposition to woman's characteristic compassion (*Locura* 304). True courage in the active protection or recuperation of honor is a male prerogative, as the wife states in *Veneciano*: "Un hombre era menester, / Porque valor de mujer, / ¿Cómo podrá resistir?" ("A man is needed, for woman's courage, how can it resist?") (546).

Masculinity and Honor

Honor, closely related to sexual predation and the aggressive display of martial ability, is the most essential masculine gender attribute. Donald Larson examines the relationship between "adventitious" or "horizontal" honor and *hombría,* or "overt masculinity" (7). For the Old Christian caste, *hombría*

> was not just *a* great value, but, except for their religion, the *only* great value. Thus, by the end of the fifteenth century, . . . the only way for a man to be truly a man was to exercise to the fullest the masculine attributes of fortitude, bravery, and domination. (9)

Developing Américo Castro's theory of the "imperative dimension of the person," Larson defines *hombría* as the index of the individual's assertion of will. This concept explains the "dependence of the honor of the male on the chastity of the female" (9):

> For if honor depends on the ability to impress one's will on others, it is clear that nothing could be so dishonoring as a man's not being able to exert authority over those whom he is most obliged to control and should most easily control: the women of his family. This holds true whether the man is husband, father, son, or brother. (10)

To the conflation of honor and *hombría,* Larson adds the category of blood purity: "if purity of blood was a cause for honor . . . then all heads of family who believed their lineage to be 'clean' would do everything . . . to prevent that lineage from becoming . . . defiled" (10–11).

In his appendix, Larson refers to the gender specificity of honor when he contrasts the texts he defines as "honor plays" with the texts featuring the falsely accused queen:

> These works . . . are the obverse of honor plays: whereas honor plays focus upon, and extol, the masculine value of honor, these focus upon, and extol, the corresponding feminine value of *vergüenza.* (170)

Shame in women corresponds to honor in men, not complementarily but in a relationship of subordination. Woman's *vergüenza* functions to protect and augment man's honor in a way that his honor does not function to protect or augment her shame. These texts present the paradoxical situation in which a woman's sexual conduct determines whether a man has or loses honor, an honor which, like the phallus, she cannot possess, but which only passes through her.

Lope's honor plays dramatize conflicts of honor/*hombría,* in which male subjects display a wealth of attitudes towards honor, sexuality, and gender roles. The husband in *Indicios* believes the wise man should be superpunctilious when it comes to honor: "que en lo que puede ser piensa, / reparar debe la ofensa / aunque no crea el agravio" ("he should think of what could be, and repair the offense, even though he may not believe it") (279).[37] For the son who thinks his mother has dishonored him, a man without honor ceases to be a man (*Nacimiento* 521). Even the king in his absolute power can suffer dishonor through woman because he is a man:

> Rey: ¿A un rey se puede afrentar,
> Que no comprehende ley?
> Don García: Sí, porque es hombre, si es rey,
> Y dió, como hombre, lugar.
> Rey: Ya sospecho quien me afrenta,
> Porque un hombre con mujer,
> Aunque rey, puede temer
> Cualquier género de afrenta.
> (*Testimonio* 408–09 [3])

Although many texts construct masculinity as the ability to take bloody vengeance, in *Galán* the act of pardoning is equated with both manliness and nobility. In this text, Celio returns from war to find his lover, Ricarda, about to marry another man; when he confronts her and shows her father their love letters, she denies everything. After many turns of the plot, Ricarda begs for forgiveness. Since her father has murdered the rival, Celio can afford to be magnanimous and accepts Ricarda's redefinition of manhood as the ability to pardon. In her persuasive speech, Ricarda shifts the desire for vengeance to the feminine realm by insinuating that if Celio "imitates" her by denying her as she denied him, he loses his status as man. Through the association of femininity and "lowly" vengeance, Celio is constructed as a man at the expense of woman (152).

Other attributes usually associated with ideal femininity appear as positive masculine traits in some plays, revealing the protean nature of these constructs. In contexts that depict woman as inconstant, man can define himself through the virtue of constancy, in opposition to other texts which define masculinity in terms of sexual fickleness.[38] For the husband of *Toledano,* his name, Constante, defines man, as obedience defines woman (596). In the texts analyzed in Chapter Six, which depict the husband as powerless against the rival-king, the appropriation of the feminine virtues of loyalty and constancy replaces the aggressive defense of honor and masculinity.

As was the case in the construction of femininity, masculine gender ideals are often fused with class distinctions. In *Discreto,* the rival's cowardice calls not only his masculinity, but also his nobility into question (218). Noblemen are by nature grave, as is fitting the objects of veneration that they are, while lowborn men laugh at anything (*Portugués* 384). While some texts support the notion that men of all classes are bound to protect their honor (*Carlos* 473), a common topos defines honor as the patrimony of the ruling group. *Nacimiento*'s king is amazed at Valentín's fury: "¿Posible es que hombre tan ruin / Defienda tanto su honor?" ("Is it possible that such a lowborn man defend his honor so?") (519). Such situations may reveal the ideology of social determinism, in which the individual's attributes are inherited with his (noble or plebeian) "blood," as the supposed "lowborn" turns out to be noble. In other cases, cross-class bonding and Old Christian blood justify plebeian males' concern for their honor.

The class status of the rival harshens the offense to the husband's honor. When the rival is of higher rank, his social advantage influences the wife's choice of him over the husband. The wife's decision in *Locura* to continue seeing her lover (the prince) after her marriage to the count is linked to her evaluation of their respective social weight and the value a liaison with one or the other confers on her: "pensé yo llamarme Alteza, / señoría apenas soy" ("I planned on calling myself Your Highness; now I am hardly Your Ladyship") (303). Her *social* misrecognition of her equally status-conscious husband, taking him for the steward when he returns secretly to the house, together with her *sexual* misconduct prove a fatal combination. *Laura*'s rival schemes to kill the duke so he can marry the duchess. The duchess connives with him, believing her husband to be unfaithful, but rejects him when she thinks she may

31

be able to marry the king: "Si he de casar, ¿no es mejor / un Rey que un Conde bastardo?" ("If I am to marry, is not a king better than a bastard count?") (369).

On the other hand, the rival's lower rank heightens the husband's shame and rage. In these cases, the husband has been doubly caught out: not only has he allowed another man to gain mastery over him, he is exposed as having less *hombría* than a man whose social rank supposedly bestows a lower degree of manliness. In *Porfiar*, the husband phrases the offense to his honor in terms of the rival's inferior social position: "ni es razón que un hidalgote / se tome tanta licencia" ("it is not right that a piddling hidalgo take such license") (712). Although he is referred to as well-spoken (594) and cuts a manly figure (597), the rival of *Toledano* plies the lowly trade of carver in the service of a rich man. The husband characterizes his position as "poco menos . . . que paje / y poco más que lacayo" ("a little less . . . than a page, and a little more than a lackey") (600) and his lineage as ". . . de hombrecillo / habido de ayer acá" ("that of a little man, fabricated only yesterday") (609). The depth of the husband's humiliation is plumbed in his need to characterize the dead man to passersby as "un medio paje" ("half a page") (618). In *Laura,* the rival takes both social and sexual revenge on the duchess by telling the king she is betraying him with her jester (369).[39]

Power and the Performance of Masculinity

These examples provide a notion of the complex and at times contradictory constellation of properties and behaviors that defined masculinity for a seventeenth-century Spanish audience. The male subjects of Lope's honor plays find themselves in situations which test their performance of masculinity as understood in their culture, often in opposition to a challenging male figure. These confrontations, real or imagined, bring the masculine identity of the husband into crisis, which can resolve in the direction of triumphant proof of manliness or disgraced failure to adequately perform according to his society's conception of manhood. The crisis of masculinity represented by Lope's honor plays stems in part from the early modern state's construction of the male individual through discourses of individuality, autonomy and loyalty and the repression of the feminine (El Saffar 177). Anxiety and hypervigilance escalate as the pressure exerted by the repressed grows, making it increasingly difficult to control woman and keep her at a distance.

This crisis also relates to the contradictory demands of masculinity as it is put into play in the system of male traffic in women. As Donald Larson points out, the Spanish understanding of manliness originates in the historical conditions of the Reconquest during the fourteenth and fifteenth centuries, making conquest and domination the supreme values for Old Christians, and justifying privilege and preeminence through military prowess and defense (8–9). Masculinity, for the male aristocrat, involved an aggressive, predatory ability to impose his will on others and others' property, while simultaneously demonstrating his ability to protect his own property. The masculine ideal both encouraged predatory sexual behavior (every husband is a potential rival of another husband), and demanded absolute control of every man over his own private sexual property.[40] For Larson, the possibility of regaining lost honor through violence is explained by this imperative of control over one's property:

> The wife who committed adultery seemed to declare that she was not subject to the rule of her husband, just as the man with whom she sinned indicated his belief that he could prey on another man's "possessions" without fear of reprisal. In acting quickly to eliminate the enemies of his honor, the cuckolded husband gave the lie to such suggestions. (12)

The loss of control over private sexual property spells the loss of masculinity and honor in the crises represented in these texts, paralleled by the husband's loss of control over the narrative, which is manipulated by wife and/or rival. The narratives of Lope's honor plays establish clear male/female bipolarities at the beginning and then proceed to disorder and displace masculinity and femininity, breaking down clear distinctions. Since these texts conflate gender and sexuality, in the period of gender confusion the wife's femininity is often called into question by her abandoning the passive position in her active desire or independent actions. Both husband and rival are feminized for their immoderate involvement with one or the other term of the bipolarity governing the exchange of women (for example, collective versus private property). The prevailing pattern of these narratives is the final movement to order, in which one of the male characters is restored to the position of subject. The conflation of order/male/subject/justice to restore masculine dominance depends on the negation of the corresponding series disorder/female/object/transgression that includes not only the female but also the feminized male.

Dramatic irony, a device highly recommended by Lope in the *Arte nuevo* as "deceiving with the truth," signals who is in control of the narrative. The complicity established between dominating character and viewers, who know the "truth" that the deceived one does not, most often shifts in the course of the action to realign the spectators with the husband. Dramatic irony abounds in those texts in which the husband invents elaborate scenarios to avenge himself in secret, signifying a kind of metacontrol of the narrative. After drowning his rival in the river, the husband of *Toledano* answers his wife's question "¿No cenaréis?" ("Will you dine?") with "Yo he cenado / de un barbo que era extremado" ("I have already dined on an excellent river fish") (619). When alerted by an anonymous letter to the love affair between his wife and his son, the duke in *Venganza* speaks of their governing in his absence in terms which his wife interprets positively, the audience negatively:

> Ya sé que me ha retratado
> Tan igual en todo estado,
> Que por mí le habéis tenido;
>   De que os prometo, señora,
> Debida satisfacción.

(267 [4])

Discreto's husband fakes an excuse to leave in order to return disguised as the rival and beat his wife. He sees through her masquerade of grief at his departure, speaking on one level for his wife, who persists in her belief that she is deceiving him, and on another for the spectators:

> Deja, Casandra querida,
> el llorar y el suspirar,
> que bien tendrás que llorar
> después que yo me despida.

(211 [5])

The ability to stay in control and maintain honor and masculinity in these plays depends on a clear distinction between property and property owners as well as between collective and private property. A rhetorical device that points to the status of woman as property in male homosocial exchange is the blazon, or "conventional poetic description of an object praised or blamed by a rhetorician-poet" (Vickers 95). In Lope's honor plays, the blazon takes the form of a part-by-part description of a woman's body based on conventional Petrarchan imagery, deploying a dual discursive strategy of merchandising and dominion. While constructing a relationship that involves "an active buyer, an active seller and a passive object for sale" (Vickers 97), this mode of discourse, by taking inventory of the female body, also takes control of it, "by making it . . . the engaging 'matter' of male discourse, a passive commodity in a . . . male exchange in which the woman herself, traditionally absent, does not speak" (Parker 131). The woman thus excluded and commodified becomes the "gendered sign of the territory to be conquered and occupied" (Parker 131).

In *Portugués,* the lackey's description of Mayor simultaneously stakes out the territory to be conquered and provides an opportunity for the duke's eroticized "looking":

> Ortuño: Divide con un perfil
> La nariz con línea igual,
> Campo de nieve y coral,
> Juntando á Enero y Abril.
> Tiene dos corales finos
> Entre murallas de piedras
> De los dientes. . . . .
> . . . .
> Del cuello, ¿qué te diré?
> ¿Qué marfil será bastante?
> . . . .
> Duque: Que me vas poniendo fuego,
> . . . .
> Doña Mayor será mía.[41]

(375 [6])

In *Halcón,* Perote the fool makes the merchandising context of the blazon explicit when he mocks poets whose praise turns woman into a ". . . mercader / De joyas y de alpargates" ("merchant of jewels and shoes") (452), on the heels of Federico's speech describing Celia's beauty in metaphors of precious metals and gems (444).[42]

When the triangular structure of the blazon is abandoned in favor of direct address to the woman as a strategy of seduction, the inclusion of the woman as speaking subject instead of passive object described has potentially negative results: "Ese clavel colorado, / . . . / Volvedlo luego al jardín / De donde lo habéis hurtado" ("Return all those red carnations . . . to the garden you stole them from") (*Testimonio* 405). But in other situations, in which the blazon displays the woman for another man, the consequences can be potentially disastrous for her (Parker 129). *Celauro*'s rival uses the blazon as a discursive strategy in male homosocial exchange to dominate the husband. After the rival's sister reveals to him that the wife has a beauty mark and a few hairs on her breast, he shows the husband a forged love letter to the wife that refers to these intimate physical features. Here the controlling division of the female body into discrete parts enables the rival to provide the husband with the "evidence" of his dishonor. His narrativizing inventory takes the place of sex, converting private property into public.

Since these plays consistently represent male anxiety surrounding men's performance of masculinity in controlling their sexual property, it is not surprising that several texts foreground the negotiation of the Oedipal arrangement with the father or a father figure. George Mariscal points out important differences between the bourgeois nuclear family that the Freudian narrative evolved to explain and its seventeenth-century Spanish counterparts (*Contradictory Subjects* 67–68). While recognizing the need for caution in studying the Spanish family, I find the Oedipal model useful in exploring representations that figure the social dynamic between absolute monarch and individual male householder within the father/son relationship, and vice versa. As perceptively analyzed by El Saffar, this dynamic, in which the male householder acknowledges the absolute power of the monarch, hinges on a social contract ensuring his power and autonomy in the home.

In some texts, the husband wins paternal approval by "acting like a man" and regaining control over his private sexual property, murdering adulterous wife and/or rival. This paternal approval can be meted out by the king (*Comendadores, Fuenteovejuna,* and *Peribáñez*), the father-in-law (*Locura* and *Vitoria*), or the father-king in *Testimonio*. Other texts successfully resolve arrested or problematic Oedipal arrangements. In *Celauro,* the son has kept his ten-year marriage to Fulgencia a secret from his father. When the play opens, the father is beating the son for continuing to see Fulgencia, whom he rejects as a suitable match for his son because of her poverty. After the husband lies about seeing her, the father gives him money. Infantilized and feminized by the father, who refuses to recognize his son in a position of power with respect to a woman, the son is further dominated by the rival, who makes him believe Fulgencia is unfaithful. He is not "man" enough to stab her, but instead opts for the feminine response of fleeing to the countryside where he wanders about in a state bordering on madness. At this point the wife instrumentalizes herself to effect the exchange of women necessary for her husband to finally enter manhood. In disguise, she allows herself to become the object of desire of the father. The news of his father's impending marriage to Fulgencia engages the husband in an aggressive posture, and he arrives, indignant, in time to stop the wedding. In a reversal of the usual scenario, the father must relinquish his desire for his son's wife, thereby recognizing his son's male entitlement and rights in a woman.

The text of *Carlos* insists on describing the relationship between the duke and his *camarero,* or valet, as father and son. Like *Celauro*'s husband, Carlos is married in secret, and therefore enjoys no public patriarchal status, continuing in a position of infantilized subordination to the duke. Without the mediating body of a woman, Carlos is feminized in relationship to the duke, and their homosocial bonding borders on the homoerotic.[43] His full entry into the symbolic order, exteriorized in the public recognition of wife and offspring and his ascension in social rank, is accomplished through his successful renunciation of his "father's" love object. When the duke's wife reveals her desire for him and pursues him actively, Carlos respects the private property of another, more authoritative male in exchange for official acknowledgment of his own patriarchal ownership.

Other texts represent the disastrous fulfillment of fantasies of paternal rage and punishment. In *Ferias* and *Galán,* the husband is killed by his father-in-law. While continuing to participate in the flow of women after marriage, *Ferias*'s husband has been unable to withdraw his own wife from circulation. After being cuckolded, he does not dominate his rival "like a man," but rather opportunes his father-in-law to take vengeance for him. Unlike the husband's, the father-in-law's actions are consistent with the masculine ideal. He simultaneously protects his own honor and eliminates a man who is lacking in sufficient masculinity to protect his rights in a woman. In *Galán,* the husband's inadequacies are not limited to his inability to regain control over his private sexual property; he is also lacking in the *hombría* defined as having pure blood. Suspecting his wife of adultery, he visits her father, who casts aspersions on the husband's blood purity and kills him. These "sons" who fail to perform their proper role in relation to the symbolic and the Law are eliminated from the male order by the wrathful "father."

The homosocial bonding of mutuality between father and son in *Venganza,* like that of *Carlos,* occurs in the absence of a woman as medium or conduit of the relationship. Their self-sufficiency threatens the continuation of the social order, since the duke has neglected the forging of exogamous bonds through marriage and the production of a legitimate heir to the throne. His libertine use of women in heterosexual circulation has served mainly as a field for further male homosocial bonding, as in the opening scene. The duke's illegitimate son, Count Federico, has also delayed full assumption of the patriarchal role; his cousin Aurora takes the active role in offering herself to the duke as object of exchange in marriage to the count. Unlike Carlos's, Federico's Oedipal journey goes terribly awry. Rather than renouncing his desire for the father's love object and channeling homosocial desire through the exogamous exchange of women, Federico submits to his desire for union with Casandra, which returns him to a pre-Oedipal state of undifferentiated sexuality: "Que entre morir y vivir, / Como hermafrodita eres" ("For between dying and living you are like a hermaphrodite") (251); "Yo me olvido de ser hombre" ("I forget to be a man") (262).[44] His desire for the "mother" evokes the father's vengeance, resulting in the complete loss of self in death.

Texts such as these portray the cost of extreme gender polarization. In seventeenth-century Spanish culture, the achievement of status, wealth, and power is based on a social contract between father in the state and king in the family. These plays reveal the individual male subject's fear of failure to live up to the terms of the contract, bringing down the power of the father-king upon the transgressors of his law, a punishment clearly not confined to criminal female subjects. At the same time, they reveal a lingering fascination and identification with the feminine, as if the inability to control woman either as private property or as medium and object of exchange among men leads to the inevitable sinking into the maternal, the feared and desired loss of identity itself.[45]

Lope's honor plays would appear to uphold the canonic interpretation of the *comedia* as vehicle of the dominant ideology. Many texts ostensibly exemplify the program of social control compressed in the seemingly tautological phrase "to be who one is." As Leo Spitzer and José Antonio Maravall (*Teatro*) have shown, this formula subordinates the individual to the hierarchical dictates of the social contract. For Donald Larson, it "implies recognition . . . of one's social configuration, that is, of one's place in society and of the behavior expected of one as a certain member of the social hierarchy" (523). This interpretation seems especially pertinent in those plays defining the "real" man as he who not only protects his sexual property, but stoically transcends personal attachment to the love object in the service of a higher social duty. But an examination of these texts also yields the possibility that they represent the *crisis* of the definition of masculinity as aggression, domination, separation from, and repression of the feminine, as well as the crises provoked for the male subject by embracing this ideal of masculinity within this particular social order. Lope's honor plays reveal a profound insecurity about sexual identity, of which the conventional restoration of male dominance and clear gender roles at the end could be a symptom and not a cure.[46] This anxiety is reflected not only in the ambivalent representation of woman and the feminine but also in the ambiguous exploration of masculinity and the father/son relationship. The paternal role is recognized as both absolute power and crushing authority; there is pride in belonging to the world of the fathers as well as resentment at the price to be paid.

Chapter Two

Sexual Outlaws

Although the wife-murder plays receive the lion's share of critical attention because of their sensationalism, only a handful of plays feature wives punished for their transgressive desire:[1] *Carlos, Comendadores, Toledano, Discreto, Contienda* (in which the conjugal-honor conflict constitutes only a small part of the action), *Vitoria, Locura,* and *Venganza.* The vast majority of the wives in the honor plays penned by Lope represent the feminine ideal. In those texts, the virtuous wife's elaborate strategies of self-erasure, necessary to avoid becoming the object of the rival's desire, amount to the erasure of sexuality itself. This equation of wifely virtue and the lack of sexual desire harmonizes with other seventeenth-century cultural practices constructing woman as "the defective portion of humanity . . . more capable of sexual pleasure than men" and hence in need of the gender-specific virtue of chastity (Vann 199). The prescriptive literature of the time conceived of marriage as a way to safely contain sex, which would "otherwise erupt in violent antisocial behavior" (Perry 52). The depiction of the ideal wife's sexuality in Lope's honor plays is limited to procreation and separated from pleasure. The virtuous wife is permitted very few expressions of even legitimate sexual desire within the sanctioned context of marriage.[2] As Richard Vann points out, the marriage manuals of preindustrial Europe considered it the "husband's responsibility to ensure his wife's . . . libidinous urgings were never aroused" (199).

The unequal punishments leveled at men and women for illicit sex reinforced the gender ideology "that saw female sexuality as more dangerous and more in need of control" (Perry 59). Adultery was a gender-specific crime that could only be committed by the wife.[3] A husband, or even a man officially engaged to a woman over twelve, had the legal right to kill her and her lover if they were caught in the act. This was not common, since his was the burden of proof; it was advisable to leave the bodies in the incriminating circumstances until witnesses could be procured (McKendrick, *Woman and Society* 36).[4] If the husband chose to turn wife and rival over to the law and they were found guilty, they were returned for punishment to the husband, who could execute them publicly.[5] The wronged husband acquired the possessions of his wife's lover, if he had been killed with permission of the law (16).[6] As adultery was a gender-specific crime, the wronged wife could not accuse her husband of it and could seek redress only from the other woman, not the husband (16).

Although wife murder was not unknown, when the husband did take action, murder was less common than confiscation of the wife's goods, or prosecution of her and her lover. Perry notes that far more numerous were those "who simply left or took lovers" (73). The wronged husband could also withdraw the charge and take the "perdón de cuernos," or cuckold's pardon, whose name indicates the low social value attached to it (McKendrick 37). Melveena McKendrick states that "many husbands profited from rather than punished their wives' infidelities, although the literature of the time is relentless in its representation of the consenting cuckold." Contrary to what Lope's honor plays may lead us to suppose, social pressure was actually against wife murder. Public sympathy was with the victims, "especially when it was obvious that the husband would not be brought to justice because of influence or wealth, or that honor was not the true motive" (McKendrick 38). In the case of a scribe who killed his wife with little cause, McKendrick reports that women created such a disturbance that a hasty hanging of the perpetrator was necessary (39). Such a possibility of female solidarity is discarded by Lope's honor plays.

Profile of the Sexual Outlaw

Not surprisingly, the wife who fails to live up to the feminine ideal and reciprocates adulterous desire embodies female sexuality itself. Female sexual desire in general is charged with negative value and eliminated or controlled. The representation of these "sexual outlaws" responds to what Raymond Bellour sees as the profound necessity to represent both aspects of femininity for the male subject. The semiotic chain "female desire—transgression—punishment" portrays both the threat posed by female sexuality that escapes the limits of patriarchal control and the consolation supplied by the subsequent reimposition of that control. Certain patterns emerge in the representation of the female outlaw's character and sexuality. These patterns unfold along with more individualized responses to specific dramatic situations.

In *Comendadores,* a description of Beatriz's physical beauty is embedded in a context of sexual availability despite close kinship ties. Her cousins, the future rivals, associate her with incest even as they refer to her virtue; they speculate that she may refuse to receive them in her husband's absence in order to appear chaste, "Que con hermanos lo han hecho / Otras del mismo lugar" ("For others in her position have done it with their own brothers") (264). She first appears at her window, looking at men, rejecting some and approving of others. As desiring subject, she is obviously attracted by *hombría:*

> Harto lindo todo es,
> Si no fuera lindo y vano.
>   Don Pedro, que es más robusto,
> No me ha parecido mal.
> . . . .
> Y lo contrario te asombre;
> Que no es bien que tenga el hombre
> Semejanza de mujer.
>
> (266 [7])

This initial characterization sets the stage for the immediate declaration of mutual attraction between the rivals and the women (the wife and her niece through marriage). While "love at first sight" is one of the *comedia*'s conventions, it usually occurs in situations that permit the proper social channeling of erotic desire in marriage. In the case of a married woman, at least some modicum of resistance is expected. Not only does Beatriz fail to think of her husband's honor, she makes him the butt of her contempt (269), the victim of her ironic double entendres ("V: En tales manos cayese / Siempre mi honor. B: Ya lo está" ["V: May my honor always fall into such hands. B: It already has"] 275) and even her curses (295). Beatriz's speech reflects her impetuous character. When the rivals are at the door and her husband tarries in welcoming them, her desire spills out in short spurts of speech: "¡Jesús! Entren: ¿qué reparas?" ("Jesus! Let them enter! What's keeping you?") (275); she expresses her anticipation in a series of exclamations: "¡Alargaos, horas dichosas! / ¡Deteneos, lágrimas mías! / . . . / ¡Ay, sangre! ¡Ay, amor! ¡Ay, fuego!" ("Stretch out, happy hours! Stop flowing, tears! . . . Oh, blood! Oh, love! Oh, fire!") (281). The wife's lack of concern with her honor or even her personal safety contrasts with her niece's lingering uneasiness (281).

The frank representation of Beatriz's desire culminates in the intensely erotic preparations for her lover's arrival, filled with images that appeal to the senses of touch, smell, and taste:

> . . . Enjuga presto
> Cuatro sábanas de holanda.
> Saca pastillas, pues sabes,
> Del escritorio pequeño,
> Haz fiestas al nuevo dueño.
> . . . .
> Perfuma esta cuadra toda,
> Echa aquella colcha indiana.
> . . . .
> Haz perfumar
> Una camisa también,
> Y apercibe colación.
>
> (295 [8])

Whereas the absence of sexuality in the ideal wife is to be read positively, Beatriz's sensuality signifies transgression and moral degeneracy. Donald Larson is correct when he says that of the three planes of morality in the text, the wife occupies the lowest (43), but he does not address the place of gender in this particular configuration of desire and immorality.

Dorotea of *Toledano* also yields easily to the rival's advances. She allows him to talk to her on the street, over her maid's protestations (594). When her husband asks her the identity of the man he saw them with, she pretends that the rival is interested in her maid. She communicates this ruse to the rival when he comes to her window. These activities—speaking with a man in public and permitting a conversation at her window—are culturally encoded as transgressive feminine behavior (McKendrick, *Woman and Society* 31). Like Beatriz, Dorotea is volatile and impatient. She pushes her husband to read the rival's letter, supposedly meant for the maid (603), and fumes when he declares that he will answer the letter himself (604). When the menacing presence of the husband frightens the rival away from their tryst in the park, Dorotea explodes in anger and then is reduced to tears (612). She as quickly changes her tune when her husband reveals that the rival already has a mistress. Alone, she gloats over her success in deceiving her husband, anticipating their next meeting (605).

Unlike these two, Leonor of *Vitoria* is aware of the obligations of her station as a married noblewoman. Nevertheless, she gives only tepid expression to her love for her husband and her duty to protect his honor: "es honrado caballero; / con justa razón le quiero / y le debo ser leal" ("Valdivia is an honorable gentleman; with just reason I love him and must be loyal to him") (419). The relationship between them is not particularly harmonious (the husband is depicted as excessively jealous), and her sexual desire for the rival gradually undermines her honorable resistance.[7] Initially impressed by the rival's manliness when he saves her from a bull, she refers insistently to his physique, or "talle" (18–19, 22, 33, 46). In spite of her attraction to him, she still perceives herself as "married and noble" (425), as does her husband, in spite of his jealous doubts (428). When the rival surprises her in her room, she still resists, convincing him to leave.

The turning point coincides with the rival's achievement of the habit of the military order of Santiago: "mas, como Antonio ha salido / con la roja cruz al pecho, / ventaja notable ha hecho . . ." ("since Antonio has worn the red cross on his breast, he has gained a notable advantage . . .") (443). She is actually deluded in awarding the rival the edge, since he fails to keep the promise of manliness held out by the cross of Santiago. It is her husband who ultimately behaves "like a real man," according to the construct of masculinity that she herself upholds and that dictates her destruction. But at this point, the meanings attached to the habit are enough to tilt the balance towards the fulfillment of illicit desire. She agrees to see the rival, admonishing him to live up to the ideal of masculinity signified by the cross and not be a coward, ". . . que es muy vil testimonio / de la cruz que trae al pecho" ("which is a vile perjury of the cross he wears on his breast") (443). At the moment of the rendezvous, fear for her reputation still combats her desire, but she justifies her action by saying that love conquers all resistance (448). She is deluded in this as well, for other texts illustrate the lengths to which the wife must go to protect her honor, even if such resistance is ultimately futile or results in self-cancellation.

The wife of *Venganza* shares the character traits of these other sexual outlaws. Casandra is impulsive, active in the pursuit of her desire, and reckless in her determination to keep her lover at all costs. She repeatedly encourages the rival (her husband's illegitimate son, Federico) to declare himself (254, 258), and incites him with a lascivious image (Kossoff 299n1492): "Toma mi consejo, Conde; / Que el edificio más casto / Tiene la puerta de cera" ("Take my advice, count, for the most chaste edifice has a door made of wax") (254). Erotic tension charges the air as the future lovers take advantage of social customs to touch each other as often as possible (Kossoff 290n1303), and culminates in an explosive image at the end of the second act, when Casandra refuses Federico her hand: "Todo principio condeno / Si pólvora al fuego aplico" ("I condemn the consequences, if I apply fire to gunpowder") (260).

Casandra is unique among the transgressive wives in that her desire is fueled by the sexual neglect of her libertine husband, the duke, who has married her in response to pressure from his vassals to produce an heir:

> Sola una noche le vi
> En mis brazos en un mes,
> Y muchas le vi después
> Que no quiso verme á mí.
>
> (249 [9])

The text associates her adulterous desire with revenge for this sexual abandonment (249, 250, 254–55), especially in the *quintillas* whose energetic rhythm, short lines and accentuation aptly capture her character:

> Entre agravios y venganzas
> Anda solícito amor.

> . . . .
> En el ánimo que inclino
> Al mal, por tantos disgustos
> Del Duque, loca imagino
> Hallar venganzas y gustos
> En el mayor desatino.
>
> (257–58 [10])

Even though the play appears to justify her adulterous desire, her fate communicates a different message. Just as falsely accused wives are expected to endure years of exile in sanctified resignation and celibacy, the sexually frustrated are to remain exemplars of wifely virtue, seeking no satisfaction of the desire that does not even enter into the definition of "wife."

Venganza's Casandra, like Leonor in *Vitoria,* struggles against her desire; her concern with honor is accompanied by fear of punishment and death (254–55, 259). But once she chooses, she throws all caution to the winds. Even after the duke returns, she wants to continue seeing her lover as before, refuses to dissimulate, jealously rejects Federico's ploy to marry Aurora to cover himself, and makes a scene when she learns he has requested Aurora's hand (354). When Federico resigns himself to her will, she declares: "Pues no haya amor imposible. / Tuya he sido y tuya soy; / No ha de faltar invención" ("No love is impossible. I have been yours and I am yours; we will find ways") (268). Although this is the last time the audience sees her or hears her speak, her last moments become visible and audible in the duke's monologue. The reimposition of the husband's control over her body and the closing of her transgressive openness reveal the delusion of her belief that she could live out her desire:

> La infame Casandra dejo
> De pies y manos atada,
> Con un tafetán cubierta,
> Y por no escuchar sus ansias,
> Con una liga en la boca.
>
> (269 [11])

In *Locura,* the prince was Flordelís's first object of desire, but the king arranges her marriage to Count Floraberto, hoping to marry his son more favorably. Flordelís is prepared to sacrifice her desire to her role as wife, to accept her fate and live, if without love, at least with the honor of a respectable noblewoman. Her husband is sexually attentive to her: his servant tells his former lover that they sleep together every night (291). In public, Flordelís's words are ambiguous and can be interpreted to signify approval or displeasure ("Es exceso. / Loca estoy de sus caricias" ["It is excessive. I am mad from his caresses"] 297), but in the privacy of her home, she confides her real feelings to her maid: "Si tristes paso los días, / las noches infiernos son" ("If sadly I pass the days, the nights are hell") (303). The prince continues to pursue her, and forced to choose between her desire and her honor, she chooses desire and dies.

The wife who reciprocates adulterous desire signifies criminal transgression and punishment; she who initiates it evokes monstrosity and madness. As figures of aggressive female desire, they threaten masculine control. The representation of their active pursuit followed by their subsequent punishment mirrors the disorder and subsequent restoration of order characteristic of many *comedias*.[8]

In her love letter to her husband's friend Felisardo, Casandra's language in *Discreto* is explicitly erotic: "cosas que un hielo encendieran, / y que poderosas fueran / a abrasar la nieve fría" ("things that would set ice on fire, and would be capable of making the cold snow burn") (198). She also appropriates the male prerogative of exchange of women:

> "Fatigábase en pensar
> que si una hermana tuviera
> para mujer os la diera:
> yo me ofrezco en su lugar . . ."
>
> (198–99 [12])

Her husband uses the euphemistic term *gozar* ("to enjoy"), meaning "to have sexual intercourse," which usually takes a male subject, to describe the obvious objective of his wife's criminal desire: ". . . le escribe / que loca amándole vive / y que le espera gozar" ("she writes him that she is madly in love with him and that she hopes to enjoy him") (200).

The action of the play is structured by the binary opposition between *locura* ("insanity") and *cordura* ("sanity"). References permeate the text, tracing the trajectory of the male subject from *loco* (for his love for an unmarried woman, for the praise of his friend that inspired his wife's passion) to the *discreto* ("discreet man") of the title. This process involves recuperating the control of traffic in women (marrying his friend to the former object of his extramarital desire) and controlling his wife's sexuality. Disguised as his friend, he beats Casandra, then arranges to leave her alone with Felisardo. Ignorant of what has transpired, Felisardo can only conclude from her rantings that Casandra is crazy. At the end, the positive term, *discreto,* has triumphed, and the negative one, *loco,* is displaced and projected onto woman, signifier at once of female sexuality and madness.

The transgressive wife of *Carlos* is characterized against the feminine ideal for her rejection of *vergüenza* as an obstacle to the fulfillment of her illicit desire (441). Her desire is doubly transgressive, because it is adulterous and because the object of her desire is of low rank (442). Although aware of her honor and fearful of punishment, she quickly dispatches her dilemma, calling on love to give her courage (441–42) and daring to pursue her desire even if it costs her life (451). As in *Discreto,* this sexual outlaw usurps the male erotic lexicon as well as the role of active desiring subject (451), promising Carlos the object of his desire: "Ama, adora una mujer; / Que te prometo de hacer / Que la poseas y goces" ("Go on, love and adore a woman; for I promise to see to it that you possess and enjoy her") (451).

In this reversal of roles, Carlos assumes the feminine position, as the title insinuates (*Carlos the "Pursued"*). He articulates his "honorable resistance" in terms of the impossibility of the sexual aggressor achieving the ends of desire, a rhetoric often found on the lips of the ideal wife: "Que primero habrá en el suelo / Sol y estrellas, y en el cielo / Arboles, que tal consienta" ("For before I consent to such a thing, first the sun and stars will be on the earth and trees in the heavens") (445). The wife, on the other hand, uses the imagery of hardness and impenetrability usually employed by male rivals to complain of their love objects' virtuous beauty: "No importa, no, cruel Narciso, avaro / De la hermosura que te ha dado el cielo, / Tan duro y frío como el mármol paro" ("As hard and cold as Parian marble, you care not, cruel Narcissus, for the beauty Heaven has given you") (475).

This transgressive, because active, desire is figured in the text through recurring metaphors of poisonous treachery and bestiality. The wife herself utilizes these comparisons ("Y este veneno y pasión / Que me abrasa el corazón" ["And this poisonous passion that inflames my heart"] 442). Carlos compares her to poisonous snakes, the Hircanian tiger, a bloodthirsty wolf, and Herod's executioner (444, 452, 471, 483). When she avenges herself of his rejection by telling the duke that Carlos is trying to cuckold him, she is presented as a monster of unrequited desire, capable of destroying the love object she may not possess: "Que menos que en beber de su enemigo / La misma sangre, no queda vengada" ("She will not feel avenged until she has drunk the very blood of her enemy") (464).

To achieve their desire, these wives lie, invent false narratives, and manipulate reality. But in the discourse on femininity of Lope's honor plays, duplicity characterizes *both* signs for woman, ideal wife and sexual outlaw. In Chapter Four, I explore the doubling strategies of good wives who disguise themselves as men or as women of a lower social class. The transgressive wife never disguises herself, but does cultivate another form of duplicity: that of masquerade. Masquerade, or "the mask of excessive femininity," involves the exaggerated performance of the feminine ideal. Joan Riviere believed that women affect ultrafeminine behavior to hide the possession of what are considered masculine attributes and to avoid reprisals.[9] But as Luce Irigaray has pointed out, to deliberately assume the feminine role "means already to convert a form of subordination into an affirmation, and thus to begin to thwart it" (76). For Mary Ann Doane, masquerade is subversive because it creates distance between the female subject and the image of femininity demanded by patriarchal orders, calling into question the "natural" status of femininity and drawing attention to it as a masculine construct.[10] Masquerade provides a means of ridiculing this construct while appearing to submit to it, of conforming to the definition of woman as spectacle and undermining masculine control at the same time.

For Lope's sexual outlaws, masquerade is a failed strategy, with the exception of Fabia, to whom I will return at the end of this chapter. Having just witnessed her adulterous desire in his absence, the audience of *Comendadores* easily reads the wife's hypocritical welcome of her husband as an act (270–71). Even the husband recognizes the exaggeration in her joy at his home-coming ("Dejad ya tantos excesos" ["Leave off such excesses"]), and her own asides call attention to it as performance (271). The wife of *Toledano* plays the role of the virtuous married woman cognizant of the least threat to her honor (602). Hoping that Carlos will assume the active role, the sexual outlaw in *Carlos* speaks indirectly of the desire of "a certain important lady," but when he fails to take the bait, she abandons the masquerade of passivity and *vergüenza*: "Ahora bien, quitarme quiero / La máscara de la cara" ("All right then, I intend to drop the mask") (451). When he continues to reject her, she chooses the role of wifely virtue for her husband, tearfully feigning shame and hesitance in revealing to him that Carlos is pursuing her and dishonoring him (453). Casandra's inability to masquerade terrifies Federico in *Venganza,* for he knows that it is necessary to the survival of the wife who chooses to live outside the law.

In spite of their recourse to masquerade, all these wives undertake a deceptive path to power. For a time, they succeed in inverting the assignation of passivity and activity by gender, dominating their husbands and controlling the narrative through their lies and machinations. In some, the rejection of the passive role is explicit. *Venganza*'s Casandra refuses the wife's position as object and adornment in the home:

> El Duque debe de ser
> De aquellos cuya opinión
> En tomando posesión,
> Quieren en casa tener
> Como alhaja la mujer,
> Para adorno, lustre y gala,
> Silla, ó escritorio en sala;
> Y es término que condeno.
> . . . .
> La mujer de honesto trato
> Viene para ser mujer
> A su casa, que no á ser
> Silla, escritorio ó retrato.
>
> (249 [13])

Her error lies in wanting something more for herself than the objectified status of property, in thinking that "woman" can mean something besides possession or object.

Casandra and the other transgressive wives are pseudo-
subjects in their quest for selfhood. In spite of their attempts to
organize their sexuality independently, it is ultimately defined
within a male symbolic system of honor and masculinity that
rewards or punishes according to respect for or deviation from
the norm. After disorder and role reversal yield to the restoration of masculine control and the redistribution of "proper"
gender roles, they emerge much more powerless than they were
before.

The Spectacle of Punishment

Lope's honor plays, and the *comedia* in general, assign positive value to female energy only when it can be channeled successfully within the confines of marriage (leading up to it or
working to save it). In the texts under consideration here, illicit
sexuality is a trope for female aspirations that transcend social
limits. When the restraints designed to contain this energy fail,
"death enforces the restrictions on female behavior" (DuPlessis 16):

> death comes for a female character when she has a jumbled,
> distorted, inappropriate relation to the "social script" . . . de-
> signed to contain her legally, economically, and sexually. In
> narrative, then, death is the second line of defense for the
> containment of female revolt. . . . Death is the price extracted
> for female critique, whether explicit or implicit. Death
> occurs as the price for the character's . . . destabilizing
> of the . . . equilibrium of respectable female behavior.
> (15–16)

The enforcing aspect of the destabilizing wife's death stems
from the nature of punishment in precapitalist society. In his
analysis of penality, Michel Foucault traces the itinerary of the
body from a socially visible object in the old regime to one
which can no longer be seen in the bourgeois order. In sixteenth-
and seventeenth-century Spain, the "horrifying spectacle of
public punishment" derived its effectiveness "from its visible
intensity" (9), and the physical pain of the body itself (11).[11] A
crime attacks the king personally, since the body politic *is* the
body of the king (Barker) and the law a direct representation
of his will; for this reason, revenge figured prominently in the
retribution, which is both public and personal (Foucault
47–48).

The murder scenes of these texts amount to a kind of theatrical public execution, given the continuity between the stage and the penal scaffold (Barker),[12] and the correspondence between father/king in the family and king/father in the state. Even if the murder takes place in the privacy of the home, the presence of the audience effectively transforms it into a public act of retribution. In this dramatic ritual, the force behind the husband's sword is the force of the law, that is, of the sovereign, and the offense to the husband's honor is at the same time an offense against the king. Like the public executions, the wife-murder plays are ceremonies reconstituting the injured husband/sovereign. The punishment, while executed in the private sphere, is also made public within the action itself. The discovery of the corpses, the narration to the king (*Comendadores*) or to the father-in-law (*Locura*), the letter to the father of the rival (*Vitoria*) all form part of the public restitution of the husband. As Foucault points out, sovereignty is restored "by manifesting it at its most spectacular" (48).[13] On the other hand, while the truth of the punishment is affirmed (the husband did have the legal right to kill wife and rival if caught in the act), what is established is not merely justice but power.[14] The social function of the ceremony of punishment in these honor plays is to provide an "exercise in terror," effective in its very excess and imbalance (49).[15]

In these texts, power is not just *exercised* on the body of the wife; according to Foucault, "power relations have an immediate hold on it; they invest it, mark it, train it, torture it, force it to carry out tasks, to perform ceremonies, to emit signs" (25). The wife's cries, her flight, her pleas for mercy, her request for confession, her speech, never claiming innocence at the moment of reckoning, but acknowledging her crime and the justice of her punishment, are all signs of her subjection. Before her death, she acknowledges her crime or accepts the justice of her punishment: "Conozco que os he ofendido" ("I know that I have offended you") (*Comendadores* 297).[16] The death of the wife on the public stage reveals the truth of her guilt and shows the operation of patriarchal power, making "the body of the condemned . . . the place where the vengeance of the sovereign was applied" (Foucault 55).

In his analysis of the Jacobean theater, Francis Barker discusses the visibility of the body in pain in a semiotic system that privileges the image over the word, as opposed to Shake-spearean texts (16). Although the importance awarded language in Lope's *Arte nuevo* would seem to draw the *comedia* closer to the verbal than to the specular pole, it would be unwise to under-estimate the importance of the actor's body as spectacle, given the scarcity of props and the absence of painted scenery in the *comedia*. Certain graphic stage devices establish the visual as the dominant plane of signification and center on the actors' bodies. Their appearances and disappearances and their spatial dispositions on the stage were controlled by stage design and a variety of stage machinery (Shergold 294). The clothing of the actors, for example, besides its iconic and eye-pleasing func-tion, also signaled social status.

Lope proscribes stage violence and the depiction of "mon-sters" in the *Arte nuevo,* but in some texts the murder of wife or rival does take place onstage, as in the stabbing of the wife in *Locura* or of the rival in *Contienda* (487). But even when the actual murders take place offstage, certain conventional devices continue to mark the body as site of the exercise of patriarchal power, such as verbal narrations, the flight offstage of wife and rival pursued by the armed husband, or the display of the corpses of wife and rival.

Locura presents the most prolonged scene of punishment. The text repeats the usual scenario in which the suspicious husband (Floraberto) absents himself to allow wife and rival time to tryst, then returns unexpectedly to collect the proof that he needs. When Floraberto returns during the night, he locks the doors, blocking all paths of escape (307). The first person he and his servant encounter is the wife's maid. When she tries to warn her mistress, he orders his servant to throw her over the railing. Alarmed by the noise, Flordelís enters, "algo desnuda" ("somewhat undressed") (307). Her scanty clothing and her loose hair throughout the scene signify her transgres-sive sexuality but also her vulnerability. Her pathetic masquer-ade at this point ("¡Dos mil abrazos te doy! / . . . / ¿Qué buena venida es ésta?" ["Let me embrace you two thousand times! . . . What a welcome arrival!"]) has no chance of success. The audience shares her terror through her asides ("¡Helada estoy de temor / y entre mil peligros puesta!" ["Fear has turned me to ice and placed me among a thousand dangers!"]) and her desperate questions. When the servant announces her maid's death, Flordelís's disoriented and unbelieving query ("¿De quién dices?" ["Who did you say?"]) brings a response that only augments her intense fear: "Sesos y sangre esparcidos / las piedras han esmaltado" ("Scattered brains and blood have painted the stones") (307). Hearing her husband killing the rival's servant offstage, Flordelís tries to call out to her father, but is paralyzed with fright (307–08). She invents the story that the man and her maid were lovers, but the husband counters with a series of questions taken from a well-known *romance,* asking after the identity of the horses, arms, cape, and finally the feet he sees in his house.[17] She evades with her answers all but the last, undeniable proof of her guilt, at which point she accepts her fate. Later, the rival helps the audience re-create the sight of Flordelís's dead body when he says ". . . muerta / la vi, teñida en su caliente sangre" ("I saw her dead, bathed in her own hot blood") (318).

Comendadores is perhaps the most famous of Lope's wife-murder texts for the excess of the husband's punishment. Not only are the murdered wife and rival doubled (two commanders, wife and niece), but the husband kills all the inhabitants of the house, including servants, slaves, dogs, cats, monkeys, and even a parrot (299).[18] Foucault relates the disproportion between the injury inflicted on the criminal and the injury committed by the criminal to the power dissymmetry between subject and sovereign, or here, between wife and husband (48–49). The very atrocity of the expiation plays an important role in the "ritual destruction of infamy by omnipotence" (57). The scene is orchestrated in a series of movements on- and offstage, where the actual killings occur. The husband arrives at the house with his slave, and announces his assumption of the role of executioner. He first addresses himself to the rival, who responds offstage: "¿Qué es de mi espada? ¡Ay de mí!" ("Where is my sword? Woe is me!") (296). The husband exits with his sword drawn as the rival comes onstage; with the husband behind him, they both exit again. Offstage, the condemned man recognizes his guilt as the husband stabs him. While the rival prays for his soul, the audience hears, still offstage, the cries of the niece and her lover as they are killed. The husband then comes onstage with his slave and his wife. Pleading for time, she faints. The husband declares that he prefers to wait until she comes around to kill her, because he wants her to feel her death ("Quiero que sienta la muerte" 296). Her senseless body remains onstage while husband and slave exit again and kill the animals and male and female servants and slaves. The wife recognizes her error and asks for confession, a request the husband grants. The incorporation of the outward signs of religion and repentance into *Comendadores* helps establish the ceremony in its entirety as a "long, public confession" (Foucault 44).[19] Later, in his report to the king, the husband narrates her end: "Y ya de su culpa absuelta, / La misma espada que ciño, / . . . / Pasó su pecho seis veces" ("Once she was absolved of her guilt, this same sword I am wearing . . . stabbed her through the breast six times") (299).

During this scene, the rivals' servant and the wife's female slave come onstage wrapped in mats in an attempt to hide from the husband's vengeance; their comic dialogue alternates with that of the husband and his slave as they go after their other victims one by one. The scene has a festive air, a result not only of the comic presentation of the servant and slave but also of the husband's puns and conceits as he goes about his grim business (296–97). Foucault speaks of the carnival aspect of public executions (61), and Barker of the conflation of terror, violence, and celebration of the public spectacle of corporal punishment. Donald Larson also comments on the carnivalesque tone of the scene, explaining it in terms of the collective celebration of the Veinticuatro's "fall and restoration" (62). While both the excess of the punishment and the celebratory air surrounding it can be interpreted in the context provided by these critics, McKendrick proposes another reading linking the comic tone of the scene with ridicule of the husband ("Celebration or Subversion"). In Chapter Five, I explore the relationship between the disproportionate reassertion of masculinity and the high degree of feminization to be redeemed.

Vitoria offers variations on the same conventions: the secret return, the flight and pursuit on- and offstage, the recognition of guilt and (rejected) plea for confession, and the husband's puns: "La roja cruz de Santiago, / . . . / sirvió a la espada de blanco" ("The red cross of Santiago . . . served as the sword's target" [*blanco* meaning both "target" and "white"]) (448). After locking the room harboring the corpses, the husband sits down to write to the father of the dead man. The rival's servant has hidden under the table, which the husband pounds with his fist as he writes. After the husband leaves, the female slave enters, "covered with flour," having hidden in a flour bin. In addition to the conventional comic device of the "enharinamiento" (a character covered in flour) and the beating unwittingly administered to the servant by the husband, the scene of corporal punishment ends on a note of scatological humor: the servant swears he was so afraid he "perfumed" the writing table (450).

In other texts, the husband decides to avoid making both dishonor and recovery of honor public by concocting intricate scenarios that make the deaths of wife and rival look accidental or as if they were caused by someone else. But while the majority of the other characters in such texts may be deprived of their "right" to be witnesses and guarantors of the spectacle of punishment (Foucault 58), the audience is always privy to the fundamental exercise of power that is taking place.

After he has left his wife gagged and bound, the duke of *Venganza* tells his rival, his own illegitimate son, that he has captured a nobleman who was plotting against him, and asks that Federico kill him. After some hesitation, Federico exits and stabs the hooded figure offstage. The duke observes, sharing the offstage violence with the audience: "Aquí lo veré. Ya llega..... [sic] / Ya con la punta la pasa" ("From here I shall see it; now he's arrived..... now he stabs her with the point of his sword") (271). Then the duke shouts for help, saying that Federico has killed his stepmother upon learning that she was pregnant and he would be disinherited.[20] The marquis enters and stabs Federico when he comes back onstage. Besides the audience, Aurora, abandoned by Federico for Casandra, seems to be aware of the punishment disguised by the duke's scenario. The duke warns her that she, and by extension the audience, should take what has happened as an example (363). Her response indicates that she has been sufficiently terrorized by the spectacle to forego any like offense against her future husband and patriarchal law.[21]

In *Toledano,* the husband pretends to pardon his wife and rival when he surprises them embracing in his house. Determined to keep his vengeance secret, he bides his time until he catches the rival swimming in the river alone. He strangles him and then calls for help, saying that the rival drowned. The stage directions describe how the husband confronts his rival with his knowledge of the offense and overpowers him; the actual murder takes place offstage (617–18). In a tearful confrontation with his wife, the husband tells her he intends to punish her adultery by killing her. He leads her offstage, and the maid enters and reveals that she has heard everything. Like Aurora in *Venganza,* the maid perceives the husband's metatheatrical orchestration of his wife's death. After the maid's brief speech, which positions her and the audience as witnesses of the spectacle of punishment, the husband enters "lleno de tierra y la mujer en los brazos ahogada" ("covered with dirt, and his wife, suffocated, in his arms") (620). The corpse remains onstage while the husband calls servants and neighbors together to hear his false story (he says she was crushed by a falling beam of the house). Counting on the efficacy of the spectacle of his vengeance, he asks for the maid's hand in marriage:

> me he quedado con luto,
> porque trayéndole yo
> se acuerde la mujer nueva
> . . . .
> que no hay hombre tan valiente
> que, viendo la horca presente,
> se atreva a matar otro hombre.
>
> (623 [14])

The display of the wife's corpse stands in stark opposition to the secluded lives of respectable Spanish women, symbolizing the rupture of the enclosure enforced by iron grills and of the feminine-gender attributes of chastity and *vergüenza.* This public exhibition converts the body into a visible sign of the vengeance of the husband/king. Barker's remark concerning "The Anatomy Lesson" by Rembrandt could serve as epithet to these plays: "A life has just been extinguished; but a body is being made to signify" (73). These scenes partake of the "overt, celebratory bodiliness" of the penal scaffold (73) and share in the moral sanction that surrounds such scenes.

The presentation of the corpses is achieved in some texts through a stage mechanism that was very popular in the *comedia:*

the *apariencia,* or discovery.[22] In some of these plays, a curtain covering the back part of the stage was drawn to reveal a tableau composed by the corpses of wife and rival. In *Vitoria,* Valdivia sends the father of the dead rival the key to the room where he can find their bodies: "Descubren un tafetán, y vese Don Antonio, y Doña Leonor muertos en un estrado" ("A cloth is drawn and Don Antonio and Doña Leonor are seen dead on a platform") (452). The corpses are displayed in a similar fashion at the end of *Venganza*: "En tanta / Desdicha, aun quieren los ojos / Verle muerto con Casandra. (Descúbrales.)" ("In so much misfortune my eyes still see him dead with Casandra. [They are revealed.]") (271).

The Persistence of Female Desire

The warnings directed at *Venganza*'s Aurora and *Toledano*'s maid in the presence of the disgraced wife's corpse highlight the enforcing function of the spectacle of punishment, restricting female behavior to the feminine ideal through terror. But at the same time, such endings also make evident the *need* for such control and the difficulty, if not impossibility, of completely annihilating or absorbing female energy. The elimination of the transgressive wife and the remarriage of the male subject at the end of *Comendadores, Vitoria,* and *Locura* signify the exchange value of woman in the phallic economy: the murdered wife and the new wife are literally exchangeable.[23] Yet the very system of exchange of women that founds patriarchal culture and establishes the male subject necessitates entry into a precarious situation in which each wife may escape the control of her husband.

The replacement of one wife with another implies that the slippage from good to bad just represented and punished could happen again. Such a pernicious cycle would necessitate the reconstitution of the husband's sovereignty in a ceremony of punishment repeating itself *ad infinitum.* As Ruth El Saffar points out, the repression of the feminine in early modern Spain leads to a constant state of hypervigilance and fear for the individual male subject (174). And the repressed does return. In these honor plays, force masters the body of the criminal wife, re-imposing the fundamental dissymmetry between subject and sovereign. But *Locura* suggests that even this does not completely assuage the fear that female sexuality may ultimately escape patriarchal control. After he has murdered his wife, the husband is beside himself when he sees a woman who looks like her: "¿Todavía os inquieta? / ¿Muerta amáis? ¿Muerta sentís? / ... / ¿Aun muerta viene a ofenderme?" ("You are still agitated? Dead you still love? Dead you still feel? ... Even dead she comes to offend me?") (319–20). The male subject's perception that female desire persists even beyond death leads to a spiral of violence, as the husband pursues his wife's double: "Pero, ¿qué mal puede hacerme, / que otra vez muerte la doy?" ("But what ill can she do me, for I can kill her again?") (320).

The profound ambivalence towards femininity that manifests itself in the need to split the sign for woman into her consoling, controllable aspect and her threatening, controlling one eventually contaminates the strict division between the two, blurring the line between ideal wife and sexual outlaw. In *Carlos,* as in other texts of this type, the female outlaw, Casandra, is represented alongside the virtuous Leonora, to whom Carlos has been married in secret for many years and with whom he has had a son. There is a disquieting similarity between these two female characters that is not dispelled by the end of the play. The transgressive wife is banished, but in spite of her willing embrace of punishment, the threat she represents has not been completely assimilated or expulsed. The text associates Casandra with Medea, in plotting to revenge herself on Carlos by murdering his children: "Que en crueldades venceré á Medea, / ... / Que hoy bañaré de sangre tuya el suelo" ("In cruelty I will surpass Medea, ... for today I will bathe the ground in blood that belongs to you") (475). Yet there is something skewed in this association, since Medea's crime lies in murdering her own children. In effect, the real Medea in the play is Leonora, whose monstrous desire is displaced onto the transgressive wife. When Leonora learns that Carlos has betrayed their pact of secrecy by telling the duke they are married, she threatens to kill their son in language that is as bloodthirsty and violent as Casandra's: "¡Su sangre me ha de teñir / El vientre donde le tuve[!]" ("His blood will stain the womb that held him!") (479). Since she partakes in the feminine, Carlos believes her capable of the most heinous deeds, even parricide:

60

Que es hembra, quiere bien, de celos llora,
Y cuando su venganza solicite,
Ni al hijo mirará, padre ni hermano,
Sino teñir en sangre espada y mano.

(479 [15])

The discourse on monstrosity, then, is not confined to the female outlaw, but is generalized as an attribute of femininity itself ("Que es hembra" ["For she is female"]). The contextualization of such a trait in the realm of motherhood reveals how close to the surface the repressed maternal lies in the idealized image of the virtuous wife.[24]

Although she secretly remarried after the death of her first husband, Leonora masquerades as inconsolable widow to prevent her brother the duke from arranging another marriage for her (476–77). Just as Casandra's masquerade ultimately fails, Leonora is made to appear ridiculous when Casandra unmasks her and casts her in another role that associates her maternity with a lack of respectability, the use of the verb *parir* underlining a crass physicality that Leonora attempts to idealize in her masquerade: "Que yo sé una melindrosa / Que ya dos veces parió" ("I know of an affected prude who has already borne two children") (477). In spite of the overlapping characterization of Casandra and Leonora, they continue to be opposed at the end: "Y de rodillas agora, / . . . / Pido perdón, perdón pido; / Que su bondad me ha vencido" ("And on my knees now . . . I beg pardon, for their goodness has conquered me") (487). The contradiction is never resolved, and Casandra's punishment is undermined by the presence of the same qualities in Leonora.

Locura offers another example of how the representational tactic of doubling woman into her consoling and threatening aspects fails to punish female desire or bring it completely under masculine control. Princess Blanca does not conform to the feminine ideal of *vergüenza;* she is aggressive in the pursuit of the object of her desire, Floraberto. The king has married Floraberto to Flordelís to prevent Blanca from marrying him, a match the king judges inferior to his daughter's station. Even after the forced marriage, Blanca tells Floraberto that if he had wanted, he could have found a way to remedy the situation: "Puertas tienen los jardines, / ventanas los aposentos" ("Gardens have doors, bedrooms, windows") (289). Floraberto fears her desire, which he characterizes as excessive (296). When his servant reports to Blanca that not only does Floraberto say he loves Flordelís but also sleeps with her every night, Blanca plots her revenge. Yet after Flordelís's death motivates the king to punish Blanca's brother, Floraberto's rival, Blanca turns against the prince and defends Floraberto, who has lost both sanity and honor (312). She swears to pressure the king into helping Floraberto (313), and the machinery does in fact get set into motion to return Floraberto to the court and restore his sanity, indicating that Blanca controls the narrative behind the scenes.[25] At this point in the action, all seem to be fulfilling their desire except Blanca (317). Yet at the end of the play, she gets exactly what she wants: the king names Floraberto both Great Constable of France and his son, giving him Blanca in marriage (323). The fact that Blanca has no lines at this juncture reveals woman's role as object of exchange between the king and Floraberto, but it also heightens the sense that female desire may slip through the cracks of narrative and patriarchal control.

These texts' contradictory representation of woman subjected by the all-powerful sovereign/husband and woman who evades total control gives special force to one of the topoi in sixteenth- and seventeenth-century discourses on femininity, namely, the futility of trying to contain it. In *Discreto,* Alberto finds himself frustrated in his attempts to traffic in women with Leonelo, exchanging his virgin sister Hipólita for Leonelo's widowed sister. When he tries to convince Hipólita that Leonelo is a better match for her than Felisardo, to whom she is attracted, Hipólita tells him she knows why he prefers Leonelo, and leaves the house disguised as a man to thwart her brother's plans. Immediately following this scene of gender confusion and role reversal, Alberto ponders the futility of safeguarding woman in the face of her desire:

> No por guardar a la mujer se puede
> tener segura; que en el agua escribe
> quien de cuidado y celos se apercibe,
> y mayores sucesos le concede.
>   Y así es razón que de su industria quede
> burlado el que su gusto le prohibe;
> que es animal que en confianza vive,

y, en queriéndole asir, al viento excede.

. . . .

    que mientras más la aprietan más se huye;
porque es como tomar puño de arena,
que por cualquiera dedo se desliza.

(217 [16])

Although applied to an unmarried woman whose desire can be licitly channeled by the end, the elemental images of water, wind, and sand that resist permanence, capture, and enclosure speak to a general failure that haunts these texts, the failure to rid woman of her desire.[26] The husband can kill the woman to end her desire, but it may resurface in another woman or persist in his imagination after her death.[27]

Los embustes de Fabia

Even though the feminine is never utterly incorporated or expelled, even in Lope's wife-murder plays, *Fabia* is unique among them in the wife's systematic and unpenalized challenge to male authority.[28] *Fabia* reverses the scenario of male dominance that characterizes Lope's honor plays in general. In Lope's other honor plays, the wife's relationship to male authority determines her fate: in the majority of texts she is rewarded or punished for recognizing or spurning the law. The few wives who evade the physical penalty for adultery (in *Ferias, Rústico,* and *Cuerdo*) do so as a by-product of male homosocial relations. The triumph of these unfaithful wives has less to do with their own desire than with the dynamics of cuckoldry played out in a male hierarchy. They suffer neither death nor flogging nor banishment only because another, more masterful male dominates their husbands.[29]

Fabia is the female outlaw who stays beyond the reach of the law. Her adultery and silence surrounding her honor transgress two of the mechanisms that would contain her within the social order: marriage and the feminine ideal.[30] Although Fabia escapes the confines of male desire, she is still in some sense defined by it. She represents, not the "real" woman in contradistinction to the signs for good or bad wives in Lope's other honor plays, but male fantasies and fears concerning the "enigma" of femininity, oscillating between "wholeness" and "lack," "active" and "passive." The unease stimulated by the "enigmatic"

63

character of woman usually leads to her domination and the reinforcement of sexual boundaries. A text like *Fabia,* which undertakes this move but never successfully concludes it, supports the thesis that the project of assimilating woman within the boundaries of patriarchal law can never be complete or final, "for reasons which have to do in part with the nature of male desire itself" (Modleski 117).

Fabia obstructs her husband's "right" to take the lives of both wife and rival by plotting to have him killed first. At the beginning of the first act, the aged senator Catulo suspects his young wife of adultery with Vitelio. Fearing for her life, Fabia promises herself to another suitor, Lelio, in payment for assassinating her husband. Usually, when the transgressive wife controls the narrative in this way, her enjoyment of power is short-lived and even fatal; the ideal wife, on the other hand, influences the development of the story line with the goal of restoring male ascendancy. Fabia guides the action towards the realization of her own desire, and in this text, it is the male characters who are in charge only temporarily. When Catulo learns of Fabia's scheme to have him murdered, he persuades Lelio to slay Fabia instead by informing him of her intention to marry Vitelio once free. But Catulo is incapable of permitting Lelio to enact the text he has authored, and stops him before he stabs Fabia. In the second and third acts, Fabia continues to outwit Catulo by playing the part of the perfect wife, preventing him from drinking a glass of poisoned wine and resisting the emperor's desire for her (all the while dallying with a third suitor, Belariso). It is even insinuated that the author engineers the intervention of Nero (who hears of Fabia's beauty and orders her to be brought to the palace) to counterbalance a feminine narrativity negatively marked as "wrong" or "without reason."[31] The emperor's efforts to gain the upper hand are as abortive as Catulo's. At the end of the third act, Catulo poisons himself to avoid being dishonored by Nero; Fabia pretends to follow his example, only to return to life once she is left alone with Vitelio. She stages this false suicide to prevent the fulfillment of the emperor's desire and ensure that of her own for Vitelio.

Many of Lope's honor plays set up similar triangular situations in which the husband's rival is the king or heir to the throne.[32] When the husband's loyalty to the Crown ties the hand that would strike out in vengeance, the wife is trapped between husband's honor and sovereign's power. In those cases in which death removes the husband as blocking figure of royal desire, the wife has no other recourse but that of marrying her king. Fabia slips through this knot, transforming the mutually exclusive "either/or" of narrative into "neither/nor" by inventing a middle ground not programmed by the play's beginnings.[33] Her *representation* of the act of self-negation leads in fact to the constitution of herself as subject.

The male characters in the text are unsettled by Fabia's traveling between the positions of object and subject of desire. Virtually all the men in the play desire her, while it is her desire for her lover Vitelio that sets the plot in motion. The fact that she acts on her desire wins her the epithets of lascivious, crazy (82), false, unchaste, cruel (83), and frivolous (93). At the same time, her facile changing of partners usurps the usual male prerogative of objectification, commodification, and circulation of love objects. In *Vitoria,* the husband warns the father of his rival that if he is forced to slay the adulterers, the father could never replace his son, whereas the husband could find a thousand women in exchange for his wife (443). Fabia's servant Camila turns this statement around, proclaiming that all women, and especially Fabia, will find a thousand men for one they can't stand (95). In the course of the action of the play, Fabia transfers her erotic attention from Vitelio, to Lelio, to Belariso, and back to Vitelio.

It is not only through her desire that the text constructs Fabia as subject, but also through her knowledge. Both knower and active subject of desire are male-gendered subject positions in Lope's honor plays; in the representation of woman, "sexuality and knowledge are usually mutually exclusive" (Modleski 61). The entrance of the male subject into the symbolic order is the result of his quest for knowledge concerning origins and sexuality. If the activity of knowing both defines masculine identity and constructs woman as the object of man's knowing, the woman who knows is threatening. Catulo's description of Fabia's knack for "softening" his resolve suggests that her knowledge emasculates him: "y de su ingenio y celestial tesoro / sacara tales cosas que decirme, / que al lince ablande cuando esté más firme" ("she will produce such things to tell me from her trove of celestial wit that could soften the lynx when he is most firm") (83). While the reversal of gender roles is a constant in the plots of many of these texts, they generally end with the reinstatement of the "proper" distribution: male ascendancy and female subordination. This second reversal never takes place in *Fabia;* she becomes neither "proper" nor "proper-ty" by the end of the play.[34]

The text attempts to maintain the opposition between knowledge and sexuality with the figure of Brisena. In the emperor's later rejection of Brisena, he will enunciate a criticism of intelligent women which discloses the uselessness of the unattractive woman as object of male heterosexual desire, as well as the underlying fear of the woman who knows his secrets and weaknesses:

> no es cuerdo el hombre, antes loco,
> que busca mujer discreta.
> . . . Porque se sujeta
> a quien ya le tenga en poco.
> Entenderá su flaqueza,
> y con su bachillería
> le ofenderá noche y día.
>
> (106 [17])

The woman of more than moderate wisdom endangers male dominance: "que quieren luego mandar / y ser cabeza de todo" ("then they want to give orders and be the head in everything") (106). The thinking woman appropriates the male franchise to be the "head," with its dual associations of "leader" and "brain"; the sexual woman is content to be a body. The separation of the two characteristics in different women—one desirable, the other not—is designed to soothe male fears and insecurities, a comfort destroyed by the existence of Fabia, at once sexual and wise. Although in comparison to Brisena, Fabia stands out as "la cifra de las bellezas" ("the embodiment of beauty" 89), the text privileges her mental qualities, unlike the majority of Lope's honor plays. When Nero sees Fabia, he is confirmed in his desire by her physical perfection (108), but he errs in viewing her only as a body, the object of his desire. It is Fabia's "head" that enables her to elude him.

As the title of the play indicates, Fabia excels in the fabrication of ingenious tricks or deceptions ("burlas," "embustes," or "industrias").[35] The ability to manipulate reality and others through "burlas" can be a double-edged sword in Golden Age literature, ultimately turned against the perpetrator ("el burlador burlado"). At the end of Lope's other play with "embustes" in the title, Celauro the trickster is unmasked and punished. The protagonist of *Caballero,* who lives off his inventive deceits or "milagros," meets the same fate. But not Fabia. Following Fabia's assault on his life, Catulo tries to protect himself by having her taste his food and wine for poison before dining, which prompts Fabia to concoct an elaborate trick. She proposes a toast, drinking first from the cup in which she has placed roses from one side of her coiffure. Before Catulo can drink, she reveals that she has added poisoned roses from the other side, and explains the trick's purpose: to show man's ignorance and powerlessness compared to woman (97). Verbal explanations of the ruse do not suffice to convey the lethal power of Fabia's knowledge: she forces a slave who has been condemned to death to drink the poisoned wine; his grimaces and contortions signify Fabia's power visually as well.

With her fake suicide, Fabia converts her own body into a signifier of her proficiency with poisons. To her able willingness to take others' lives she adds the simulacrum of her own death. As in the scene of the poisoned toast, the subterfuge is followed by its exegesis: "que aquella muerte fingí / por que el traidor me dejase" ("I feigned that death so the traitor would leave me alone") (110). Fabia's hoax blurs the boundary between life and death in order to control sexual access to her body and to preserve the right to organize her desire independently of efforts to transform her into passive object.

The unfolding of Fabia's powers consolidates the male characters even as it dominates and intimidates them. Her plot to assassinate Catulo, in particular, draws the male characters together against her. Fabia's cognitive domination of the surviving male characters at the end dislodges them from their status as subjects in the relationship of exchange. While it is not unusual for an old man married to a young woman to be ridiculed in Golden Age literature, in this text *all* the male characters are dominated and deceived by a female subject, including the young rivals Lelio and Vitelio, and Nero, representative of absolute male power. None succeeds in regaining his masculinity in relation to Fabia.

Fabia's hovering between life and death prolongs the anxiety of the male characters. Catulo imagines Fabia's divine features bloody and cold in death, as he watches her and Lelio, wanting and not wanting the death he has contracted (86). A second description belongs to Nero, who invites all present to observe the physical changes taking place in Fabia's body after she has taken poison:

> El alma salir porfía
> . . . .
> y el hermoso cuerpo agravia.
> Ved vueltos los bellos ojos
> . . . .
> Ved muerta la viva grana
> y ved la nieve amarilla,
> y en una y otra mejilla
> la de la muerte inhumana.
> Mirad cárdeno el rubí,
> la mano ya helada y floja.
>
> (109 [18])

In other texts featuring transgressive female desire, the husband tries to arrest woman's oscillation between active subject and passive object of desire by putting his wife to death. For Sarah Kofman,

> to make a dead body of woman is to try one last time to over-come her enigmatic and ungraspable character, to fix in a definitive and immovable position instability and mobility themselves. . . . For woman's deathlike rigidity . . . makes it possible to put an end to the perpetual shifting back and forth between masculinity and femininity which constitutes the whole enigma of "woman." (223)

Here, Fabia's "dying" and return to life further extends the unbearable movement between poles, just as Nero's description captures a transitional moment between a live body and a corpse. The ending of the play does not halt this movement: she is Vitelio's object of desire once more, but a Vitelio who offers himself to her in bondage to her superior knowledge and power. She has exploited appearances to win the object of *her* desire, a dynamic project underlined by her words: "Vitelio, mucho me cuestas; / mas ya de nuevo te gano" ("Vitelio, you cost me a great deal but now I win you again") (110).

The image of Fabia as phoenix mirrors the unsuccessful endeavor to either subdue or eliminate woman: "F: Ya como el fénix me mira. / V: . . . / que de la ceniza muerta / a nueva vida respira" ("F: Behold me now, like the phoenix. V: . . . breathe new life from the dead ashes") (110). But the idea of rebirth implies not only the physical return to life but a change of morals as well: "Ya murieron mis costumbres; / otra soy, y siempre tuya" ("My old ways are dead; I am a different person, and yours forever") (110). The dualistic definition of woman's nature at the beginning of the play—she is either very bad or very good—seems to call for this moral rebirth at the end.[36] The "new" Fabia supposedly negates the "old" Fabia, as the traits of the former presumably take the place of those of the latter (private sexual property versus circulation, object versus subject, faithfulness versus many love objects, etc.). But in her fluid passage between extremes throughout the play, Fabia escapes the rigid binary positions.

Given her subversion of binary oppositions up to this point in the text, it is more likely that Fabia's claim to moral rebirth exemplifies her expert masquerade, or "performance" of the feminine ideal. Fabia is the only female outlaw in Lope's honor plays for whom masquerade is not a failed strategy ending in death or punishment. From the beginning, the shameless Fabia impersonates the ideal wife. Catulo's accusation of adultery inspires her indignant response: "¡Oh, Senador, sabe Dios / que te sirvo humilde y casta!" ("Oh, Senator, God knows that I serve you humbly and chastely!") (77). Camila knows that no matter what her mistress does, Fabia will be able to placate her husband with false tears (77). The (untrue) news of Catulo's death furnishes the opportunity for a counterfeit fainting spell, followed by plans to don hypocritical mourning ("luto fingido" 87). Camila is eager to publicize this image of Fabia as "ejemplo de mujeres casadas" ("exemplar of married women") (85). Later, Fabia announces that she devised the toast trick to demonstrate her faithfulness (96). The culminating act in her masquerade is of course the sham suicide. Her self-annihilation seems to resemble that of the wife in Lope's *Corona,* who disfigures her body with a torch to quench the king's desire, but

Fabia only mimes a gesture taken from the repertory of the "constant wife" persona that she assumes with such skill.

Does she not merely continue the masquerade with Vitelio, motivated by his negative reaction to her open pursuit of her desires? Vitelio's words, calling Catulo's presumed death the "espejo de tus infames costumbres" ("mirror of your infamous ways") (86), echo in her own: "Ya murieron mis costumbres" ("My old ways are dead") (110). Her careful phrasing would seem to indicate that Fabia is playing the part of the passive, subordinate wife to quell the fears that her independence aroused in him. The adoption of this role does not necessarily mean the negation of her other selves. When Fabia contemplates the public dissemination of her image as bereft widow, she replaces the imminent "death" from sorrow with the idea of her dying of laughter at her deception: "que la muerte del infame / me tiene muerta . . . de risa" ("for the death of that vile man is killing me . . . with laughter") (85). At the end, the irrepressible mirth of female plurality bubbles once again under the masks of grief and constancy. As Luce Irigaray puts it,

> the force and continuity [of woman's desire] are capable of nurturing repeatedly and at length all the masquerades of "femininity" that are expected of her. . . . (Re-)discovering herself . . . could only signify the possibility of sacrificing no one of her pleasures to another, of identifying herself with none of them in particular, *of never being simply one.* (27, 30)

Fabia's pleasure in her multiplicity erodes the binary programming of this narrative, and resists the confinement of woman and her desires within the boundaries of male desire.

I have dedicated so much space to this text because of its anomalous character. *Fabia* is an early experiment which was not repeated. Lope could have written it as early as 1588, a date which would make it one of his earliest honor plays. Perhaps the young Lope identified with the female outlaw who soars above social strictures, because he himself felt marginal and insecure in the dominant culture for his lack of noble blood, and possibly for his "impure" blood. Fabia was an ideal figure for the displacement of the escapist fantasies of the audience, stifled by the demands of a suffocatingly repressive society. As the national crisis deepened and anxiety at the decline of

Spanish hegemonic power escalated, the need grew for representations of a secure identity, constructed as both national and masculine, that required the incorporation or destruction of woman, and the transformation of masochistic suffering into sadistic control. Yet even in the majority of the later texts, the feminine is never totally absorbed or eradicated. This analysis of *Fabia* merely documents the most daring of ways in which woman escapes the places to which the seemingly monolithic structure of the honor play consigns her.

Chapter Three

Secular Saints

The remaining thirty-eight texts that comprise the pool of honor plays examined in this study depict wives who conform to the feminine ideal. The complexity of the sign of the "good" wife has to do with the split status of woman within the phallic economy: her use value in private ownership—physical attractiveness and procreative capacity—and her exchange value in male homosocial circulation (Sedgwick). Once the exchange between men has been transacted in the marriage contract, the wife's beauty continues to be an asset in private ownership, but it also represents the liability that she can be put back in circulation by becoming other men's object of desire. *Alfreda* dramatizes this dangerous schism in female beauty. Pressed by his vassals to provide heirs to the throne, the reluctant king is finally convinced by a portrait of Alfreda. Sent to verify her beauty, Count Godofre usurps the king's legitimate access to his bride by marrying her himself. He explains her reclusion in a remote village by inventing a false verbal portrait of her monstrous ugliness. When the king sees Godofre's wife six years later, he tramples the rights of his vassal by taking her for himself. In the havoc that ensues when everyone learns Alfreda's true identity, her beauty bears the blame rather than illicit male desire: "ella es la misma Medusa, / todos nos transforma en piedra. / . . . / Ella es monstruo de hermosura" ("she is the very Medusa; she transforms us all into stone. . . . She is beauty's prodigy") (245). Alfreda's monstrous beauty, the cause of "so much misfortune" (241), excuses the behavior of the male characters, including Alfreda's former suitor Selandio, who tries to stab the king to prevent him from possessing her ("¡Gran rigor / tiene de Alfreda el amor!" ["Love of Alfreda demands these extremes!"] 245).

An apparent solution to woman's problematic bodiliness, captured in her dual status as private and exchangeable property, is the cultivation of the virtues that constitute the feminine ideal. *Peribáñez* works through this dilemma, transforming the wife's "beauty" into "virtue" on the discursive level of the text. The peasant Casilda is a paragon of feminine virtue, recognizing her subordination to her husband ("Ya sabes que la mujer / Para obedecer se casa" ["You already know that woman marries in order to obey"] 114). The text stresses Peribáñez's rejoicing in the prospect of having her beauty for himself (110). But he soon becomes aware of the difficulties involved in attempting to withdraw such great beauty from circulation for private use, as Casilda becomes the commander's object of desire: "¡Que un tosco villano sea / Desta hermosura marido!" ("That a crude peasant be the husband of this beauty!") (113). Peribáñez ponders the dilemma of the socially inferior man with a beautiful wife:[1]

> Erré en casarme, pensando
> Que era una hermosa mujer
> Toda la vida un placer
> Que estaba el alma pasando;
> Pues no imaginé que cuando
> La riqueza poderosa
> Me la mirara envidiosa,
> La codiciara también.
>
> (130 [19])

The Commander's judgment ("¡Dichoso el hombre mil veces / A quien tu hermosura ofreces!" ["A thousand times blessed is the man to whom you offer your beauty!"] 113) is reversed by Peribáñez in the *estribillo,* or refrain, of his lament: "¡Mal haya el humilde, amén, / Que busca mujer hermosa!" ("Cursed be the humble man, amen, who seeks a beautiful wife!") (130). As in *Alfreda,* the woman's beauty, and not male homosocial rivalry, causes the problem:

> Pero á tu gracia atribuyo
> Mi fortuna desgraciada.
>   Si tan hermosa no fueras,
> Claro está que no le dieras
> Al señor Comendador

Causa de tan loco amor.

(131 [20])

Immediately after this exposition of his predicament, Peribáñez hears that Casilda has been chaste and constant, rejecting the advances of the commander. The substitution of "beautiful" with "good" is accomplished by echoing the refrain of his previous lament: "¡Oh, cuánto le debe al cielo / Quien tiene buena mujer!" ("Oh how indebted to Heaven is he who has a good wife!") (132). This text illuminates how the wife constantly struggles to cancel the liability represented by her body through the practice of the feminine virtues of chastity, constancy, and *vergüenza*. The exaltation of the virtue of shame in particular means that the moral superiority of the good wife over the bad depends on her having "no self, no distinguishing characteristics" (Modleski 50).

The dramatic situation shared by all the virtuous wives of Lope's honor plays is that they have been placed in jeopardy by the pursuit or lies of their husbands' rivals or by their husbands' false perception of their infidelity. Paradoxically, only through these life-threatening scenarios, that may lead to the definitive extinction of their subjectivity, can they prove their adherence to their culture's definition of ideal womanhood. Casandra in *Cardona* even declares herself grateful to the rival for pursuing her (the direct cause of her and her family's banishment), since who she is ("quién soy") is defined by his existence: "porque no hay casta mujer / hasta ser solicitada. / Por él se sabe quién soy" ("For a woman is not chaste until she has been solicited. Because of him people will know who I am") (662).

The Double Bind

In their representation of the feminine ideal, these texts necessarily depict the predicament of women in patriarchal orders. Being a perfect wife means total obedience and subordination to the husband's wishes. Yet, it is no simple task to navigate the complex and contradictory waters of masculine desire.[2] Many texts portray the difficulties of the wife in complying with her husband, in spite of her willingness to do so. Teresian scholar Alison Weber, in her study of the mystic nun of Avila, clarifies that the term *double bind* refers not to "a difficult choice but rather the illusion of choice within a relationship" (45). As important as the paradoxical injunction that cannot be obeyed without disobeying is the context in which it occurs: "an intensely important relationship that is essential to the subject's self-definition" (45). Faced with an either/or situation, the good wife can choose neither without negating the masculine desire that defines her identity.[3]

An example of the double-bind situation of the ideal wife occurs in *Resistencia*. Before the rivalry with the king develops, the count is already enmeshed in the opposition between love and duty. His desire to be with his new bride conflicts with his obligation to support the king in battle against the English. His speech makes it clear that he considers staying away from the battle dishonorable and feminizing:

> ¿y yo en Belflor metido,
> como conejo tímido escondido?
> . . . .
> y que digan que el conde Gesualdo,
> muy cobarde, reposa
> entre los brazos de su amada esposa.
> . . . .
> que está haciendo labor con sus criadas,
> cuando a su Rey le obliga
> la furia de las bárbaras espadas.
>
> (203 [21])

Matilde encourages him to go, recognizing the undercurrent of violence in the count's fear of feminization: "¿Qué enojo es ese? / Salga mi lengua al paso / y ese discurso belicoso cese" ("What wrath is this? Let my tongue intervene and that bellicose discourse cease") (203). In light of Ruth El Saffar's analysis, this passage figures simultaneously the escape from the world of the mothers and the connection between military aggression and masculinity.

Ironically, the count's participation in the war brings the king and his followers to Belflor, creating the occasion for Enrique to see and desire Matilde, much to the count's consternation. When he arrives at the royal tent at the battlefield, the count is told that the king is asleep, but he suspects Enrique is with Matilde. Before, her willingness to allow him to depart for war earned her the title of "strong woman" and "matron" (204). Now the count heaps abuse on her for not preventing him from going, taking her willingness as a sign of her adultery: "Mujer que de su marido / se despide secamente, / . . . / es falsa, es fiera, es traïdora" ("A woman who dryly takes leave of her husband . . . is false, a wild animal, a traitor") (216). He channels the aggression he is unable to direct at the rival-king against Matilde in a fantasy of devouring and dismemberment:

> Y luego con estos dientes
> matar la que está en sus brazos
> y enviarla hecha pedazos
> a sus infames parientes.
>
> (216 [22])

Since in the double-bind situation, the wife cannot speak without being wrong, she may opt for silence upon finding herself besieged by the rival on one side and fearful of her husband's reactions on the other. In *Hungría,* Leonor keeps silent to prevent her husband's murder of the rival, which would result in public dishonor (30–31).[4] After a nobleman saves her from being raped by the rival, the wife of *Indicios* begs him not to tell her husband, "porque aun dudas no consiente / la pureza de mi amor" ("because the purity of my love does not consent to any doubts") (264). Pursued by the king, *Corona*'s Sol vacillates between revelation and silence, opting for the latter (587). At the end, she justifies her silence: "Callé, porque mi marido / No sospechase la infamia" ("I was silent, so that my husband might not suspect the infamy") (601). These wives are damned if they speak and damned if they do not, for their silence also leads to further dishonor.

The wife's dilemmas trap her within her relationship to her husband, and between husband and rival. By showing that *both* husband and rival are threatening to her, Lope's honor plays succeed in representing her as "radically outside the law . . . caught within a structure that needs her to ensure 'human communication' (men's dealing with other men . . .), but at the price of negating her own language and experience" (Modleski 28). While the resolution of her dilemmas leads to her negation, these texts at least delineate the paradoxical predicament of woman in the social order.

Chapter Three

The Feminine Ideal as Self-negation

As Julia Kristeva points out, the bipolar oppositions that structure narrative are represented as mutually exclusive and in need of resolution. But that resolution (narrative closure) is merely a pseudo-synthesis, since the exclusivity of choice set up from the beginning requires the absorption or negation of one of the terms. The husband's dilemma, inspired by the wife's unfaithfulness, suspected or real, requires a choice between honor and love: to choose one is to cancel the other. Since the contradiction established by the opposition of terms demands resolution, his story moves inexorably towards one or the other. Yet alternatives to bloody vengeance or sacrificing honor to love did exist in seventeenth-century Spanish society. These humane options are excluded by the "nonalternating negation" of the honor-play narrative pitting love against honor.

Narrative's potential to produce choices that preclude middle options has different consequences for male and female characters. The husband is actually constituted as male/hero/subject by this exclusivity of choice and the establishment of hierarchical difference (honor is valorized above love, male above female). The formula "I am who I am," articulated in the process of resolving his dilemma, means putting honor and his social obligations as a nobleman before all else. The affirmation of self is active, indicating his willingness and capacity to choose honor above love. On the other hand, such exclusivity of choice functions to the detriment of the female subject, for either option she chooses amounts to self-negation. If she yields to or initiates adulterous passion, she ensures her elimination at the hands of her husband. Resistance, on the other hand, involves marshaling strategies to make her "self" disappear. For the wife, "to be who she is" means putting the defense of her husband's honor above all else; the affirmation is passive, indicating her willingness to go to any lengths to negate herself.

In effect, the construction of the ideal wife in Lope's honor plays entails the perverse willingness to suffer in a context of abusive male authoritarianism. The wife is faithful to her husband, even if it means dying to defend his honor:

> y si de algo está corrida
> el alma, es sólo de ver

que no tiene que perder
por su honor más que una vida.

(Indicios 263 [23])

These characteristics are particularly exaggerated in falsely accused wives who suffer extreme and unjust punishment at their husbands' hands. Although her husband has stabbed her repeatedly and left her for dead, Laura declares: "Aunque me has muerto, Roberto, / te quiero más que a mi vida" ("Even though you have killed me, Roberto, I love you more than my life") *(Laura* 360). Hyperbole becomes fact: in this discourse on femininity, a woman's life is literally less dear than a man's honor.

It is not enough to imprison woman in a structure that negates and victimizes her; she must also give her consent to being negated and victimized. As de Lauretis notes, masculine desire "requires in its object . . . an identification with the feminine position . . . women *must either* consent *or* be seduced into consenting to femininity" (134). Those wives who are not susceptible to seduction and refuse the passive feminine position are coerced into assuming it through physical abuse and mental manipulation *(Discreto)*, eliminated *(Comendadores, Vitoria, Locura, Venganza, Toledano)*, or banished *(Carlos)*. Most wives, however, willingly embrace the standards of feminine behavior as codified in the virtues of constancy, chastity, and shame. This means effectively accepting their exclusion from the subject position, welcoming their condition as Other defined in terms of the Same. Honor plays that gravitate towards the euphoric pole reconfirm man's faith in womanly virtue, as he himself has interpreted it. Her virtues and strategies of resistance add up to self-negation; the more ab-negated and abject, the more virtuous she is.

A significant topos in the discourse of the ideal wife is her self-sacrificial consent, although innocent, to her own murder at the hands of her husband. In *Cortesía,* the husband's servant, hoping to have her himself, lies to the wife, telling her that her husband has ordered him to kill her because he thinks she is unfaithful and he wishes to marry another woman. The wife adjusts herself to the measure of her husband's supposed desire, as if he were requesting a trifle:

> Que me mates
> es justo, pues que mi esposo,
> viva yo, no ha de casarse.
> Démosle, Claudio, ese gusto.
>
> (342 [24])

Even without knowing the reason, the falsely accused queen of
Nacimiento accepts her death (496). The good wife's virtue lies
in freely choosing self-erasure.

The Heroism of Powerlessness

Faced with the onslaught of the rival's unwanted attentions, the
ideal wife mounts a campaign of "honrada resistencia" ("honorable resistance").[5] She is characterized by imagery of hardness and impenetrability that participates in the construction of
the feminine ideal as corporeal and topographical (en)closure.
In *Indicios,* the rival compares her to a stone without a soul
(255), and associates her with inviolable fortifications: "¿Qué
murallas diamantinas / tengo sitiadas yo [?]" ("After all, are
these ramparts I besiege made of diamond?") (256).[6] In the
texts featuring a falsely accused queen, this discourse of honorable resistance is supplemented by divine intervention. Powerless to defend herself when the king believes the lies of the
rival, the queen survives a long period of exile that tests her
constancy and chastity. The prevailing of her innocence at the
end, programmed in the initial oppositions of the narrative, is
represented as the result of a pressure which is at one and the same
time teleological and theological (Kristeva). In *Animal,*
Teodosia's survival in the wild is attributed to Providence (423).
After hearing her story, Lauro, a typical nobleman, urges her
to vengeance, which she rejects. He then appeals to her faith in
supernatural remedies: ". . . el Cielo te vuelva / a tu marido a
tus brazos, / la corona a tu cabeza" ("may the Heavens return
your husband to your arms, the crown to your head") (424). The
end of Act I of *Hungría* sums up the point of marshaling heav-
enly forces on the side of the queen's honor and innocence:
"que no ha de ofender el hombre / lo que Dios defiende y
guarda" ("for man must not offend, what God defends and safe-
guards") (36).

The intervention of divine forces on the part of the falsely
accused queen depends on her embodiment of the feminine

ideal. Leonor is characterized from the first moment of *Hungría* as an exemplar of virtue (28), and in spite of all her trials, she remains loyal to her husband (and celibate for twenty years). Subordinating her desire for even divine vengeance to her constancy, she criticizes the count for waging war against the king in her defense, preferring the prudent tactic of awaiting providential restoration (40–41).[7] What is being underwritten by the theological teleology of these texts, posited on passive feminine virtues, is woman's absolute obedience and subordination to masculine desire. This pressure, that is at once narrative and supernatural, indirectly authorizes woman's place in another way as well, since the instruments of her return to grace are either her sons, reinforcing her reproductive function (*Hungría, Testimonio,* and *Nacimiento*), or the acknowledgment of sexual difference and "proper" gender roles (*Animal* and *Discordia*).

In three of these texts, the falsely accused queen does finally assume an active role in her restoration,[8] in apparent contradiction to her declared faith in Providence. But the wives of *Testimonio* and *Nacimiento* are confined to passive resistance. In *Testimonio,* Mayor is merely the ground on which the conflict between the king and his sons is played out.[9] She saves the life of the son who slandered her; by prostrating herself before him and baring the breasts that nursed him, she redeems the physicality of the female reproductive body through idealized self-effacement (414). It is only when she is able to substitute a "good" son for the "bad" ones that she repudiates García and his brothers: "Mi hijo sea no mas él que me honra" ("Only he who honors me may be my son") (415). Mayor also remains loyal and submissive to the king. Before the duel between García and Ramiro, she humbles herself at the king's feet, then takes her place by the pyre on which she will burn should her defender be defeated. Her role is ever that of compliant victim ("culpada víctima inocente" ["accused innocent victim"] 419), trusting in God to punish her treacherous sons and grant Ramiro victory.

In *Nacimiento,* Queen Margarita suffers the conventional twenty-year exile, during which she remains completely inactive. The title of the play and its recapitulation at the end (". . . la historia verdadera / de *Ursón y Valentín,* Reyes de Francia" ["the true story of Ursón and Valentín, kings of France"] 525) highlight Margarita's subordinate role of providing successors to the throne. Her reinstatement is also achieved entirely through male characters, and, like Mayor, she trusts passively in the Heavens to avenge her. This confers on her son, Valentín, the status of divine instrument of revenge (503, 517). At the end she refers to the king who put her out to die as "just" for restoring her to favor (523). Described as a saint, a martyr (515) whose holy body is viewed as a relic (517), and "exemplum of women" (518 and 523), Margarita joins the pantheon of secular saints made up of wives who suffer unspeakable torment in the performance of the feminine ideal. The patient faith in God of the falsely accused queen is another facet of her "honorable resistance," as deserving of eternal glory as other wives' refusal to give in to the insistent desire of the rival: "esperando un claro día / que, para más gloria mía, / premie el cielo mi inocencia" ("awaiting the illustrious day when, to my glory, Heaven will reward my innocence") (*Pleitos* 512).

The possibility exists that the representation of feminine behavior perfect in its passivity may actually be subversive of male power. In "The Powers of Silence: The Case of the Clerk's Griselda," Elaine Tuttle Hansen examines how Griselda achieves restoration to the position of honored wife of a wealthy lord and co-ruler of his kingdom through submission and silence (231). As in the case of Lope's falsely accused queens, Griselda fulfills her culture's definition of perfect femininity "by willfully accepting, even reveling in, the powerlessness of her position" (232). The negative side of their willing embrace of subordination is readily apparent: it is "by definition both punitive and self-destructive" (232) and implies that the more they suffer the better they are; it brings the problematic reward of permanent union with a sadistic tyrant; and it presents a resolution troubling in its suggestion that "the end of the heroine's suffering must in a sense spell the end of her virtue" (233).

On the other hand, Hansen teases out other implications of Griselda's paradoxical position as a woman: "the fact that she is strong, in other words, because she is so perfectly weak" (232). Hansen proposes that a "perfectly good woman" is in some sense both insubordinate and threatening to men and to the "concepts of 'human' identity upon which patriarchal culture is premised" (232). The emphasis on the saintly virtue of the wife-queen at the beginning of Lope's texts would seem to support her thesis that virtue in a woman provokes male aggression (234), not only in the spurned rival, but on some level in the husband-king himself. Although I am wary of any suggestion that a woman can be empowered by embracing her powerlessness, or that she subvert male tyranny by refusing to resist it (234), there is a sense in which the celebration of the perfection of woman's submission in these plays entails the representation of the imperfection of male power. The husband-king, in spite of his omnipotence, is, after all, unsuccessful in imposing his will on his virtuous wife. His failure to destroy her in avenging his honor reveals the limits of his power vis-à-vis the perfectly virtuous woman. He must ultimately recognize the error of his perception and the validity of her perfect virtue. [10]

The Body's Betrayal

But in some plays focusing on the feminine ideal, no amount of virtuous self-negation can overcome the liability of the body or remove it from jeopardy. Wives who adopt passive strategies of resistance are often met with the limits of feminine virtue, since the actual remedy of their situation is male-gendered. As the title indicates, Matilde of *Resistencia* is a model of honorable resistance. She staves off the king's advances during his visit to Belflor, and when he returns later and dupes her into opening the door by saying he is her husband, she escapes him once again. She pretends not to believe that he is the king, for the king would never neglect his kingly duty or betray a vassal. This deception allows her to threaten force in her rejection of him (214). But after the death of her husband, she has no power to stop the king, who forces her, dressed in mourning and in the presence of her husband's corpse, to promise to marry him within the year. Honorable resistance in itself, as represented by the very plays that extol and demand it, is clearly insufficient, hence the dependence on divine intervention in certain texts.

The female body is, in a sense, betrayed by the social relationships that define it. According to Judith Butler, "the body" cannot be separated as natural biological reality from the cultural meanings mapped onto it: "Bodies cannot be said to have a signifiable existence prior to the mark of their gender" (8). Desire and the body do not exist in opposition to culture and gender, but are spoken by and through them in a discourse that then presents female desire and the female body as "essential" or "natural." As Kaja Silverman phrases it,

> the structuration of the female subject begins not with her entry into language, or her subordination to a field of cultural desire, but with the organization of her body. That body is charted, zoned and made to bear meaning, a meaning which proceeds entirely from external relationships, but which is always subsequently apprehended as an internal condition or essence. (*"Histoire"* 66)

Narrative plays an important role in the construction of the female body. For Teresa de Lauretis, "the work of narrative . . . is a mapping of . . . sexual difference into each text," a sexual difference conceived as "male-hero-human, on the side of the subject; and female-obstacle-boundary-space, on the other" (121). Two basic functions are assigned in the "two-character drama" of dominant narrative: "mobile characters, who enjoy freedom with regard to plot space, . . . and those who are immobile, who represent in fact a function of this space" (118). In Lope's honor plays, the hero engages the rival in a struggle for possession of an object which is at the same time the site of their struggle:

> her body . . . has become her battlefield and, paradoxically, her only weapon and possession. Yet it is not her own, for she too has come to see it as a territory staked out by heroes and monsters (each with their rights and claims); a landscape mapped by desire, and a wilderness. (de Lauretis 132)

Because the body is at the same time her only weapon and not hers to possess, the tactics of the good wife to withhold her body from the rival do not always meet with success, or succeed only at the expense of that very body.

Clothing captures the dual status of woman's body, both hers and not hers, both unmistakable materiality as privately owned object of desire as well as transparent mobility as sign of exchange. In *Batalla,* the body persists stubbornly as object of desire in spite of the wife's attempts to make herself less attractive to the rival-king by dressing in shabby clothing. The plan backfires as the king proceeds to remove the wife from the husband's house on the grounds that he is not maintaining her as befits her lofty station. While clothing can signal social status or the lack of it, it cannot conceal the wife's physical desirability that cuts across class. In *Rosambuco,* a piece of clothing underlines the interchangeability of women in circulation. Her husband and the viceroy surprise the heavily veiled wife in conversation with a man. The husband attempts to enforce the legislation prohibiting the use of veils to oblige the woman to uncover herself; the unknown man defends her and the viceroy decides in his favor.[11] Terrified that her husband will recognize her by her attire, the wife asks a friend to exchange clothes with her. Later the wife denies that she has been out, but at that moment the friend's servant returns the wife's clothing, establishing her guilt in the eyes of the husband.

The ease with which one woman can stand in for another in the stream of exchange is represented comically in two texts and tragically in another. In *Peligros,* the wife's cousin desires the man who is pursuing the wife. With the aid of a female servant, she lets him into the house and allows him sexual access to her, letting him think she is the wife. Both husband and father are prepared to kill the innocent wife upon gaining proof of her adultery. The husband sets up the conventional trap, absenting himself to catch the lovers in the act. As he and his father-in-law await the appropriate moment on the street outside, the wife appears, and the identities of the lovers within are revealed. The husband in *Bella* achieves mastery over his rival by replacing one woman with another. After proclaiming to his disgruntled in-laws that his wife has kept her honor intact, he reveals that he has punished his rival by arranging for him to have sex in a dark room with a crone the rival thought was the wife. Not only are women replaceable, in this text sexual coupling with an old woman is figured comically as suitable punishment for a would-be cuckolder.

In *Estefanía,* the exchangeability of women's bodies proves fatal for the wife. The husband believes his wife is being unfaithful, but in reality it is her maid who, dressed in the wife's clothes, is trysting with the rival at night. The husband pursues the maid to his wife's bedroom and stabs his sleeping wife to death. Even though the wife's body was absent from the scene of guilt, her clothes suffice to place it in ultimate jeopardy, underlining the fundamental equivalence of women in circulation and the transparency of the sign of exchange. Estefanía's fate exposes the social construction of the body as well as of gender, especially in its public display. At the end of the play, references to the curtains surrounding the bed indicate that they were drawn to reveal Estefanía's fatally wounded body ("Estefanía en la cama, herida"). Like the sexual outlaws murdered for adultery, Estefanía's corpse signifies the visible vengeance of the sovereign/husband on the flesh of their subjects, even when that flesh is innocent of transgression.

In *Príncipe* and *Dina,* power is written on the female body through rape.[12] In these two texts, the woman's efforts to deny access to her body are simply overcome by force. As in *Resistencia,* the wife's honorable resistance in *Príncipe* is ultimately dependent for success on the physical presence of her husband; in his absence, Blanca is raped by the rival-king. The scene of the rape constructs woman and the female body as "site of male pleasure" (de Lauretis 149–50) and power: when she asks why he has entered her room, the king replies "a gozar una mujer" ("to enjoy a woman") (145), reflecting woman's reduction to the level of object and the underlying interchangeability of women.

Just as her body is hers and not hers, the wife's rape is her and yet, more importantly, her husband's dishonor. For his homecoming, Blanca drapes house and servants in black and destroys the gardens. Astonished at the evident signs of mourning, knowing of no death in the family, the husband expresses his reluctance to acknowledge its possible cause in the recurring refrain, "¿Cómo tanto luto negro / Si no es muerta doña Blanca?" ("Why so much black mourning, if Doña Blanca is not dead?") (147–48). When Blanca enters, completely enveloped in black, the husband fails to recognize her, and asks who she is. She replies simply "una mujer" ("a woman"), echoing the rival-king's instrumentalization of her and indicating that she has lost the status of wife in her failure to protect her husband's honor: "M: ¿Cuya? B: Tuya solía ser" ("M: Whose? B: I used to be yours") (148).[13] Declaring that she now is "worth less" ("¡Menos valgo!"), she reveals that it is the death of his honor that requires the mourning. At first he refuses to believe her, because he has confidence in the efficacy of her chastity. But as she narrates how she was raped at knifepoint, he is made to understand that feminine virtue is not enough, given the liability of the body. Since only through woman could such a man as her husband be dishonored (148), and only blood can wash away the stain of dishonor, Blanca tries to kill herself with her husband's sword (150). She takes upon herself the guilt and responsibility for her rape and her husband's dishonor, caused by another man using his sexual property. When she persists in her desire to die for her "sin" even after the death of the rival (158), her husband and brother-in-law insist on her virtue and swear they have restored her good name through vengeance. While she can be convicted of her bodiliness, no action of hers can suffice to redeem it; this can be accomplished only by the male subject, since her body has been constructed in terms of his honor in the first place.

Even though she upholds and ultimately represents the sanctity of marriage and kinship, the wife may have to "die" (symbolically as in *Príncipe* or literally as in *Estefanía*), sacrificed on the altar of her husband's honor, since the rival's desire lies outside her control, and her only recourses in avoiding the threat to her husband's honor are passive and reactive. These texts point to the sameness underlying the euphoric plot (continued marriage) and the dysphoric one (death). If the euphoric plot signals the "ability to negotiate with sexuality and kinship" (DuPlessis 3) and the dysphoric "inabilities in this negotiation" (4), Blanca has "failed." She signals her "death" by dressing the body which has occasioned her disgrace in mourning and asking her husband to kill her. The logical extension of this blending of the euphoric and dysphoric would be the wife's suicide to maintain the sanctity of the marriage contract, a solution forbidden by Catholic dogma.

Unlike the husband's dishonor in *Príncipe,* in *Dina* that of Jacob and his sons caused by the rape of their daughter and sister can be repaired by marrying her to the man who has raped her. Jacob, who is satisfied that Dina's marriage to Prince Siquen restores his honor (228), believes that ". . . la venganza es bárbara en los sabios / Cuando tienen remedio los agravios" ("vengeance is barbaric in wise men when offenses have remedies") (229). Jacob's sons insist on bloody vengeance, viewing Jacob's position as cowardly expediency. Their opposition

is also related to the fact that Dina's rapist is a "mancebo
idólatra" ("idolatrous youth") (230). The religious difference
between them and their enemy becomes a crucial component
in their ruse to avenge themselves. Pretending to agree to
Dina's marriage if the prince and his male subjects accept cir-
cumcision, they take advantage of their adversaries' weakened
state to massacre them in their beds. Through this conflation,
the brothers claim superiority on the grounds of both masculinity and religion.

Dina aligns herself with her brothers, rejecting the prince's
offer of marriage and threatening him with revenge. The material compensation of queenly status can never compensate for
her hatred of Siquen (232). Faced with her father's plan, she
contrasts his "cowardly remedy" with her brothers' manly
readiness:

> . . . hermanos tengo:
> Yo sé que me vengarán.
> . . . .
> Padre, yo estoy deshonrada:
> Donde ha de cortar la espada
> No es necesario el consejo.
>
> (226 [25])

After relating the inadequacy of her resistance ("Qué llanto, qué
resistencia / Acompañaron mi honor / Hasta el fin de su trage-
dia" ["What weeping, what resistance accompanied my honor
until the end of the tragedy"] 225), Dina swears that she prefers death to remaining, unavenged, the permanent signifier of
her male relatives' dishonor: "Tu honor y mi afrenta venga, /
Si no en Siquen, en mi sangre, / Para que la tengas buena"
("Avenge your honor and my offense, if not on Siquen, then on
my blood, so that yours may be good again") (226).

Dina's complicity in her brothers' bloody vengeance needs
to be interpreted in light of the blame laid on her by her father
for her rape. Like Blanca in *Príncipe*, Dina is implicated in her
own rape because of her very bodiliness, but Dina's fault is
further specified as having to do with her active looking. In
psychoanalytic theory, with its restricted focus on the socio-
sexual journey of the boy child, the same dynamic that makes
woman the "Other" against which the male subject defines

himself operates to relegate her to the status of "to-be-looked-at-ness."[14] The woman who looks threatens the male subject's sense of identity, secured through the Oedipal quest that posits woman as object of both looking and knowing. Male anxiety about female voyeurism and the prohibition of women's pleasure in looking at other women are related to the impossibility of fixing her enigmatic identity, for example, as either active or passive (Modleski 6).

Feminist theory has disputed male ownership of the gaze by asking the question "what happens when the woman looks" (Modleski 73)? The implications of this question for female spectatorship will be addressed in Chapter Eight, which explores the feminist response to the exclusion of the female subject from the active structures of looking by examining a "wide range of gazes and forms of address" conditioned by multiple variables (Pribram 9).[15] Male monopoly of the gaze, as the editors of the provocatively titled anthology *The Female Gaze* point out, "replicates the structure of unequal power relations between men and women" (5). Texts such as *Dina,* in its punitive linking of Dina's looking and her rape, reveal the need to police the female gaze in order to enforce women's exclusion from the active looking position.

On arriving at the city of Siquen, Dina disguises herself to go out with the express purpose of seeing its women:

> Pero con justo deseo
> Veré estas damas; que creo
> Que el cielo en ellas formó
>   Una copia natural
> De su divina hermosura,
> Fuera de la compostura
> De su traje artificial.
>   Sin esto alaban también
> Sus bailes, música y danzas.
> Tal donaire en las mudanzas
> Y en las canciones se ven.
>
> (211 [26])

For Dina, all women have the desire to look: "Somos, Leazar, las mujeres / Amigas de ver" ("We women, Leazar, are fond of looking") (211). The insistence on Dina's pleasure at looking at women prepares the presentation of her rape as punishment for appropriating the male gaze. Her companion's first question when they arrive at the city is "¿Agrádante las mujeres?" ("Do the women please you?"), to which Dina replies:

> Por todo extremo me agradan;
> Y más aquestas del baile
> Con hábito de gitanas.
> . . . .
> Lindos trajes me parecen,
> Lindos talles, lindas caras,
> Lindos movimientos, Zelfa;
> Que bien sabes que la gracia
> De la mujer es el aire,
> Y aquel compás en que anda
> El movimiento del cuerpo.
>
> (214 [27])

Dina's looking leads to mutual pleasure and solidarity. The women ask her to remove her veil so they can enjoy seeing her, too: "¡Qué resplandor! / No parece el sol tan bien" ("What a glow! The sun is less brilliant") (220). Dina's response expresses her appreciation and emulation of their grooming and her aspiration to form bonds of friendship:

> Gran gusto me ha dado el veros:
> ¡Qué bien en Siquen vestís!
> ¡Qué lindos trajes usáis!
> ¿Qué os ponéis? ¿Con qué os laváis,
> Que tan gallardas salís?
> . . . .
> Muy amiga quiero ser
> De las dos. . . .
>
> (220 [28])

Siquen is attracted by Dina's looking, but he distinguishes between their gazes: "Que ella con los ojos mira / Por vana curiosidad, / Y yo con la voluntad" ("For she looks with her eyes out of mere curiosity, and I look with my will") (215). The male gaze leads to objectification and the imposition of will through sexual violence, justified by the inclusion of woman in the category of male property:

> Una mujer que me anima
> Con su hermosura, ¿qué debo

A los cielos que la crían?
Cuantas cosas Dios crió,
Son para el hombre. . . .

(218 [29])

When Dina tells her father she has been raped, stressing her desire to see the women of Siquen and her pleasure in looking at them, he immediately blames her, not only for transgressing the enclosure required by *vergüenza* ("El salir fué tu deshonra" ["Going out was your dishonor"]), but explicitly for her active looking: "Pues bien sabes que, por ver, / La más honesta mujer / Corre peligro en la honra" ("For you well know that, through looking, the most honorable woman endangers her honor") (226). Woman must not look, for, looking, she attracts the male gaze as object of desire:

No hubiera casos tan feos
Y excusara mil enojos,
Nacer la mujer sin ojos
Y los hombres sin deseos.
    Fuiste á ver, sin acordarte
Que allá te habían de ver;
Como si pudiera ser
Querer mirar sin mirarte.
    No te libras del engaño
Ni excusas de la traición,
Porque quien da la ocasión,
Ese es la causa del daño.
    Y del tuyo no te asombres
Si fuiste á ver las mujeres,
Sin mirar que, si lo eres,
Te habían de ver los hombres.

(226 [30])

Jacob's fantasy of reconstructing woman without eyes exposes the futility of reducing woman to passive object of the gaze, while the corresponding fiction, "men without desires," reveals the underlying link between the scopic drive and desire. Women, as objects of desire and the gaze, should be sightless and desireless.

Not only must women looking at women be prohibited and punished, their looking at each other must be recuperated within the heterosexual dynamic of male rivalry, honor, and revenge. Although Dina energetically refuses to bear the blame for the rape that outrages her, her desire for revenge is part of the transformation the play effects in her, leading her away from female homosocial desire and into line with masculine desire, which she makes her own. And, because the female body also bears negative meanings equating "female" with sexuality, characters such as Dina and Blanca are guilty and deserving of punishment for having a body, one that can be desired and raped.

La corona merecida

Unlike female characters whose bodies are their undoing, Sol, the wife in *Corona,* finds a solution to the seeming incommensurability of the feminine ideal and the female body. In other texts, the female characters' practice of the feminine ideal is thwarted by the body; in spite of their virtue, they experience the violation of their bodies' borders, Dina and Blanca through rape, and Estefanía through the sword of an avenging husband. In *Corona,* when honorable resistance fails to keep the body out of harm's way, it functions as a weapon turned against itself. Sol pretends to give in to the rival-king to save her husband's life, but before their meeting she burns her body with a torch. Reversing the ploy of the besieged wife in *Batalla,* whose shabby attire failed to conceal beauty or put an end to desire, Sol removes her beautiful clothes to reveal her mutilated body. She redeems her bodiliness by extinguishing the king's desire through the willing sacrifice of her body. It is not surprising that this solution is represented in only one of Lope's honor plays; although other ideal wives embrace self-negation, their bodies remain intact for the pleasure of their husbands, whereas Sol's act of self-erasure effectively ends her career as object of desire, whether licit or illicit. While other wives' bodies are marked with their guilt by male representatives of the law, Sol's glory lies in inscribing that law on her body with her own hand.

Playing with the double meaning of *fuego* ("fire" and "leprosy"), Sol pretends to have the dread disease:

> Estoy llagada de fuego,
> . . . .
> Que aunque bizarra y vestida
> Me veis, y tan adamada,

Soy manzana colorada,
En el corazón podrida:
    Mire estos brazos Su Alteza
Llenos de la sangre y llagas.

(599 [31])

The king's physical revulsion at Sol's sores resonates with the negative value attached to the female body constructed as sexuality itself:

¡Quedo, quedo! No me hagas
Más asco. . . .
    Quita estos paños sangrientos,
Que el estómago me mueven.
. . . .
    ¡Ved lo que yo deseaba!

(599 [32])

The series of metaphors contrasting a deceivingly beautiful "outside" with a dirty, empty, or black "inside" (inspired by Sol's own image of the red apple with the rotten heart) activates the topos dating from the high Middle Ages of woman as "both seductive and physically corrupt" (Gilman, "AIDS and Syphilis" 95):

¡Espada sucia y mohosa,
Con la guarnición dorada!
. . . .
    ¡Casa famosa desierta,
Con excelente portada!
¡Oh pared negra y borrada,
Con tela de oro encubierta!

(599–600 [33])

In this tradition, as Sander Gilman notes, "female beauty only serves as a mask for corruption and death" ("AIDS and Syphilis" 95–96).

As in the truth-producing ritual of torture, the wife of *Corona* marks herself with the ineffaceable signs of power, the power to punish (Foucault, *Discipline and Punish* 34), aligning herself with those characters whose raped and murdered bodies signify the sovereign power to punish the female body for its transgressive desire or for its mere bodiliness. But other meanings besides power attach themselves to Sol. By branding herself, the wife of *Corona* converts the female body itself into a monstrous sign of feminine virtue, productive of eternal fame and glory for the Spanish empire. The transformation of the guilty materiality of the female body into the transparent sign of virtuous self-negation in this text parallels the propagation of the religious symbols of virgin martyrs in seventeenth-century Spanish culture. As Mary Elizabeth Perry points out, in the face of women's increased participation in society, the discourse of the virgin martyr preserved the gender ideology that stresses woman's passivity, obedience, piety, and chastity (12, 37). In this way, women's "passion and yearning" could be channeled into a kind of "respectable" heroism which not only did not challenge the gender order, but also reinforced the devaluation of the female body (37). Mary Beth Rose also refers to the virgin martyr as a model for "a feminine mode of negative self-assertion," one of the few forms of self-assertion deemed appropriate for women ("Gender, Genre, and History" 267).

Lope's text secularizes the discourse of the virgin martyr and yokes it to the national program of surpassing classical antiquity. When the king despairs of possessing Sol, he cites classical examples of women who went to extreme lengths to defend their chastity, including one who resembles Sol: "Y si Espurina se afea / El rostro con mil heridas, / . . . / ¿Qué habrá que posible sea?" ("And if Espurina disfigures her face with a thousand wounds, what possibility is there?") (591). A courtier encourages him to keep up his siege, declaring that his examples are of Greek and Roman women, "Pero españolas, jamás / A príncipes poderosos / Hicieron ese holocausto / De sus vidas" ("But Spanish women never made such a sacrifice of their lives to powerful princes") (591). The king's reply places the spectator in the proper position for the correct reading of Sol's self-mutilation:

> Ni menos merece gloria
> Por sus mujeres España;
> Que hay muchas, como esta hazaña,
> Dignas de eterna memoria.
> Mas cuando ninguna hubiera,

Doña Sol sola bastara
Para que Roma callara
Y Atenas enmudeciera.

(591 [34])

The theme of national glory was already introduced at the beginning of the play with the mention of heroic deeds by Castilians that exceed those of Rome (568). In effect, Sol's feat is immediately assimilated into the Spanish imperial objective of competing successfully with classical antiquity in honor and fame. The wife's servant is the first to elevate her deed to this level (600), and the queen explicitly establishes Sol's eclipse of classical precedents, to the glory of Castile, at the end of the play:

Callen romanas y griegas,
Porcia, Evadne y Artemisa;
Que tú sola á todas llevas
Laureles, palmas y olivas.
España queda obligada
A la virtud peregrina
. . . .
Tú y cuántos de ti desciendan,
. . . .
Se llamen desde este día
Coroneles para siempre.

(601–02 [35])

While the discourse of Spanish competition with classical prestige seems to overshadow the Christian discourse of the virgin martyrs, the queen's reference to "Coroneles" effectively relates the two through the nexus of feminine self-sacrifice. Like Sol, Doña María Coronel disfigured her face with boiling oil to escape the desire of the king; in 1376 she founded and endowed a convent where she held the position of abbess until her death (Perry 78). If El Saffar is correct in her assessment that Spanish national identity was built on the exclusion of the female body as Other, *Corona* illustrates just what is required of women to be included in the definition of "Spanishness."

95

Chapter Four

Duplicity and Disguise

Chapters One through Three discussed wives' passive strategies of honorable resistance to adulterous desire, efforts to
redeem the liability of the body that meet with qualified success or disaster, and sexual outlaws' failed attempts to escape
the feminine position. In this chapter, I examine the duplicitous
strategies of ideal wives and their manipulation of the body
through disguise. As I pointed out in Chapter One, sixteenth-
and seventeenth-century discourses enjoining (en)closure
attempted to control women and confine them to the private
sphere. Duplicity and disguise offer the possibility of resistance
to ideological or literal containment.

Some wives resort to duplicity to subvert masculine control
of the narrative. Joan Ferrante observes that given the

> limited opportunities to exercise real power over their own
> or others' lives, women in medieval literature . . . find subtle
> or hidden ways to exercise such power, to manipulate people
> and situations and to spin out fictions which suit them better
> than their reality, by which they can or hope to control
> reality. (213)

Outwardly the perfect widow, Leonora in *Carlos* relies on masquerade to protect her secret marriage to Carlos and on her wits
to concoct opportunities to communicate with him. In the presence of Carlos and the count, who is courting her, she pretends
to drop something. While the count gropes around for the non-
existent item, she gives Carlos her glove. Carlos's reaction
indicates that such tricks are not uncommon in her (447).

In *Indicios,* when the husband's friend Felipe tells the wife,
Clara, and her cousin Inés that he is in love with a woman in
Barcelona, they decide to intercept his letters, hoping that he

will forget his lover and fall in love with Inés. The duplicity of the wife and her cousin Inés creates a chain of events that causes the husband to suspect his wife of adultery. Falsely informed that Felipe is trying to cuckold him, the husband misinterprets all the "evidence" ("indicios") of his dishonor: the two women's nervousness when he surprises them talking, Felipe's defense of Clara when he accuses her of impropriety, her reluctance to let Felipe move from their house to an inn, and the discovery of one of the intercepted letters, which he believes to be from Felipe to Clara. Whereas the attempts of transgressive wives to usurp the male role in the traffic in women end in punishment and death, the deviousness of this wife culminates successfully in Felipe's marriage to Inés.

Femininity Disguised

In other texts, wives hide behind heavy veils or change their identity by disguising themselves as rural plebeian women, beastlike creatures, and men.[1] While such devices help to resist containment, under these disguises lingers a conformity to the feminine position that tampers only partially with the codes that require the (en)closure of woman. Those female characters wearing disguises do violate the requirement of a closed mouth, by controlling the action as narrativizing subjects spinning tales of their own, and they do reject the enclosed life in the home, venturing out into the public sphere. But their bodies remain closed as male property. No text represents the independent organization of her desire by the disguised wife.[2]

In some texts, the disguise is imposed by the husband or the circumstances leading to exile in the wilderness or countryside. In *Alfreda,* the husband designs the rural disguise to conceal his usurpation of the king's bride-to-be (227). Alfreda clearly resents it, for the insult to her nobility, and also because she thinks he is motivated in keeping her from the court by doubts concerning her virtue (228). When the king arrives unexpectedly and her husband tells her to hide, she refuses with obvious delight in her play-acting ability: "que yo sé muy bien que puedo / con mi habla y mi vestido / tener un mundo escondido" ("for I know very well that I can hide a whole world with my speech and my dress") (237).

Because of the ragged clothing the king gave her when he drove her out of the palace, and her apparent lack of a husband,

Queen Margarita in *Nacimiento* is considered a "pobre ramera" ("poor prostitute") when she is found in childbirth and taken in by shepherds. Margarita bears this shameful label in silence during the long years of her exile. One day the king happens upon her while hunting, and she agrees to go to his bed. As in all the plays that engineer a meeting between husband and disguised wife, *Nacimiento* plays her true identity, known only to the audience, against the wife's double entendres ("Muy poco puedo perder, / Que ya le he dado otro sí" ["I can lose very little, for I have already said to him 'I do' "] 515). When the son arrives with news that the rival has confessed to slandering the queen, the text juxtaposes praise for the virtue of the supposedly expired queen (518) and condemnation of the supposed shepherdess's infamy (518).[3] Margarita comes full circle at the end when she and the king appear "vestidos de corte" ("in courtly attire") (522). Her costume underlines her social role, guaranteeing proper succession to the throne. Whether in rags, shepherdess disguise, or queenly raiment, Queen Margarita of *Nacimiento* signifies only passivity and use value for male sexual pleasure and procreation.

Having escaped the death ordered by the king, Leonor in *Hungría* lives disguised as a peasant for twenty years. The king, heavily besieged by the defenders of the queen's honor, flees to the countryside, where he meets his disguised wife. Struck by the resemblance between his "murdered" wife and the peasant woman, the king relives his offense. He insists on his wife's treachery, while the queen defends her virtue and condemns his rash jealousy. As she feigns fear of the harm that may come to her for her resemblance to his dead wife, the king grows in awareness that his jealousy led him to kill his wife and newborn sons unjustly (52).[4]

In her opening narrative, Teodosia of *Animal* declares that her wild appearance is a direct result of the king's power: "Fiera soy, pues que me envían / a que entre ellas viva y muera" ("I am a wild beast, for they send me to live and die among them") (429). She presents her choices as exclusive: either continue to live as an animal or be killed by the king. But when she pulls back her tangled mane, signifier of freakish animality, she discloses her beautiful face, foreshadowing her restoration to value-filled status for her use value in "making kings." In spite of her passive faith in God to restore her honor and her explicit rejection of revenge, Teodosia does take control of the narrative when she steals Faustina's newborn daughter and raises her as an animal.[5]

Unlike the falsely accused queens in *Nacimiento, Hungría,* and *Animal,* the wife of *Celauro* does not disguise herself reactively, to hide from her husband's wrath. The husband has kept knowledge of their union from his father because of his wife's poverty. When the rival leads him to believe that his wife has been unfaithful, the husband takes their children and goes off to the wilderness. The wife follows him, exchanging her clothes for those of a *serrana,* or highlander. In this disguise she enters the service of her father-in-law, who falls in love with her and wants to marry her. She agrees, hoping this new deceit will bring her husband around (130). She reveals her true identity upon hearing (false) news of her husband's death, and when he arrives on cue, indignant at the prospect of the wedding, she manages to soothe her father-in-law's hurt feelings so that by the end he recognizes their marriage and awards his grandsons a hefty annuity.

The wives of *Bella* and *Desposorio* conceal their identity with veils, in order to leave the enclosure of the home to spy on their unfaithful husbands. Their entry into the public sphere attracts a rival, initiating the process through which the husband reassumes his conjugal obligations through defense of honor.[6] Although the wives appear to be the active subjects of this process, their actions serve only to "correct" the male gender attributes of their husbands.[7] Their apparent assumption of the subject position ultimately reveals their exclusion from it, in that their very purposefulness is already constituted by male symbolic systems in which they are the sign and object of exchange.

The options for the female character sketched by Teresa de Lauretis illuminate the limitations of the wife who assumes the active position through disguise.[8] When the wife appears to take a public role, "the narrative is patterned on a journey ... whose possible outcomes are those outlined by Freud's mythical story of femininity" (139). The end of the wife's itinerary signifies not *her* fulfillment, but the fulfillment of the promise made to the "little man" (that he will find a woman waiting at the end of *his* journey): "And so her story like any other story, is a question of his desire" (de Lauretis 133). The wife of these texts is a pseudo-subject undertaking a pseudo-quest which places her in the space where the male subject might find her at the end of *his* quest, as de Lauretis suggests. He recovers honor and masculinity so that she might reassume the feminine position. Ultimately, her story always turns out to be his story.

Carolyn Heilbrun and Rachel Blau DuPlessis study this same question in terms of the gender specificity of certain narratives, namely, the masculine monopoly of quest and the restriction of the feminine narrative to romance and marriage/death plots. DuPlessis notes that in nineteenth-century narrative,

> quest and love plots were intertwined, simultaneous discourses, but at the end of the work, the energies of the Bildung were incompatible with the closure in successful courtship or marriage. Quest for women was thus finite; we learn that any plot of self-realization was at the service of the marriage plot and was subordinate to . . . the magnetic power of that ending. (6)

The passage from quest for self-realization to marriage, or, in Lope's honor plays, the reintegration of marriage, is mediated by the "proper gender role" (6).

Cross-dressing and the Theater

The same dynamic is evident in scenarios in which the wife assumes "masculine" gender attributes. The wife's masculinization, and by this I mean the assumption of the active role and other attributes monopolized by the male gender, forms part of the gender disorder that characterizes Lope's honor plays, portraying "images of ambiguous sexuality that threaten to destabilize the identity of protagonists and viewers alike" (Modleski 5). The masculinization of the ideal wife is very different from the sexual outlaw's appropriation of the active role leading to her punishment. Active female energies are tolerated if provisional and expended in the service of the male subject. Although order is eventually restored through the redistribution of proper gender roles, "female power is for a while expressed," incorporating "back into romance some of the boldness and aggression of quest, making romance temporarily the repository of female will" (DuPlessis 14).[9]

Whereas the animal-body or rural plebeian disguise signifies a step down, either from personhood or from privileged class, by cross-dressing, woman participates in the signs of the higher-valued gender.[10] Cross-dressing is by far the most subversive strategy invented by the wife to influence the course of the narrative and achieve her goals. Since she herself fabricates the body that best suits the achievement of her desires, the cross-dressed woman in Lope's honor plays contests the definition of woman as male property. Cross-dressing frees her from the restrictions, enclosure, sexual vulnerability, and passivity that define the feminine position. It empowers her to move freely in the public sphere and to act effectively to influence people or their decisions.[11] In an age in which sex roles were considered "ordained by God or nature" (Woodbridge 149), cross-dressing can call attention to femininity and masculinity as cultural constructions rather than natural essences belonging to the stable entities of "man" and "woman." For Juliet Dusinberre,

> the masculine woman and the woman in disguise are both
> disruptive socially because they go behind the scenes and
> find that manhood describes not the man inside the clothes,
> but the world's reaction to his breeches. . . . A woman in
> disguise smokes out the male world, perceiving masculinity
> as a form of acting. (244–45)

As Judith Butler points out, cross-dressing offers "sex and gender denaturalized by means of a *performance* which avows their distinctness and dramatizes the cultural mechanism of their fabricated unity" (138).[12] The woman dressed as a man reveals the inequities of gender construction, as well as the ease with which woman invades the male province and assumes attributes assigned to the "superior" sex. If the Other can be so successfully impersonated, and the borders segregating sexual categories so porous, "how secure are those powers and privileges assigned to the hierarchically superior sex, which depends upon notions of difference to justify its dominance?" (Howard 435).

In *Women and the English Renaissance,* Linda Woodbridge correlates the theatrical treatment of female cross-dressing to an actual social movement of women wearing men's clothing. In the 1570s, women in London began wearing masculine attire, complete with dagger or pistol, and even attended church dressed this way (142). Citing documents of the time, Woodbridge shows that the phenomenon, which cut across social barriers, was perceived as going beyond fashion to constitute a "deliberate challenge to the immutability of sexual distinctions" (139). After waning between 1590 and 1606, the debate peaked in intensity around 1620.[13]

While no corresponding movement of female transvestism transpired in Spain during this period, roughly corresponding with the production of Lope's honor plays, Melveena McKendrick cites the examples of Catalina de Erauso, who served in the Spanish army in America for 18 years before her sex was discovered, and of Feliciana Enríquez de Guzmán, who followed her lover to Salamanca disguised as a man, where she studied and won literary prizes before reassuming her feminine identity.[14] The female actor Bárbara Coronel wore nothing but men's clothing onstage and off (McKendrick 41). That Coronel was not an isolated case is suggested by Mary Elizabeth Perry's discussion of moralists' condemnation of "actresses who dressed as men both on and off stage" (22).[15]

Jean Howard distinguishes between cross-dressing on the public streets and in the theater, where it was "mediated by all the conventions of dramatic narrative," while recognizing that these various practices form "an interlocking grid through which we can read aspects of class and gender struggle" (418). In spite of its conventional nature, the theater, in which lowborn men and women regularly donned the clothing of the highborn and women the attire of men, helped destabilize the highly regulated "semiotics of dress," designed "to keep people in the social 'places' to which they were born" (421–22). Carmen Bravo-Villasante documents the abundance of *comedias* in which a cross-dressed woman appears and the enormous enthusiasm of the public for her appearance. J. Homero Arjona estimates that she appears in a good quarter of Lope's *comedias* (121),[16] a figure that holds true for his honor-play production as well.[17] By simply changing clothes, characters become unrecognizable. For example, Alfreda fails to recognize her former suitor Selandio disguised as a peasant (*Alfreda* 227–32), illustrating the power of the signifiers to denote both sex and status, and the ideological equation between identity, gender, and social position. Disguise makes transparent "those fixed and immutable barriers" between the sexes and social classes, blurring distinctions and "rais[ing] questions about how they are maintained" (Wheelwright 28). The veritable mania for disguise in general and female cross-dressing in particular led some female actors to specialize in this role.[18]

The interest in both real-life and theatrical transgressions of sexual boundaries as well as the persistent but unsuccessful legislation to prohibit or restrict female transvestism (McKendrick, *Woman and Society* 35) suggest a Spanish preoccupation paralleling the English with the "nature" of men and women and the fate of traditional gender roles in the early modern world (Woodbridge 153). The questions concerning Shakespearean texts raised by Howard can be fruitfully applied to Lope's honor plays as well:

> If women off the stage seized the language of dress to act out transgressions of the sex-gender system, did the theatre effectively co-opt this transgression by transforming it into fictions that depoliticized the practice? Or was the theatre in some sense an agent of cultural transformation, helping to create new subject positions and gender relations for men and women in a period of rapid social change? (428)

Lope's ten honor plays featuring female cross-dressers cluster between the years 1598 and 1613, encompassing the signing of humiliating peace treaties (1598 with France, 1604 with England, and 1609 with Flanders). This supports Woodbridge's theory that the portrayal of the woman dressed as a man may have been related to the social perception of "martial manliness" versus "peacetime effeminacy" (147). The gender confusion in so many of Lope's honor plays may have been motivated in part by the widening gap between an ideal of masculinity rooted in military performance and the peacetime lifestyle at the court. Francisco de Quevedo, in his "Epístola satírica" ("Satiric Epistle"), longs for the "good old days" when men were men and women were women, clearly relating martial pursuits to masculinity and the courtly lifestyle of his contemporaries to effeminacy. In a period in which the culture's ideal of masculinity was in crisis, fascination with and fear of aggressive women in literature does not necessarily mean that gender roles were changing or that women were becoming more assertive, but that men may have felt more threatened by the possibility (Woodbridge 262). An analysis of the exaggerated representation of the "virile woman" in Calderón's successors, including sexual desire between the cross-dressed or "masculine" woman and another female character, would illuminate attitudes towards gender in the second half of the seventeenth century.[19]

The increasing efforts to confine respectable women to the home and the increasing visibility of nonrespectable women in public places may also have contributed to the appeal of the woman dressed as a man, who claims male space for female spectators. Lope and other dramatists had to take women playgoers seriously. As Woodbridge points out, the presence of women in the theater made it necessary to produce plays they would like, but it did not make it easy (252). Different kinds of women attended the *comedia,* and different kinds of men also needed to be flattered.[20] The solutions explored in these ten texts are nothing short of ingenious. They provide women in the audience with female characters who depart from the feminine stereotypes of weakness and passivity, moving with the freedom of a man through the world, yet whose energies and decisive actions are recuperated within the narratives of romance or marriage. The sexual outlaw was too dangerous to depict with any great frequency; the aggressive woman who poses no challenge to the patriarchal order and ultimately reassumes the feminine position was the perfect complement to the passive wife whose stoic resistance might have become rather bland fare if not occasionally spiced with the woman dressed as a man.

While many Shakespearean critics point to a similar strategy in his texts,[21] the Shakespearean cross-dresser discussed by Howard who faints at the sight of blood or cannot wield a sword is conspicuously absent in Lope's honor plays. As Annette Kuhn notes, when woman fails to perform the masculine role signaled by her masculine attire, cross-dressing intensifies, rather than blurs, sexual difference (55–57). For the majority of Lope's transvestite female characters, who effortlessly perform the male role, cross-dressing is a "vehicle for assuming power" (Howard 433), however recuperated it may be by the end.

Cross-dressing is gender specific in Lope's honor plays. Men never appear dressed as women, although they do assume disguises of other kinds and do cross-dress as women in other plays by Lope and his successors.[22] As Susan Gubar points out, "the asymmetrical status accorded to men and women in our culture is provocatively illuminated by the different attitudes we inherit toward cross-dressing in the two sexes" (483).[23] In her discussion of "sexual rebels" in sixteenth- and seventeenth-century Seville, Perry remarks that while men dressed as women were ridiculed for being effeminate, cross-dressed women were considered to be lewd (127).[24] In literature, the man dressed as a woman is the subject for farce (Wolfson 609–10) or depicted as "pathetically weakened or emasculated . . . unless he is using his disguise for effecting escape or for seducing women" (Gubar 483). Within the confinement of cross-dressing to female characters, other restrictions apply. Neither the peasant wife nor the sexual outlaw ever cross-dresses or disguises herself in any way. The transgressive wife uses masquerade to achieve her goals, or simply pursues them directly, an option that is not tolerated. A text such as *Discreto* demonstrates that cross-dressing was not always the site of resistance to the sex-gender system, in that, like Shakespeare's *Twelfth Night,* it seems "to applaud a crossdressed woman who does not aspire to the positions of power assigned to men [Hipólita], and to discipline a non-crossdressed woman who does [Casandra]" (Howard 431). The key difference appears to lie in the *permanence* of the sexual outlaw's aspiration to "masculine privilege and prerogatives" as opposed to the ideal wife's transitory assumption of masculine garb in her husband's service, a disposition that partially deflects the danger signaled by her clothes (432).

The Unmarried Woman as Cross-dresser

While the majority of the female cross-dressers in Lope's honor plays are wives whose freedom of movement increases as their husbands' diminishes, in several texts an unmarried female character launches an offensive to disrupt masculine control of the exchange of women in marriage. In *Discreto,* Hipólita and her maid leave her brother's house dressed as men, complete with sword and shield (214), to subvert her brother's plans to marry her to Leonelo. Although she justifies the assumption of masculine dress in terms of women's vulnerability at night on the street (214), she also constructs the body for herself that best matches her disruptive mindset and behavior. Hipólita says she has dressed herself and her maid this way because she has divined the self-serving intentions of her brother in marrying her to Leonelo: "codicioso de su hermana, / hermosa, rica y vïuda" ("greedy for his sister, beautiful, rich, and widowed") (214). Her maid approves of Hipólita's assertive nature: "A mujer que se resuelve / no queda que aconsejar. / Animosa siempre has sido" ("It is useless to counsel a woman who has made up her mind. You have always been spirited") (214).

Hipólita thwarts her brother's plans and manages to take revenge on Leonelo as well. Passing herself off as Leonelo's rival, Felisardo, in Leonelo's presence she maliciously informs the night guard that s/he is on her way to court Leonelo's sister. Leonelo's flustered reaction reveals the subversive effect of the gender bending practiced by Hipólita and others who turn out not to be what or where they are supposed to be:

> ¡Basta que yo imaginaba
> que éste a Hipólita quería,
> y es la misma hermana mía!
> . . . .
> ¡Todo es alquimia, por Dios,
> cuanto se busca en mujer!
>
> (215 [36])

Hipólita's intervention ultimately facilitates her marriage to the man of her choice.

Catalán combines motifs from different types of honor plays: the unmarried woman who cross-dresses to pursue her recalcitrant lover, the falsely accused queen, and elements of the plot featuring a higher-ranked rival. When Count Remón returns to Barcelona after a seven-month absence, he reveals to his old love, Clavela, that he has fallen in love with Isabela, Princess of England. Although she returned his love, she has been married to the King of Bohemia. When her husband dies, Isabela writes to Remón that she still loves him, and he departs for England.

Dressing as a man to follow him ("de caballero, de camino, con espada y capotillo" ["like a gentleman dressed for travel, with a sword and short cape"] 408), Clavela soon begins to manipulate the narrative. When she learns that Remón and his servant have been taken captive, she ransoms them. Although Remón and his servant Rocabruna recognize her, they decide to go along with her ploy (411). Disguised next as a male pilgrim, Clavela tells Isabela that the count is dead. As narrativizing subject, or generator of narratives, she influences the action by fabricating an incredible battle at sea, replete with bizarre metaphors ("Ya con los pies en las manos / . . . / Que al fin los remos son pies" ["With their feet in their hands, . . . for in effect oars are feet"] 414) and even stranger similes:

> Caen á la mar cabezas
> Como por la mano tosca
> Del villano á tierra bajan
> Desde la encina bellotas.
>
> (415 [37])

She presents herself as eyewitness of the count's fate, imprisoned in a dark dungeon. Since Isabela has been postponing her marriage to the emperor hoping that the count would appear, Clavela's strategy is transparent: "Ya no tienes que aguardar, / Porque heridas y congojas / Tendrán su cuerpo en la tierra" ("Now there is no more reason to wait, for wounds and affliction will have laid his body in the ground") (415). Convinced by Clavela's fiction, Isabela decides to marry the emperor and asks Clavela to accompany her as her cupbearer.

The opening of the second act confirms Clavela's successful management of the narrative. After a month, Remón and Rocabruna are still waiting for the horses, jewels, and clothes Clavela promised to send them. By the time the count speaks with Isabela, it is too late. Meanwhile, two of the emperor's courtiers, jealous of Clavela, tell the emperor that his wife is deceiving him with her cupbearer. They take Clavela off to dispatch her in the wilderness; the emperor decides to test Isabela's innocence in armed combat. After saving Clavela from the rivals, the count decides to defend Isabela's honor, and when Rocabruna is overcome with fear, Clavela takes his place without Remón's knowledge. After Remón and Clavela kill the rivals, Clavela reveals her identity and wins the "prize" of Remón as husband. The text presents the pairing of Remón and

Clavela as the product of divine intervention, downplaying Clavela's appropriation of the masculine role. Isabela comments, "No estaba de los cielos que yo fuese / Tu esposa, pues dos veces lo ha impedido" ("It was not the Heavens' intention that I be your wife, since it was prevented not once but twice") (415). The power hierarchy alluded to in the reference to the emperor as ". . . la suma alteza / A que puede llegar un hombre humano" ("the greatest height to which a mortal man can reach") (412) further undermines Clavela's role in the marriage of a princess to an emperor instead of a mere count.

In this play, female energy assertively expressed is recuperated under the sign of the feminine virtue of *firmeza,* or steadfastness, as what could have been a quest plot is absorbed within the narrative of marriage. When Clavela first assumes masculine attire, her male servant strenuously objects to her unfeminine and hence dishonorable behavior (409). Clavela contemptuously dismisses his objections, claiming *firmeza* as a national attribute: "Tenemos los catalanes / Firmeza en nuestros intentos" ("We Catalans possess steadfastness in our intent") (409). She recognizes her usurpation of a masculine prerogative in disrupting Remón's marriage to Isabela: "Que fué varonil hazaña" ("It was a virile feat") (427). After Remón saves Clavela from the rivals, initiating her return to the feminine position, she recasts her steadfastness in terms of feminine, not national virtue: "Sepa el mundo que ha nacido / Una mujer que, olvidada, / Tanta firmeza ha tenido" ("Let the world know that a woman has been born who, abandoned, has possessed such steadfastness") (442). Clavela's participation in Isabela's trial of innocence is not presented as a "virile feat," but as her desire to live or die with the count (445), who rewards her feminine virtue with marriage: "Yo, de tu firmeza cara, / No puedo negarte en premio / Ser tu marido" ("As a reward for your rare steadfastness, I cannot deny you the prize of being your husband") (445). Narrative closure, on redistributing proper gender roles, attempts to dissolve the ambiguity presiding over the play's title, "el valeroso catalán" ("the valiant Catalan"), as to which Catalan it refers to, Remón, or Clavela disguised as a man.[25]

Less successful than Clavela is Floris of *Resistencia,* who also cross-dresses to pursue a less than ardent lover. When

Enrique, Prince of France, praises Matilde's beauty and attends her wedding to the count, Floris confronts him disguised as a page. Declaring that ". . . la ocasión / hizo una mujer varón" ("the occasion made of a woman a man") (193), she justifies not only her attire, but her aggressive behavior. When the ensuing scandal is sorted out, Floris is left prisoner. Two years later, disguised as a female pilgrim, Floris again confronts Enrique, now King of France, for having abandoned her. She offers to accompany him to war disguised as a page, praising her own gallantry and bravery (202). When Enrique visits the count and is attracted to Matilde, Floris sees her earlier fears confirmed.

After the count's death, the king brushes off Floris in a letter, ordering her to choose between marrying a page in his service or entering a nunnery. She appears, completely mad and still dressed as a man, during the scene in which Enrique forces Matilde to agree to marry him. When Floris's identity is revealed, Matilde draws a parallel between their fates:

> Si ésta, perdiéndote vivo,
> ha dado en tal desconcierto,
> yo, que pierdo al Conde muerto,
> ¿cómo me consuelo y vivo?
>
> (228 [38])

The king dismisses Floris ("que siempre aquesta mujer / fué loca" ["this woman has always been crazy"] 228), and denies their similarity, for Floris has lost a king and Matilde has gained one. In this way, the assumption of the masculine role is punitively branded as madness.

The different outcome of Clavela's and Floris's cross-dressing strategies has to do in part with the negative portrait of the king in *Resistencia,* for whom both Floris and Matilde are objects of desire to be possessed and discarded at will, but also with their different status as unmarried women. Clavela remains a virtuous virgin, while Floris is clearly "damaged goods," as she herself laments:

> Yo tengo culpa, en efeto,
> que en gozando una mujer,
> allí le viene a perder

el hombre todo el respeto.

(187 [39])

When she first dresses as a page, Enrique comments: "¡Bizarro traje!, ¡extremado!, / darte cien abrazos quiero" ("A dashing costume! In the extreme! I want to embrace you a hundred times") (196). In a martial setting, Enrique continues to single out her feminine attributes:

> que con armas defensivas
> nunca yo te pensé ver,
> que las solías tener
> por todo extremo ofensivas.

(205 [40])

Clavela creates a male persona that cloaks her sexuality; Floris's body, whether in women's clothing or in men's, is always marked as sexualized object of male desire.

The Containment of Homoeroticism

The possibility that the cross-dressed woman might be the object of desire of another woman is both evoked and denied by these texts. The convention of one female character falling in love with another disguised as a man entered Spanish literature via Fiordispina's love for the cross-dressed Bradamante in Ariosto's *Orlando furioso*. It is a constant in *comedias* using this device,[26] and appears in other sixteenth- and seventeenth-century texts as well, such as Jorge de Montemayor's *Los siete libros de la Diana* (1553). *Catalán, Laura,* and *Portugués* give the dramatic cliché a different twist: the wife is accused of adultery with the woman disguised as a man while both the wife and her accuser remain unaware that her page, cupbearer, or jester is in reality a woman.

In *Laura* and *Catalán,* the accusation comes from a jealous rival, but in *Portugués,* the duke misreads the relationship between his wife and her page. Lisarda, abandoned in the wilderness by her lover,[27] first disguises herself as a peasant woman, but soon changes the gender of the disguise because as a woman, she is still in danger (375). When the duke meets her, she passes herself off as a skilled seducer of women and cuckolder of husbands:

> Si yo tuviera un vestido
> Como ese vuestro, ¡pardiez!
> Que requebrara tal vez,
> A excusa de su marido,
> A la más bella casada.
>
> (375 [41])

She playacts masculinity so well that the duke takes her to the palace, where "Mendocica" becomes the favorite of both duke and duchess. But the duke becomes jealous of the intimacy between the two women. He eavesdrops on the following scene, notable for its polyvalent eroticism, in which Lisarda holds a mirror for Mayor:

Mayor:	¿Tocada á tu gusto estoy?
Lisarda:	Rica y gallarda.
	. . . .
	¡Qué hermosa!
	. . . .
Mayor:	De suerte, ¿que yo te agrado?
Lisarda:	Bien está esa cinta presa;
	. . . .
	¡Qué rica prisión de amor!
	. . . .
	¡Por Dios, señora, que estás
	Como el sol!
	. . . .
	¿Hay tal gracia? ¿Hay tal belleza?
	(385 [42])

In all three texts, the husband tries to kill the woman he perceives to be the object of his wife's desire, but she escapes and returns to prove the wife's innocence. In each case, the proof consists simply in the revelation of her female identity. "Mendocica" insists that the duchess is "buena, constante y casta" ("good, constant, and chaste") and when asked for verification, replies: "Que soy mujer, que esto basta; / Que no pueden dos mujeres / Ofender ninguna fama" ("That I am a woman, and this is enough; for two women cannot offend any good name") (400).[28] The following exchange occurs at the end of *Catalán*:

Enrique:	¡Qué es esto! ¿Por qué la llaman
	Dama y Clavela á don Juan?
Isabela:	Para que fuese más clara

                    Mi inocencia, si es mujer.
Clavela: Mujer soy.
Enrique: ¡Alta probanza
                    De tu inocencia, Isabela!

(445 [43])

This "proof" of the wife's sexual fidelity to her husband implies either that sex between women is inconceivable or that
such relations would not dishonor the husband. In her study
Immodest Acts, Judith Brown documents medieval and early
modern attitudes towards sexual activity among women,[29] citing prohibitions in ecclesiastical sources ranging from Paul's
Epistle to the Romans, medieval penitentials, Aquinas's *Summa
theologiae,* and later theologians' writings influenced by him.
While civil law refers to this aspect of female sexuality as early
as the fourteenth century, there is little legislation until the increased repression of sodomy in the sixteenth century. Both
Charles V's statute of 1532 and Gregorio López's mid-sixteenth-
century gloss on the *Siete partidas* include women in the death
penalty for same-gender sex (Brown 13–14).[30] On the other
hand, the scarcity of references to women in comparison with
the wealth of commentary on male-male sexual activity in law,
theology, and literature leads Brown to assume "an almost active willingness to *dis*believe," to ignore or dismiss female
homoeroticism that is related to a deeply phallocentric view of
human sexuality.[31]

   These texts contrive situations that are perceived by the husband as heteroerotic and by spectators as homoerotic, all the
while affirming the primacy of the phallus, since only the
sexual use of his property by another man could dishonor the
husband.[32] Female homoeroticism in this context can be viewed
as "harmless and pleasingly erotic" (Wheelwright 59–60).[33]
But as Susan Wolfson suggests, cross-dressing makes signifiers
that ordinarily function as "clear markers of difference" function
as "agents of sexual disorientation" (585), opening up a space
for female homoeroticism even as it is denied and dismissed.[34]

The "Double Movement" of Cross-dressing

A similar dynamic of subversion and containment attends all
cross-dressing in Lope's honor plays. Cross-dressing uses the
very signifiers of sexual difference to undermine its essentialist

underpinning; it foregrounds the artifice that informs "masculinity" and "femininity," erodes male privilege, and blurs customary lines of gender demarcation. Its unsettling effects on both social and psychological levels seem to require plots that end in the submission of the cross-dressed female and the renewal of male power. But even so, for Natalie Zemon Davis the sexual inversion so popular in literature, art, and festivity can work both ways: to "clarify" the gender hierarchy by controlling the expression of conflicts within the system, or to generate "new ways of thinking about the system" in such a way as to "*undermine* as well as reinforce" it (130–31, 142–43, 147–50).[35]

The majority of these texts play the masculinization of the female character against the temporary feminization of the husband, by which I mean his unwilling assumption of the dominated role assigned to the feminine gender and his concomitant loss of the subject position. In *Hungría* and *Animal,* the wife abandons her initial disguise as rustic woman and dresses as a male peasant to rescue her husband from the misfortunes that have befallen him, while simultaneously restoring herself to wifehood. Her active role contrasts with the passive attitude of the falsely accused queen in *Nacimiento* and *Testimonio*.

In *Hungría,* Leonor's final transformation coincides with the point of maximum feminization of the king. When he asks Leonor to help him ascertain who has deposed him, the two disguise themselves as peasant men to return to the court. Even though the king's disguise does not cross gender lines, the drop in rank signifies his degraded status; for Leonor, the change in gender compensates for the loss of rank suffered in the fall from queen to peasant woman, empowering her to help the king. In this disguise, she resolves the problem of succession, restoring the king to both masculinity and rank as she places the disputed crown on his head (56). She facilitates the exchange of women for her sons, marrying them to the faithful Liseno's daughters, and completes the redistribution of "proper" gender roles by revealing her own true identity.

As in *Hungría,* Teodosia of *Animal* sorts out the threads of the narrative in male disguise, negotiating the peace that allows her to reassume her role as woman, wife, and queen. When

Rosaura is captured and brought to the court, Teodosia pretends to be a "coarse rustic" who has befriended the "monster" (Rosaura) and can control her violent behavior. Teodosia, as narrativizing subject, exploits the exaggerated legends about herself as "animal" to manipulate the king and the treacherous Faustina. When asked what became of Faustina's stolen child, Teodosia invents a gruesome tale of child sacrifice:

> Pregúntéle lo que hacían
> de aquellas criaturas tiernas
> que robaban a sus padres,
> y díjome ¡oh, gran fiereza!
> que a un ídolo que tenían
> sacrificaban con ellas.
>
> (451 [44])

When she overhears Faustina plotting to kill the king, she saves his life with an anonymous letter (458). The revelation of Faustina's treachery puts an end to the animosities between Hungary and England and Scotland. Still dressed as a peasant man, Teodosia resolves the problem of succession by identifying Rosaura as Faustina's child, and, after she has revealed her own identity, arranges political ties by marrying Rosaura and Felipe. Before hiding to eavesdrop on Faustina, Teodosia remarked: "yo, en forma de villano, escucho y veo / hasta que llegue el fin de mi deseo" ("I, in the form of a rustic man, listen and look, until the fulfillment of my desire arrives") (456). That the fulfillment of her desire means the fulfillment of *his* is figured as usual in narrative closure: the exchange of woman repairs and strengthens relations between Hungary and England.

In other texts, the wife assumes the attire of a high-ranking male and the bellicose behavior that defines him. In *Celauro,* the rival maneuvers the husband into a compromising situation to convince the wife her husband is courting another woman. When the rival guides her, disguised as a man, to the scene, the outraged wife engages her husband in a spirited swordfight. Both husband and rival praise the unknown swordsman's manliness (109). The rival's servant underlines her confident performance of masculine behavior: "¿Supo, dime, Lupercio, que era ella / la que en hábito de hombre lo fué tanto / que osó reñir con él de cuerpo a cuerpo?" ("Did he find out, Lupercio, that it was she who, dressed as a man, was so much a man that she dared fight with him hand-to-hand?") (110). Terry Castle notes in her studies of English masquerade that one of the reasons cross-dressing was suspected of encouraging sexual as well as general freedom for women was because the female characters dressed as men assumed "not only the costumes but the social and behavioral 'freedoms' of the opposite sex" (909). As in *Catalán,* the wife in *Laura* usurps the male role in the trial of innocence. After escaping death for supposedly being the duchess's lover, Laura returns to the court with the duke, both disguised as Spanish gentlemen, "con capas y sayos vaqueros, rebozos, sombreros de plumas, dagas y espadas" ("with capes and tunics, cloaks, plumed hats, daggers and swords") (375). Laura performs the masculine role of defending an accused woman, challenging her husband to prove her own innocence (375).

The Cross-dresser as Soldier

While the "militarization" of these wives is fleeting, two other texts present female cross-dressers as full-blown soldiers. In *Amazons and Military Maids,* Julie Wheelwright studies real-life women who passed as men. She finds a commonality among them in their "desire for male privilege and a longing to escape from domestic confines and powerlessness" (19).[36] Another constant is the subsequent revision of their story "to conform more closely to prevailing understandings of sexual difference," for example justifying their cross-dressing for patriotic or romantic reasons (109). Whatever "dangerous connotations" may have adhered to women's successful appropriation of power "could be ignored in the theatre and popular literature by imbuing the warrior heroine with romantic or innocent motives" (Wheelwright 113).[37] While in other plays by Lope and his successors female characters wear men's clothing or become soldiers for diverse reasons, in Lope's honor plays it is always a reflection of masculine desire.[38] Perhaps the restriction of the motives for cross-dressing responds to the pressure exerted in these particular texts towards "proper" gender roles and the determination of the wife's fate by her respect or contempt for masculine authority.

In the cases of female soldiers and sailors examined by Wheelwright, their "awareness of female oppression doubled when their superior status was snatched away" (13); they resented their enforced return to woman's work, which they saw as a "social and economic demotion" (86). In contrast, Lope's military cross-dressers willingly embrace their subordinate role upon revelation of their true identity. In *Cardona,* a general masculinization of the female characters prepares for the emergence of the female soldier. The wife, Casandra, and the King of Sicily's daughter Clenarda gradually assume more active roles as the husband (Cardona) is paralyzed by one male homosocial bond after another.[39] At the beginning, Casandra's mourning reflects her husband's dishonor (656), but later, a spy reveals that the armada headed for Valencia includes Casandra and Clenarda "en soldados transformadas; / dagas y espadas ceñidas / amenazan vuestras vidas" ("transformed into soldiers, wearing daggers and swords that threaten your lives") (669). When incriminating circumstances lead Casandra to fear that Cardona will kill her to avenge his honor, she invents the story of her own murder and reappears disguised as Dionís, a Portuguese nobleman who has come to aid the King of Aragon.

In this disguise Casandra single-handedly resolves the military impasse. Clenarda, also dressed as a soldier, has come to surrender to the King of Aragon out of love for his son, whom her own father has captured. After Clenarda tells her story to "Dionís," who praises her bravery (690), Casandra steps forward and announces that if the King of Sicily kills the prince, s/he will kill his daughter in retaliation. The King of Sicily agrees to the marriage between the prince and Clenarda, and the King of Aragon makes "Dionís" a duke. "Proper" gender roles are restored at the end: through the exchange of Clenarda to cement bonds between the Crown of Aragon and the Kingdom of Sicily and through Casandra's surrender of all her honors to her husband (692). This gesture makes explicit what is latent in other texts: the female characters' masculinization in the service of the husband's renewed access to action, honor, and masculinity.

Even though Casandra unties the knots in male homosocial relations on the political and military level, the text represents her actions as belonging to the arena of love and sexuality. Her primary reasons for disguising herself are to recover the honor lost when it appeared she and the prince were lovers and to take revenge on her husband for believing she was unfaithful.

Cardona suffers at the sight of Dionís because s/he looks so much like Casandra, reviving his regret at having doubted her innocence. Crisply ordering Cardona to control himself, Dionís reverses the usual scenario in which the man, in control of his emotions, slaps the hysterical woman to her senses (689). Casandra secretly takes pleasure in his suffering, subordinating military victory to that of love: "La más altiva y próspera vitoria, / del enemigo la mayor venganza, / . . . / no igualan al placer de Amor vengado" ("The loftiest and most prosperous victory, the greatest revenge on an enemy . . . do not equal the pleasure of avenged Love") (689).

Discordia's contradictions reveal the ambivalence characteristic of Lope's honor plays towards femininity in general, as fascination and identification with the female character struggle with the desire to distance and control her. Elena is the most masculinized of all the falsely accused queens. The reversal of the typical scenario of these texts—here it is the king who is separated from the queen for many years—corresponds to the pervasive gender reversal in the play.

Elena's story closely allies questions of state and gender inequality, specifically the devaluation of women's capacity to govern. After her father, the duke, dies, Elena is pressured to marry. The ambitious Otón wants her to marry his son Pinabelo; others, fearing that marriage to one of her vassals will result in wars of succession, urge her to put herself under the protection of the King of Frisia. They formulate their position in terms of their fear of a woman's rule: "cuántos daños al honor / nacieron de un loco amor / y un gobierno de mujer" ("all the damage to honor that was born of irrational love and woman's governance") (125). Elena herself is extremely conscious of her station and loathe to marry beneath herself (127). Her rejection of Pinabelo shows how the intersection of class and gender situates her in a contradictory position: both superior and inferior to men. She rejects him as inferior in rank, but affirms woman's need to submit to a dominating man:

> Si bien se ha de gobernar
> la mujer ha de tener,
> no quien sepa obedecer,
> sino quien sepa mandar.

> (127 [45])

118

After her wedding to the King of Frisia, she acknowledges him as owner of both her body and her state (134).

Elena's assumption of an active role in the recovery of her good name appears to reverse these initial oppositions between woman's submissiveness and incapacity to govern and male ascendancy and rightful place as head of state and family. Otón sets the king up by telling him when and where to find Elena and Pinabelo together; when the king enters, Pinabelo calls in Elena's men to defend her against the king. The people rally around Elena, and the king must flee. The king suspects he has been deceived, but with no proof of Elena's innocence, he is prepared to wage war against her. Although she remains faithful to the king, she leads her own troops in battle against him, rules in his absence, arranges for a secret meeting with him disguised as a soldier, calls for a public duel to prove her innocence, and fights it herself disguised as a knight, defeating the king.

Elena rejects feminine gender attributes when she decides to lead her own troops: ". . . ¿Mujer? Sólo en la cara. / . . . / y que saben ser fuertes y ser fieras / adonde son traidores los vasallos" ("Woman? Only in face, . . . for women know how to be strong and cruel where vassals are traitors") (143). Her transformation is signified by her "hábito corto, con espada y daga y bastón y sombrero con una pluma grande revuelta" ("short outfit, with sword and dagger and baton and a feathered hat") (145). This masculinized appearance, however, is not a disguise, and Elena is not attempting to pass herself off as a man;[40] rather, she now represents the simultaneous presence of feminine and masculine attributes. She "acts like a man," moving freely in the military sphere, without ceasing to be a woman: "y que a mujer acompaña / tal vez viril corazón" ("at times a virile heart accompanies a woman") (145). She draws Otón's attention to her masculine dress and to her skill in performing the violent activities of war:

> ¿Viste . . .
> aquel escuadrón . . . ,
> cómo le compongo y cuadro,
> y que al que se desordena
> de un bote el pecho taladro?
>
> (145 [46])

Unlike other wives, whose masculinization compensates for their husbands' feminization, Elena's stems from her desire to defend her honor against her own husband. In doing so, she appropriates the love/honor dilemma of the male protagonist. The feminizing potential of her love for the king conflicts with her masculinizing desire to defend her honor, not through passive resistance but through active means taken from the preserve of masculinity. She swears undying love for the king even as she insists on defending her honor (145).

In the third act the king reveals that his combatant in Elena's trial of innocence turned out to be none other than Elena herself, outfitted in white armor crested with black and white plumes (149). After knocking each other to the ground with their lances, they continued on foot with swords, according to the king's narration, ending in his defeat in spite of his expert sword, ". . . robusta pujanza, / real pecho, heroicas fuerzas" ("robust strength, royal breast, and heroic force") (149–50). Elena revealed her identity, and her innocence was declared. The king's shame at being defeated by a woman, ". . . que a las armas / no obliga naturaleza" ("whom Nature does not oblige to arms") (150), was so great that upon his return to Frisia he forbade anyone to mention Elena's name.

It is highly unusual for a woman to be represented as superior in strength and skill to a man. The wife in *Cardona* who comes to the aid of the King of Aragon does not suspend the hostilities through physical prowess, but by holding the King of Sicily's daughter hostage. Part of the king's humiliation in *Discordia* has to do with his "unnatural" defeat by a woman in the masculine sphere of arms.[41] It is also unusual that the text makes no reference to divine intervention in Elena's victory. The representation of the female soldier adept in the martial arts of warfare is unsettling because, as Wheelwright points out, war is the epitome and ultimate test of masculinity in so many cultures. Warfare gives men a chance

> to assert their control, their capacity for domination, conquest and even immortality. . . . War allows men to assume their role as patriarchs; to become the defenders of the nation, the protectors of "their" metaphorical and actual women and children. (17)

Discordia represents the female soldier's superiority in arms, but it subsequently evacuates that representation of all efficacy. If the king's combatant had been a man, the play would have ended here, since the outcome of the trial of innocence signified the "truth" of God's judgment. Even though all proclaim the triumph of Elena's innocence, it appears to have no effect on the narrative whatsoever.[42] Elena's assumption of masculine gender attributes merely dissolves as the initial programming of the text reasserts itself. At the end, Elena's story is no different from the story of the other wives in this group of plays. She, too, becomes the narrative image signifying the movement of phallocentric desire towards its fulfillment.

Elena is torn between the imperatives of two genders: "La guerra me ciñe espada / y el alma me pide paz" ("War girds a sword on me, and my soul asks for peace") (145). Towards the end, the "masculine" term of the opposition is negated in favor of "feminine" faithfulness and constancy. When she learns that Otón has offered six cities for the heads of the king and his son, Elena invalidates her ability to rule: "¡Ay, gobierno de mujer, / errado cuando acertado!" ("Oh, woman's government, mistaken even when apt!") (158). She attributes her failure to have Otón and Pinabelo killed as traitors to "piedad de mujer" ("woman's compassion"), thus defining masculine rule as ruthless. The king confirms this gender norm when he beheads the two noblemen sent to attack him and orders the death of Otón and Pinabelo at the end. The gendering of the instance of power culminates in Elena's reference to phallic rule:

> [¡] pues aunque sobre el poder,
> *en no viendo espada al lado*
> se afrentan de obedecer!
> Ni puedo admitir marido,
> ni hacer que me teman puedo.
> Cuando el que ha de ser temido
> llega, Otavia, a tener miedo
> el gobierno va perdido.
>
> (158, my emphasis [47])

Elena also abdicates defense of her own honor in favor of the king's, declaring she will write him to come kill her to regain his honor (158). She exchanges the position of active subject for one of self-negation: "De todos he de vengarme / con morir" ("I will avenge myself on all of you by dying") (158). Her death at the hands of the king would provide the spectacle that will make her vassals fear and obey their ruler, at the same time allowing the king to recoup the masculinity lost through his domination by Otón and Pinabelo and defeat at her own hands. Her public responds to her "feminine" gesture of purely passive vengeance and self-sacrifice: "¡Qué raro ejemplo de amor!" ("What a rare exemplum of love!") (158).

When the king arrives disguised at court, Elena's expression of appropriate sorrow ("justo sentimiento") and willingness to follow her husband in death (159) provide the "proof" the king needs to return her to favor. The validation of purely "feminine" proofs and the invalidation of her "masculine" proof of innocence complete the redistribution of gender roles, as the king punishes his rivals. Elena's oscillation between masculine and feminine positions is arrested by the king's absorption of masculinity in his "rightful" exercise of violence in defense of his honor and sexual property. The "regendering" of Elena and the king in the heterosexual couple anticipates the elaborate ceremonies recounted by Wheelwright in which the female soldier was publicly reaffirmed in her proper role.[43] Once the business of governing and warfare has been returned to men, Elena can devote herself entirely to the queenly duty of producing heirs.

***

In spite of the multiple deceptions that constitute the action of these plays, the audience was never deceived. A fundamental characteristic of the *comedia*'s semiotic mode of production is that the play is always perceived as a *representation* of reality, unlike the captivating *illusion* of bourgeois realism or naturalism (Barker).[44] False appearances are always transparently false in relation to the True and the Real for the audience, "which accepts by convention that it can penetrate the disguise, while those within the action cannot" (Barker 27). The many social and sexual signifiers were not necessarily read as multiple and nonhierarchized differences, but in relation to a transcendental signifier. As Barker suggests, in its "*doubling of the surface* . . . the reality of this world is utterly single, however it may be folded over on itself" (28–29). For all the fluid transactions in the area of gender, these texts ultimately perform the phallocentric Same. Even though the disguised female character constructs bodies and generates narratives, these "texts" are finally signed with the Name-of-the-Father. Her strategies serve "above all to ensure the legitimacy of the lord and his ordering of society" and the revelation of her true identity means the recovery of his name, if married, or trading hers for his, if unmarried (Freeman 258).

Yet the doubling of the surface that is always the Same does leave residual traces of difference. The endings of texts such as *Hungría, Animal, Celauro, Bella,* and *Desposorio* return the wife to the passive and subordinate position, but do not successfully dispel the contradictions introduced by the active phase of the disguised female character's incursion into the public sphere. As DuPlessis suggests, the quest dimension of these plots sets forth something that the marriage or romance plot "with difficulty revokes: that the female characters are human subjects at loose in the world, ready for decision, growth, self-definition" (14). Although honor plays like *Discreto, Catalán, Cardona,* and *Discordia* appropriate and absorb woman's aspirations, they always run the risk of failing to contain the female energies released in the process.

Chapter Five

Rivalry and the Struggle for Dominance

The transaction of power between the rival and the husband in the erotic triangle is channeled through the machinery of cuckoldry. As Eve Kosofsky Sedgwick notes, " 'to cuckold' is by definition a sexual act, performed on a man, by another man" (49). In this sense, men's heterosexual relationships in Lope's honor plays function chiefly as strategies of male homosocial desire, tracing the paths by which men may attempt to arrive at satisfying relationships with other men through the bodies of women. In Sedgwick's term *male homosocial desire,* the word *desire* does not designate an emotion so much as a structure,

> analogous to the psychoanalytic use of "libido"—[not] a particular affective state or emotion, but . . . the affective or social force, the glue, even when its manifestation is hostility or hatred or something less emotively charged, that shapes an important relationship. (Sedgwick 2)

The bond of cuckoldry differs from other social conformations, such as those mutual ones cemented through marriage or forged between husband and male authority figure at the end of some honor plays.[1] It is necessarily hierarchical in structure, involving an active participant in ascendancy over a passive one. Often, the deciding factor in the struggle between husband and rival is cognitive supremacy—who knows more than whom. The rival's cuckolding of the husband entails a dimension of superior awareness ("he doesn't know I'm cuckolding him") that at times cedes to the husband's recuperation of mastery ("he doesn't know I know he's cuckolding me").[2] The bond signaled by cuckoldry, then, involves an asymmetrical relation of cognitive transcendence, of dominance and subordination (Sedgwick 66).

The rival and the husband occupy opposing but complementary positions in the system of male traffic in women. The rival demonstrates his predatory ability to use other men's sexual property, to cuckold, affirming women's exchange value in circulation. The husband demonstrates his ability to maintain his control over his sexual property, to not be cuckolded, withdrawing a woman as use value from collective to private ownership. In both cases, the ultimate goal is to establish a relationship of superiority over another man. The difficulties attending this process constitute the representation of a crisis of masculinity.

The rival understands that women have value only in circulation, a position which is not free of dangers for the male subject exclusively attached to this understanding. The husband finds himself in the precarious position of attempting to fix his wife's value in herself and keep it for his private use. As Sedgwick phrases it,

> like dealers in gold and silver who claim that the value of
> cash is merely assigned by economists while the value of
> precious metals is inalienable, [he] imagines that he can pick
> one element out of the larger stream of exchange and stamp
> it forever with the value that is really lent to it only by its
> position in that stream. (54)

The increasingly violent extremes to which the husband is driven relate to the difficulty of establishing a stable, private relationship with a woman in the context of transactive circulation. His terror of male encroachment is often directly related to his own experience of the flow of women as exchangeable property among men, either before or after marriage. To be a "man," to consolidate bonds with authoritative males through heterosexual desire, requires the instrumental use of women. Yet both rival and husband run the risk of jeopardizing their position as subject in the relationship of exchange, of being feminized or objectified in relation to other men, by their denial of one of the terms of women's status within the phallic economy. As Sedgwick points out,

> any attempt to stabilize the systems of symbolic exchange
> in terms of either private or collective ownership, either the

> materiality or the transparency of the objects exchanged,
> either the heterosexual or the homosocial aim of desire,
> brings the countervailing, denied term into play. (54)

The rival's claims of collective ownership are usually overridden in the affirmation of the husband's right of private ownership, while the husband's murder of his wife both spoils the value of the object and proclaims her public, circulable character. Only the man who is not excessively fixated on either of the terms of the schism in women's status will be successful in achieving a relation of mastery to other men (Sedgwick 51).

In most scenarios of bonding through hostile rivalry, the husband passes through a period of objectification by the rival to recover the dominant position. The husband who becomes aware of his subordination frequently employs this cognitive leverage to gain ascendancy over his actual or would-be cuckolder.[3] This transition is often figured as a movement from blindness to recovered vision. For Francis Barker, in the pre-bourgeois world, sight is the governing mode of access to reality (26); the husband's failure to "see" the truth is a most "terrible instance of debility in the spectacular kingdom" (33).

The honor plot represents the end of one Oedipal journey and the beginning of another. The attainment of a woman in marriage signals the hero's successful "passage into adult life, his advent to culture and history" (de Lauretis 126). This is the "paradise lost" the husband attempts to recapture as the action unfolds. Having been momentarily "blinded," the husband is driven in his investigation of sexuality to learn the origin and the end. His quest for (self-)knowledge moves from loss to the restoration of vision, power, honor, and manhood. The achievement of his goal coincides with the possession of woman, in the form of the original love object, cleansed of any taint, or a new wife, signaling the fulfillment of his second Oedipal journey.

***

While the majority of Lope's honor plays represent the husband's obsession with his love object as private property, other plays feature men whose temporary blindness is due to excessive participation in the collective circulation of women, leading to the neglect of their own wives and the duties and obligations of the ideal husband. These texts suggest that the husband's punishment is related to his failure to attend to important male relationships formed through marriage, and that the immature bonds formed through the shared heterosexual use of women must be superseded by those of kinship.

In these plays—*Bella, Desposorio, Venganza,* and *Discreto*— the husband's continued trade in the circulation of women after marriage fails to justify the parallel re-entry into this stream on the part of the wife. In fact, the options of the two vis-à-vis the marriage contract are differently constrained by their gender: the wife must be faithful even if the husband is not. If she does put herself back into circulation, absolving her actions by her husband's infidelity, she is eliminated (*Venganza*) or coerced back into the feminine position of passive property (*Discreto*). While the husbands are also punished for their philandering, these texts do not alter the double standard reinforced by law in seventeenth-century Spanish society (only a woman could be guilty of adultery). Woman's status in exchange is determined by male subjects; as Gayle Rubin phrases it, "the social relations of a kinship system specify that men have certain rights in their female kin, and that women do not have the same rights either to themselves or to their male kin" (177). By denying her value as private property, the husbands of these plays leave themselves open to predation by other males.

When the duke reveals that he desires Laura because she belongs to another man, his servant replies:

> que había de estar la mujer
> propia como los balcones:
> que, para que no ofendiera
> y poder verla con tasa,
> estuviese asida a casa,
> mas siempre estuviese fuera.
> (*Laura* 346 [48])

In *Bella,* the husband explains his lukewarm feelings for his wife:

> Que es celosa
> y el ser propia, que no hay cosa
> que tanto me desespere.

. . . .
. . . tener
mujer a hora de comer,
mujer después al cenar,
mujer después en la cama,
y a todas horas mujer,
. . . .
¿a quién no espanta? . . .[4]

(615–16 [49])

The rival's servant in *Porfiar* compares the variety of the single man's desire to the monotony of married life:

hay muy pocas posesiones
que no paren en desprecio.
. . . .
. . . esto de estar allí
a todas horas, es cosa,
por fácil, menos gustosa.
. . . .
En un año una mujer
es silla, es banco, es bufete,
porque como no inquïete,
eso mismo viene a ser.

(703, 707 [50])

Such passages reveal the imitative nature of male desire in the Girardian sense, but also the lessening of desire for the possessed love object in a construction of masculinity as predatory: the "warrior" quickly loses interest in "conquered territory."

Federico of *Halcón* (and Boccaccio's tale) prides himself on his role as rival.[5] He compares the lover who actually acquires the desired woman to Midas:

Todo aquello que tocaba,
En oro se convertía,
Oro comía y bebía,
Y hasta en oro se acostaba.
Lo mismo deben de ser
Los gustos de los casados,
Pues estando en casa atados,
Cuanto tocan es mujer.

(444 [51])

The husband expresses precisely these same sentiments; feeling imprisoned by marriage, he decides to visit a courtesan (450–51). However, when the husband learns of the rival's pursuit of his wife, he becomes consumed with jealousy, goes mad, and dies. In the monologue in which he decides that his only recourse is to lose his sanity, he associates himself with the Midas figure employed in Federico's description of the sated desire of the married man (465). Reduced to poverty by his extravagant courtship, Federico kills a falcon, his only remaining possession, to offer the widow when she pays him a visit. Ironically, she has come to request the falcon for her ailing son; impressed with his gesture, she agrees to marry him. The contradiction cloaked by the text's happy ending is that according to Federico himself, the achievement of his desire spells the end of that desire. He exchanges his enjoyment of the free flow of woman's "gold" for the hoarding of private ownership that this text represents as leading to madness and death.

Husbands heavily invested in woman as circulable commodity are feminized, for "the path through heterosexuality to homosocial satisfaction is a slippery . . . one" (Sedgwick 50). Only the male subject who understands that men's bonds with women "are meant to be in a subordinate, complementary, and instrumental relation to bonds with other men" (51) can maintain the role of subject in exchange and achieve a position of dominance over other men. Both the husband who neglects his private property to pursue other women and the rival who attempts to cuckold another man learn, in Sedgwick's phrase, that "there is something contagious about the ambiguities of femininity" (50). Valerie Traub notes that early modern child-rearing practices and medical literature contributed to a fear of effeminacy through an excess of erotic contact with female sexuality:

> At the age of seven or so, boys were "breeched," or put into the pants of manhood. From then on, masculinity and femininity were ideologically constructed as oppositional and hierarchical; in particular, femininity was seen as *dangerous* to the male. Unlike our own age, in which heterosexual desire is the mark of masculinity, for the Renaissance male, lust was seen as effeminating. ("Prince Hal's" 457n2)

If unable to immunize themselves in a phase of temporary contagion, these husbands run the risk of being permanently feminized or objectified in relation to other men.

Leonardo of *Bella* ignores his wife to enjoy other women with his unmarried friend Teodoro. The opening moment of the play characterizes their inordinate proximity to female sexuality as feminizing:

Teodoro:	De tanto buscar placer,
	casi he venido a temer
	el amor de las mujeres.
Leonardo:	. . . .
	Y así he venido a entender,
	. . . .
	que el que a mujer ama tanto
	por fuerza ha de ser mujer.

(612 [52])

Teodoro also calls himself a hermaphrodite ("que al fin soy hombre y mujer" ["for in effect I am man and woman"] 613). If desire for women equals effeminacy, manliness means setting femininity at a distance. The shepherd in *Veneciano* explains his refusal to reciprocate woman's desire as a fear of losing his identity: "Miedo de perderme amando / En aqueste mar de amar. / . . . / Silvia, yo quiero ser mío" ("Fear of losing myself through loving in this sea of love. . . . Silvia, I want to belong to myself") (552). In *Halcón,* the servant declares that ". . . quien ama, / Apenas hombre se llama" ("he who loves can scarcely be called a man") (448), and the rival of *Peligros* affirms that he who loves women risks losing esteem:

> que como amor es flaqueza,
> el que en ser flaco tropieza,
> ¿cómo ha de ser respetado?
> Cierto que tiene razón
> el mundo en tener en poco
> el que es con mujeres loco.

(173–74 [53])

These judgments are confirmed by the fate of those rivals who lose their footing walking the thin line between instrumental use of woman and surrender to the contagious ambiguities of femininity. In *Comendadores* the rivals are feminized by their fear of riding spirited Andalusian horses, the sword rusted in the scabbard, their clumsy falls and accidents, and finally their flight in perfumed nightclothes from the husband's sword. In spite of his superior rank, the corralled rival of *Locura* is also thoroughly humiliated by the husband's reference to his feet poking out beneath the drapery in the wife's bedroom. Half-dressed ("en cuerpo"), he grovels for mercy, reminding the armed husband of his social obligation to him as heir to the throne and swearing he offended the husband only in thought (298).

But not all male subjects tainted by female sexuality cross the line into permanent loss. For the husband, as shown by texts like *Bella, Desposorio,* and *Discreto,* the antidote is the strengthening of the bonds of kinship and the reimposition of control over the wife. In *Bella,* the void created by the husband's disregard for his sexual property attracts first a predator and then the wife's male relatives, prepared to either avenge her on the husband if falsely accused or kill her if found guilty. In responding to the threat to his honor, the husband vindicates himself in the eyes of his father- and brother-in-law (641). In *Desposorio* and *Discreto,* the husband initially feminized by his erotic involvement with another woman overcomes the threat to his private property and simultaneously forms new male bonds by arranging the marriage of his extramarital love object.

Violence as Redemption

The plays discussed above present husbands who foolishly "forget" woman's value as private property; other texts represent the dangers and dilemmas of the husband exclusively fixated on it. The degree to which the husband has lost control of his property in the period of lost vision determines the degree of violence that accompanies its recuperation. Wives whose illicit desire remains in the realm of the imagination can be brought back under control through punishment (*Discreto*) or set at a distance through banishment (*Carlos*). Murder is most likely if the wife has been used sexually by the rival, either with her consent (*Comendadores, Vitoria, Venganza, Toledano, Contienda*) or through rape (*Fuenteovejuna, Príncipe, Dina*),[6] since the threat to the husband's honor has actually been carried out. The sadism that explodes at the end of some of these texts is intimately linked to the male subject's realization that he has been victimized like a woman in the plots of men (Modleski 97–98). While he thought he had achieved the freedom of masculinity promised him in the social contract, he learns that the woman has eluded his grasp. By the end, the husband resembles the "quintessential sadist" described by Modleski: "stern, remote, and punishing, always in command of himself and the woman" (68). The husband's menacing presence after he has become aware of his dishonor communicates his power and control.

Even before he is dishonored, Constante of *Toledano* is presented as unmanly. His first appearance, tired from walking (596), works against the masculine ideal of strength and physical aptitude. His image is further undermined by his hesitance when asked for a *merienda* by his disguised wife, replying that he has to ask his spouse's permission. He is slow, failing to catch the nuances and conceits of the rival's letter. But after his suspicions have been aroused, he swears, "ya viviré con mil ojos" ("now I will live with a thousand eyes") (609).

Compensating for his earlier weakness, Constante overpowers his rival and drowns him, highlighting his physical prowess ("valedme, brazos robustos" ["serve me well, robust arms"] 618) and revealing the extent of his humiliation at being "unmanned":

> Si te pareció que yo
> soy hombre que guardo mal
> lo que en guarda se me dió;
> . . . .
> vengo a que veáis, galán,
> que basto yo para hombre
> de la mujer que me dan.
>
> (618 [54])

He tells those who answer his shouts for help that the drowned man died for competing with him. In cryptic language that conveys their struggle for mastery, Constante assigns superior strength and skill to himself: "aviséle que nadase / en otra tabla más baja / y que adonde entré no entrase" ("I warned him to swim in another less deep place, and not to enter where I entered") (618). At the end, he walks onstage sustaining the weight of his dead wife in his arms.

In *Dina,* the brothers demand bloody revenge for Dina's rape, while the father is willing to recover honor through marriage. The extremity of the brothers' reaction has to do with being dominated by another male, but also with Dina's active and homoerotic looking. Not only was another man looking while they were not looking, leading to the misuse of their sexual property; what is worse, the woman was looking while they were not. Unlike the threat to man's vision posed by the transgressive wife in her enigmatic "to-be-looked-at-ness," or power to lure another man's gaze, Dina's looking must be punished because it usurped a masculine prerogative and occurred in a lapse of male specular vigilance. The sons do not criticize their father's practical solution directly, but those brothers that support Jacob's plan are called cowards by the others (230). At the end the text gets it both ways: Jacob's paternal status is fortified by the appearance of an angel, through whom the brothers address their plea for forgiveness to the divine Father (234). The brothers have reasserted their masculinity while salvaging the respect due the patriarch.

The use of murderous aggression in *Veneciano* is not justified by Spanish law, which gave men the right to kill a rival only in cases of proven adultery. Confronted by the husband, the rival promises to mend his ways and praises the wife's virtue. When Sidonio insults him instead of accepting his apology, the rival regrets his former humility and threatens to court the wife publicly. At this point, Sidonio drops verbal taunts and reaches for his sword (543). It is enough that his *hombría* has been injured by the rival's belief that he *can* prey on Sidonio's wife. When the Venetian Senate offers two thousand ducats for his capture, he disguises himself as a shepherd in the countryside, where he lives for many years. Even though he acted out of the threat posed to honor and masculinity, his own servant believes the Senate acted correctly in punishing a grave crime committed in a public place (545).

The fact that the husband recuperates his masculinity so quickly suggests that this particular text is more interested in some of the other paradoxes inherent in the gendered construction of honor. The first act ends with Sidonio's reassuring statement that he leaves his small children "[s]in padre, pero con honra" ("[w]ithout a father, but with honor") (544). The next two acts reveal this statement to be an oxymoron: the presence of the father is necessary to ensure honor, for the poverty occasioned by Sidonio's absence exposes his daughter to predation. By defending his honor, Sidonio has placed it in danger. As long as masculine identity is defined in terms of controlling woman, woman will pose a never-ending threat to masculine identity. Since only masculine virtue can withstand poverty,[7] Sidonio must give himself up and offer the ransom money to the dead rival's son as his daughter's dowry. This selfless act wins him the title of "piadoso," or compassionate (563).

Sidonio can mend male homosocial relations with his daughter because she is his to use, unlike the sons of the banished Evandro, who befriended Sidonio with the intention of capturing him to ransom their father. Evandro rebukes them for betraying the bonds of friendship: they could give their father for a friend, but they cannot give a friend for a father, because one cannot give away what belongs to another ("dar lo ajeno" 550). What they did wrong ("compassionate foolishness"), Sidonio does right ("the compassionate Venetian"). By giving the rival's son his daughter, Sidonio replaces the dead father with himself (565–66). The legitimate channeling of the son's desire cancels the illegitimate desire of the dead rival, an exchange that also operates through the category of ownership, as the son articulates:

> Perdóname, padre mío:
> Tú me enseñaste que amase
> Lo que en esta casa hallase,
> Y es menor mi desvarío;
>   Que tú buscabas lo ajeno
> Y yo lo que puede ser
> Mío, siendo mi mujer.
>
> (561 [55])

While the split among men arose out of the dichotomy in woman's status as both private and public property, Sidonio controls both at once: he shows he owns his daughter by marrying her off and at the same time he affirms her value in exchange. Sidonio's successful manipulation of both poles of woman's status is typical of the male subjects who come out "on top" at the end of these plays. But before they achieve this position of superiority they must first be "cured" of their obsession with one or the other pole.

In *Vitoria,* the husband, Valdivia, is never unaware of the rival's attempts to cuckold him. In the place of cognitive dominance, the husband's masculinity is compromised by his failure to perform his proper role in relation to the Law. Valdivia jealously guards his wife as sexual property, but is unable to adequately protect her.[8] The action of the play is initiated when another man defends his wife from a loose bull. The taurine symbolism (besides representing the dangers posed for women by rampant masculinity) aligns the male subjects in a relationship of plus and minus masculinity.

The positions of husband and rival are further established in their first verbal exchange. Valdivia's words articulate his loss of control ("¿Entró una mujer aquí?" ["Did a woman come in here?"] 414), while the rival emphasizes the fact that he has carried out Valdivia's husbandly duties for him: "Pues defendelda por mí, / que yo con esto he cumplido" ("Well, defend her in my place, for I have fulfilled my obligation") (414). The husband attempts to shift the blame for his inaction from himself to his wife. First, he criticizes her for running from his side (414). The wife justifies her flight, reprimanding her husband for insisting that they go down into the street too soon (414).[9] Valdivia then attacks her duplicitous nature: "[¡]qué bien que tu ingenio fragua / un embuste, una quimera!" ("how ingeniously you forge a trick, a chimera!") (414). That his unfounded criticisms of her may reveal his own sense of inadequacy is suggested by her sarcastic reply:

> Si veo un toro furioso
> por una calle venir,
> ¿he de esperar, o he de huir?
> . . . .
> ¿Dirás que el toro fingí
> para que me entrase aquí?
>
> (414 [56])

The existence of the bull is beyond question; what is in question is whether Valdivia is "man" enough to protect her from it.

Even before their encounter, the husband feels diminished by the rival's able performance of masculinity. He has already distinguished himself in the tourney Valdivia and his wife came to watch. The rival's participation wins him paternal approval, from his biological father ("Hoy has honrado mi casa. / Hoy has andado muy hombre" ["Today you have honored my house. Today you have acted like a man"] 417), and from the Duke of Alba, the *comedia*'s conventional signifier of the Spanish ideal of warlike masculinity, who rewards the rival with the concrete symbol of that ideal: the habit of a military order (416). The rival's manly physique and youth increase the husband's discomfort, as the wife informs her slave (418). After their humiliating confrontation, the husband tries to restore his lost stature in the eyes of his wife by reminding her of his successes in the past:

> . . . que había muerto
> indios, cocodrilos, fieras
> en las playas y riberas
> del nuevo mar descubierto,
> y que supiera mejor
> de un torillo defenderme.
>
> (418 [57])

The list has something of the comic to it; the diminutive of "bull" and the echo of the verb *defender,* damagingly placed in the mouth of the rival earlier, establish verbal excess as supplement for scarcity of action.

Valdivia's problematic social status aggravates his sense of inferiority. The wife refers to him as a noble and honorable gentleman; Valdivia prefers to add to his identity as gentleman that of soldier (429). But when the rival asks his servant about "Captain" Valdivia, the reply undercuts this masculinity-conferring title with the low prestige of "indiano" (418), since Valdivia made his fortune in America.[10] In this way, the husband's subordination to the rival is related to the social disesteem of earning one's fortune through commerce rather than inheritance.[11] George Mariscal analyzes discursive efforts to "accommodate the 'new' peoples born of the contact with indigenous groups in America" ("*Persiles*" 100); because of the nature of their wealth, the *indianos* represented a more immediate threat than the *mestizos:*

> While the *mestizo* problematized the blood-based social
> body, the *indiano* figured an entirely separate domain of

> subjectivity premised on the accumulated capital acquired
> through contact with the new world. (100)

The husband in *Vitoria* resembles the figure of Antonio *hijo* in
Cervantes's *Persiles,* who according to Mariscal, is "doubly
marked as both a barbarian [*indiano*] and a deficient male"
("*Persiles*" 100). Valdivia himself associates his return to Spain
as a rich man with pacific passivity: ". . . medré, / y en menos
tiempo volví / donde en un templo que vi / de paz, la espada
colgué" ("I prospered, and in less time I returned, and hung my
sword in a peaceful church I saw") (440). When Valdivia threatens to shoot the rival, the latter's father tells his son that all his
masculinity and honor would be of no avail against a man
armed with a pistol (438). But this manner of eliminating a rival might not be the ultimate proof of manhood that Valdivia
seeks, since the Spanish ideal closely associated masculinity
with the sword.[12] In effect, during Valdivia's visit to the rival's
father, he threatens over and over to avenge his honor with his
sword. Still, his willingness to negotiate in writing and then in
person with the father rather than confront the rival directly
continues to cast Valdivia in a less than manly light. His weak
position is underlined by his persistent failure or reluctance to
actually take out his sword. At the beginning, the wife tells her
female slave that Valdivia let go of her hand to move his toward
his sword, while the rival waited for the bull with sword in hand
(418). Later, Valdivia remarks,

> con esta medio envainada,
> que ayer casi la saqué,
> para lo que hacer pensé.
> Vuelvo a sosegar la espada.

(441 [58])

Valdivia's bloody vengeance makes up for his earlier sense
of inferiority, as he proceeds from shamefully sheathed sword,
to half-unsheathed sword, to sword in hand during the murder
scene. This trajectory parallels the shuffling of his subject positions, as he counters the *indiano*'s "hanging up the sword"
with the noble soldier's manly readiness to use it. In his interview with the rival's father, Valdivia spoke of his "heredado
valor" ("inherited courage") (440), and at the end, reconstituted

as male subject, he refers to both his inherited noble blood and his heroic action on the battlefield as marks of honor:

> Con la sangre generosa
> que heredé de mis abuelos,
> y aquel honor que se compra
> en Flandes con mil heridas.
>
> (453 [59])

In his analysis of *El médico de su honra,* Paul Julian Smith points out the contradictory composition of Calderón's dramatic subjects:

> the action of the play suggests that human identity is an arbitrary juxtaposition of incompatible discourses or subject-positions. Wife and lover; husband and killer: neither of these contradictions can be resolved in a single person. (162)

Valdivia never ceases to be both *indiano* and noble soldier, confirming Mariscal's conclusion that the "barbarous *mestizo* and the *indiano* may enter the domain of culture but only as undecidable figures" ("*Persiles*" 100). *Vitoria* shows the negotiation of the relative value of these subject positions through discourses of masculinity and honor.

Like *Venganza,* which eliminates the inadequate son in a replay of the Oedipal scenario, *Vitoria* removes a son who is too caught up in the circulation of women to accede to real manhood by taking one as his private property in marriage. Valdivia, on the other hand, plays the whole gamut of woman's value, exercising his control over his wife by murdering her and receiving a new wife in exchange.[13] When the dead rival's father gives him his daughter in marriage, he receives the paternal approval previously awarded the rival. The text contradicts Valdivia's statement about the irreplaceability of sons:[14] the compensatory behavior re-establishing his participation as subject in the male traffic in women positions him in the place of the dead son, as the father proclaims to his relatives at the end (454). The mature Valdivia's ultimate power over the younger male and the bloody resolution of his crisis of masculinity in terms of father/son bonding represent male homosocial relations as fundamentally patriarchal.[15]

A common device depicting the cognitive domination of the male subject overinvested in woman as private property is his effusive praise of matrimony while the audience knows he is being deceived. In *Comendadores,* as critics have pointed out, the husband's happiness at returning to his home and his delight in domestic pleasures expose him to ridicule (McKendrick, "Celebration or Subversion?"). The scene of his humiliation is extensive. First, he expounds on the joys of the married man, criticizing the single life and embracing all those of his household as "family" (271–72). In an aside, the wife echoes his "[r]eventando de placer" ("[b]ursting with pleasure") to express her displeasure at his arrival: "Rabiando estoy de pesar" ("I am raging with sorrow") (271). The complicity between audience and wife makes the husband's blindness even more laughable as he goes on to praise his wife in terms that incarnate Luis de León's "perfecta casada," or "perfect wife," (272). On recovering his "sight," the husband remembers this moment, now "bursting" with poisonous rage: "¡Reventaré como preñada víbora! / . . . / ¿Que dije bien del casamiento?" ("I will burst like a pregnant viper! . . . I spoke well of marriage?") (291). The stinging recollection of his degradation surely fuels his revenge, as he massacres all those he embraced as "children," including the animals, with the exception of his faithful slave. The excess of violence employed to recover honor provides "superproof" of his (lacking) masculinity.[16] *Comendadores* becomes an emblematic text, recalled by other husbands under similar pressures.

Marital Mis-perceptions

The ironic praise of domestic bliss also occurs in texts in which the wife's adultery is only apparent, revealing the threat to masculine security inherent in marriage itself. Regardless of the virtue of the wife, private ownership necessarily places the husband in jeopardy of being subordinated, if not through actual incursions on his property, through cognitive dominance.

At the beginning of *Cortesía,* the husband's servant reveals his desire for the wife in an aside. When the husband waxes eloquent on the joys of matrimony, the audience already knows there is a snake in this paradise. His references to marriage as a tranquil sanctuary are highly ironic, as is his comment on the blindness of his former lifestyle ("la ceguedad en que estuve" 337). The husband is so pleased with marriage that he wants to act as go-between for everyone and everything, including the fish, the birds, the sun and moon, even Time and Fortune (337). Escalating in foolishness, he extends his comic marrying mania to different parts of his body: "Tengo los brazos casados, / los ojos y los oídos, / . . . / y todos bien empleados" ("My arms are married, my eyes and ears, . . . and all married well") (337). The flip side of the husband's complacency is the ease with which he believes his servant's lies, transforming his praise into curses and regret for having married (346). As in *Comendadores,* the memory of his unknowing contentment exacerbates the husband's sense of outraged manhood, although here he persists in a state of unawareness even as he thinks his eyes have been opened (346). Only at the last moment is the husband's belief in his wife's perfidy dispelled.

In *Indicios,* this double reversal (praise/vituperation/praise) is accomplished in encapsulated form at the beginning of the play. The husband arrives home from an extended absence accompanied by a friend. Since the audience already knows that she is not at home and that she is being pursued by a very persistent rival, the husband's unquestioned assumption of his wife's expectant enclosure makes him look ridiculous (260). When no one answers, the husband's knocking becomes more obstreperous in proportion to his growing embarrassment. As neighbors hurl insults and fetch firearms, he leaps to the worst conclusion (260–61). After a neighbor tells him that his wife has gone to a cousin on her deathbed, the husband admits his error: "¡Villana imaginación / de haber ofendido ansí / su opinión!" ("Coarse imagination! To have offended her reputation in this way!") (261).

This episode predicts the movement of the entire play, as the husband falls prey to appearances manipulated by the rival only to realize he has misinterpreted all the "signs" ("indicios") of his dishonor. Yet since he failed to "see" the truth after the first incident, there is no reason to believe that the second has "cured" him of his ever-present anxiety about his ability to protect his private property. Just after the opening episode, the noble guest and his servant Gonzalo vent their spleen against marriage. By the end, the nobleman and the wife's cousin are joined in matrimony, ostensibly to suffer all the ills experienced by the husband and outlined by this same guest earlier in the play. Only Gonzalo stands firm in his resolve to avoid the dangers inherent in marriage (295).[17]

In many texts like *Indicios,* the rival blinds the husband by manipulating reality. These plays reveal a fascination with the semiotics of a system in which sight is the dominant mode of access to a reality that is always present and always single. In such a realm, misreadings of signs can be potentially fatal, but then, as the fate of the rival sometimes demonstrates, so can the manipulation of signs to make others "see" what is not real, or "not see" what is real. The restoration of the temporarily blinded husband ultimately confirms the "truth" of vision and the "singularity" of the specular realm, for all the deceptive convolutions it appears to take (Barker). The ease with which one male subject can blind another with respect to reality is directly related to the construction of masculinity as predatory and to male anxiety about loss of honor. The hypervigilance described by Ruth El Saffar as the price paid for a secure sense of masculine identity in early modern Spain leaves the husband highly vulnerable to the rival's machinations.[18] In such texts, the rival controls the narrative until he is discovered and punished near the end. In most cases, the rival is subordinated with the aid of the wife; in other texts, the husband's recovery of vision and control is effected through bonding with another man besides the rival.

In *Indicios,* the male triangle is formed by rival, husband, and pseudo-rival. The rival, supposedly a friend of the husband, tricks him into believing his friend Felipe is cuckolding him. Both rival and husband are feminized in their respective obsessions with collective and private property. Felipe masters the entire spectrum of traffic in women: he has fled from Barcelona, where he wounded a man he was cuckolding, and he marries the wife's cousin at the end. A hierarchy of bravery and cowardice is set up in which the performance of each male subject correlates not only to cognitive mastery but also to his position in the traffic in women.

Deciding to rape the wife if she will not give in, the rival declares that many men miss their chance through cowardice (259). His comment betrays his anxiety about being judged cowardly if he fails to act; the servant's reply, "Y muchos, por su osadía, / pierden también su opinión" ("And many, through their boldness, also lose their good name") (259), points to the risk the male subject runs of losing his good name through either cowardice or bravery in attempting to live up to the masculine ideal. Felipe rescues the wife, wounding the rival as he flees. Thinking that Felipe is the wife's lover, the rival returns to the scene, casting his jealousy in terms of his own perceived lack of bravery: "Mis celos hacen en mí / lo que el valor no ha podido" ("My jealousy accomplishes what my courage was unable to") (265). Surprised when the husband himself answers the door, the rival pretends to faint, making up a story about being attacked by three men. When the husband admonishes him for succumbing so easily to a minor wound and solicitously offers him a chair, the rival realizes the public damage his *hombría* has suffered (267), especially as the husband goes on to praise Felipe.

When the rival flatters the husband, saying that he ran to his house for protection, the latter pompously assumes this role, assuring the rival he will avenge him (265–66). But the husband is in fact being cognitively dominated by every other character in the play, for Felipe agreed to the wife's request not to tell him about the rival's pursuit. The husband's puffed-up statements congratulating himself on his masculinity (266) and his untimely praise of friendship (266–67) make him appear ludicrous, as he swallows his "friend's" story and all the other characters refer in asides to the real situation about which only he is in the dark. The servant comments ironically that he is "[e]l primer hombre ofendido / que a su enemigo ha vendado" ("[t]he first offended man who has bandaged his enemy") (266).

Felipe further eclipses the husband and "unmans" the rival by creating the fiction that he and his servant pursued the nonexistent attackers. He "deceives with the truth," indirectly warning the rival by telling all present that the attack was actually justified because the rival was courting an absent friend's wife. The wife also lambasts the rival, replacing her husband with Felipe as manly defender: "que el que una vez os hirió / también os sabrá matar" ("for he who wounded you once will also know how to kill you") (268). To all this the husband reacts with befuddled disbelief: "Un hombre que tan leal / siempre a mi amistad ha sido, / ¿en esta culpa ha caído?" ("Such a man, who has been my faithful friend, is guilty of this?") (268). The wife celebrates Felipe's dual superiority on the basis of incomparable force and cognitive dominance: "y que no he visto . . . / tan resuelta valentía / ni enredo más ingenioso" ("I have never seen . . . such resolute bravery nor such an ingenious deceit") (268).

The two women manipulate even the most masterful male, Felipe, in their determination to marry him to Inés, but their scheming actually helps the rival's designs at one point. He tells the husband that Felipe is courting his wife and that he himself is in love with Inés. The signs of the wife's and Inés's conspiring then become the false "indications" of the husband's dishonor.[19] Dismissing his fearful reaction upon seeing the letter denouncing Felipe, the husband declares that ". . . nadie puede saber / de mí tanto como yo" ("no one can know of me as much as I") (278). This is his error, as it is precisely what he does not know that is his downfall. He is torn between his fear of knowing and his fear that he does not know: ". . . Pero digo mal; / bien puede venir aquí / lo que yo no percibí" ("But I am wrong; it is possible that what I failed to perceive be stated here") (278). His drive to know finally conquers his fear of the unknown contents of the letter: "también me ha de dar cuidado / todo lo que no he sabido" ("all that which I have not known must also trouble me") (278).

The irony deepens as he now believes himself in possession of the knowledge that eludes him (279). Even though he plots to collect evidence of his dishonor and assumes the knowing alertness, intentioned asides, and dramatic ironies practiced by deceived husbands in other texts, he cannot play the role of menacing sadist, since he has neither cognitive leverage nor *hombría*. When he confronts his wife, she puts her finger on the sore point: "que indicios mal comprobados / . . . los introduce el miedo" ("fear introduces . . . unproven signs") (286). Felipe rushes in and "saves" her, once more establishing himself in the position of authority and increasing the husband's "fear" of losing his masculinity. The husband reveals his concern for his slipping image when the rival sets him up for a duel with Felipe: "Si replico, ha de pensar / que en mí es falta de valor" ("If I object, he will attribute it to a lack of courage in me") (292).

The rival's control of the narrative is finally broken by bonding of mutuality between the husband and Felipe. When the husband takes out his sword, announcing his intention to kill the man who has offended him, Felipe turns and looks behind him (293), comically dashing the rival's hopes that the husband will kill Felipe. Felipe then guides the unraveling of the intrigue, revealing that it was he who wounded the rival and, still in the husband's role, threatening the rival with death if he ever sees him again. The husband adopts a subordinate position, even in the moment of his restored vision:

> ¡Ay, amigo de mis ojos,
> mil veces beso tus plantas,
> perdonándome otras tantas
> mi inorancia y tus enojos!
>
> (295 [60])

Felipe appropriates the title of the play, vindicating his own virtue as nobleman: "que en mi noble proceder, / sólo pudiera tener, / *en los indicios, la culpa*" ("for only mere indications of blame could bear on my noble conduct") (295). Certain contradictions persist that undermine the neat resolution of male homosocial desire in terms of Felipe's "noble conduct": while the rival is condemned for preying on other men's private sexual property, Felipe is not. The text assuages this contradiction by emphasizing that the rival's crime lay in the betrayal of friendship, but the problem remains inherent in the construction of predatory masculinity. The power to loosen all the knots in the plot does not lie in Felipe's hands alone; only the two female characters can reveal the mystery of the intercepted letters, illustrating woman's capacity for duplicity to achieve her desire. In this sense, the dangers inherent in marriage pointed out throughout the play are double-edged: the difficulty in guarding private property against predators, as well as the impossibility of fully containing woman within marriage as passive property.

The variations on the theme of "seeing is believing" are even more complicated in *Laura*. The rival, Ricardo, juggles two triangles, one composed by himself, Duchess Leonarda, and the duke, and another formed by the duke, Laura, and her husband (Roberto). To achieve his desire for Leonarda, Ricardo generates a seemingly endless stream of false narratives which are referred to insistently in the text as "chimeras" (350, 351, 352, 354, 363) and "poetic deceits": "Bien se trazan mis quimeras; / con poéticos engaños, / finjo historias verdaderas" ("My chimeras are well plotted; with poetic deceits I feign true stories") (350). When the duke surprises him holding on to Leonarda's necklace, Ricardo says he was looking closely at it because he would like to have one like it to give to the woman he loves. Relieved, the duke declares, "¡Qué de cosas ven los ojos / que no son como las ven!" ("How many things the eyes see that are not as the eyes see them!") (340). The success of Ricardo's poetic deceit depends here on the failure of other characters to trust what they see.[20] At other times Ricardo exploits their willingness to believe what he makes them see, manipulating appearances through a combination of half-truths and outright lies. He tells Leonarda that the duke is after Laura, but embellishes this truth by saying that Laura reciprocates this desire and that together they are plotting to kill her and Roberto. He tells Laura that the duke wants to kill Roberto and Leonarda and that she should pretend to go along with his plan until Roberto returns. When Leonarda and Roberto, strategically positioned by Ricardo, "see" and "hear" Laura's complicity in the duke's supposed plot, they join in Ricardo's plan to kill their spouses.

In spite of the specular debility manipulated by Ricardo, the authority of both sight and narrative is ultimately relegitimized in the site of royal power. Leonarda tells the king the "true" story and hides him to provide proof of Ricardo's treachery, using the same ploy Ricardo manipulated earlier to produce eyewitnesses to a false reality. The king's reply, "que tu verás el castigo" ("and you will see my punishment"), emphasizes the central role of sight in the display of sovereign power. While the rival is exposed through woman's intervention, she is instrumental only in passing the narrative reins from the "wrong" male hands to the "right" ones. Leonarda justifies her deception of Ricardo as the necessary means to unmask the master deceiver (374), but she and the other characters are actually still under the sway of his "poetic deceits," believing that Laura, the duke, and the jester are all dead because of him (374). When the duke and Laura arrive on the scene disguised as Spanish gentlemen, it is they who dispel the residue of Ricardo's chimeras, by revealing their "true" identities.

In *Cortesía* and *Celauro* as well, the rival is brought down by the wife telling the "real" story. In *Cortesía,* the course of the plot is shaped by the lies of the husband's servant. First he tells the wife the husband has ordered him to kill her because he suspects her of adultery. When she rejects his offer to replace her husband, he tries to rape her. A noble Spaniard rescues her and takes her to Spain under his protection. The servant then tells the husband that the wife was kidnapped by two gentlemen and went with them willingly. Both wife and husband authorize the servant's false narratives, repeating them as fact, basing their future actions on them, and generating new false narratives because of them. The wife tells the servant's story to the Spaniard (Juan); the husband instructs the servant to spread the news that bandits killed him and his wife on the road, his symbolic "death" signifying both dishonor and loss of masculinity for being unaware. The servant's narrative control seems to recede into the background as the action concentrates on Juan's dilemma: to act on his desire for the wife or to protect a woman in distress as a noble Spaniard. But in fact, everything that Juan says and does, or chooses not to say and do, is conditioned by his belief in the servant's story. In this sense, he is as feminized by the rival as the husband. Upon learning that Juan's sister wants to marry her disguised husband, the wife takes control of the narrative by revealing his true identity and confronting the servant, who admits his guilt.

Like *Laura, Celauro* exploits the dangers of *believing* that "seeing is believing." The rival convinces his sister to let the husband court her at her window, and persuades the husband to woo a woman for him, in reality his sister. The wife agrees to witness her husband's "infidelity," because "... es poca lealtad / ... / creer de él esta bajeza / sin remitillo a la vista" ("it would be disloyal... to believe this vile deed of him, without referring it to sight") (99).[21] Although deceived by the rival, the wife counters with *embustes* of her own. While those of the rival are designed to gain superiority over another male, the wife's tricks temporarily dominate both husband and father-in-law in order to establish their mastery more firmly at the end.

In other texts the wife's chastity is not put into question by the rival's lies but by incriminating circumstances that the husband chooses to "read" as signs of his dishonor. The jealous king of *Corona* discovers his wife and the rival in what appears to be an embrace. In fact, the queen has given the rival permission to draw near to show her a letter he claims proves the king's infidelity. In their struggle over the letter, his cuff becomes entangled in her collar.[22] The queen's terror causes her to go into labor, and the furious king orders his servant to murder her and her twin sons and to kill the rival under cover of fire in battle.

In *Rosambuco,* the husband becomes suspicious of his wife when he learns she has exchanged clothes with a friend to avoid being recognized by him as the woman he saw earlier in conversation with another man. The husband's rigor in deciding to kill her on so little evidence reveals both the extreme hypersensitivity of the male subject as well as the danger it represents for the woman who ventures beyond real and symbolic enclosures. As she prays to Saint Benito, the statue moves its arm as a sign of her innocence, motivating Rosambuco's conversion. However, explaining the husband's hypersensitivity in terms of narrative necessity does not negate the dynamics of rivalry represented in the text, nor obscure its hierarchical structure. The miracle that intervenes to obstruct the husband's reconstitution of his threatened masculine identity is no less "real" than other endings that communicate basically the same ideological messages about the sex-gender system and the social hierarchy. In secular plays, the husband's power to punish offenses against the law stems from his connection to the source of ultimate power, the king, whose power in turn flows from God, who is both King and Father. In saints' plays, the subordination of earthly representatives of the Law of the Father merely privileges the transcendent level that sanctions the social hierarchy down below. In both cases, woman is the medium through which the order of supremacy is established.

In *Estefanía* and *Peligros,* the signs of the husband's dishonor are produced by another woman using the wife's identity to have sex with the rival. In *Estefanía,* the husband's readiness to "read" the female slave's body as his wife's is explained in part by the darkness of the scene, but on a psychological level, it stems from his besieged sense of masculine identity, already under attack in his intense *political* rivalry with his adversary. Feeling at a disadvantage in other masculine arenas, the husband is quick to carry this defensiveness over into the sexual domain, murdering both rival and wife. This text is unusual in that it makes no defense of the husband's actions in the name of honor. In *Laura,* even when it is revealed that the murdered wife was innocent, the duke assures the husband that he acted understandably: "¡Oh qué mal hecho! Pero no me espanto; / que es, en fin, el honor sagrada cosa" ("Oh, how badly done! But I am not surprised, for honor, in short, is a sacred thing") (367). *Laura,* however, is a comic play and the wife is in reality very much alive. *Estefanía* is a dark text that ends with no pardon of the husband's overzealous defense of his honor, and no resolution to the tragic misreading motivated by the dynamics of rivalry. In the last scene, the husband tells the king, his murdered wife's father, what has happened, recognizing his fault in the matter (363); the king announces his intention to turn the affair over to the courts (363). The play ends indecisively with the promise of a second part which was never written.

The comic structure of *Peligros* averts the violence to which misreadings of the signs of dishonor can lead, since the social rank of the wife's double allows resolution through marriage. At the beginning, Blanca is desired by three men. Her father marries her to the one of her choice, Pedro; Félix goes to America; and the third suitor, Bernardo, continues to court Blanca, arousing the husband's anxieties. The proliferation of "bad readers" adds to the humor of the text, and the fact that it is women who are manipulating the signs increases the men's domination. When the husband is awarded a position at the court, he leaves for several months without his wife, since he cannot afford to support his family with the ostentation required by his rank (183). Aware of "the dangers of absence," he prescribes an extreme practice of enclosure:

> Cierra, mis ojos, tu puerta,
> luego que la noche avisa,
> . . . .
> Echa la cubierta al coche
> cuando salieres a misa,

> y el manto al rostro en la iglesia.
>
> (186 [61])

To keep male honor alive, woman must live as the dead:

> que haya recato en tu casa,
> . . . .
> y que muestren como tuyas
> tus puertas y celosías
> que hay dentro personas muertas
> que defienden honras vivas.
>
> (186 [62])

All the husband's precautions are in vain, however, for the wife's cousin, enamored of the rival returned from America, plots with the female slave to let Félix in.

While at the court, Pedro is honored by Emperor Charles V himself and associated with the ideal of masculinity embodied by the Duke of Alba and the habit of Santiago. Under the pressure of living up to this standard, the husband is more likely than ever to anticipate offenses to his publicly recognized *hombría*. When he meets Félix on the road home, the husband assumes the role of the suspicious but crafty husband, playing along to collect evidence of his dishonor and delivering anguished monologues on the need to wash his honor with blood.

The husband offers to act as Félix's go-between, then invents a pretext to leave home again. The wife misinterprets his tepid arrival and speedy departure as signs of infidelity. Her gloss on the title of the play indicates the gender specificity of the dangers of absence (202). A wife has no legal or socially sanctioned means to redress a husband's adultery resulting from absence, but the preying on male property that occurs in *his* absence can lead to her death, whether guilty or innocent. While her husband is occupied in the public sphere, a wife must further restrict her freedom of movement, and knows that other representatives of patriarchal law are prepared to step in and mete out punishment for deviant behavior in a husband's absence. When Bernardo accuses her of adultery with Félix, whom he has seen entering and leaving her house, the wife writes an indignant letter to her father, telling him that Bernardo has offended Pedro's honor by courting her and by saying that she is unfaithful. The father confronts Bernardo with the intention of killing him to protect his son-in-law's honor; but when Bernardo repeats his accusations, the father swears he will kill Blanca if she is proven guilty.

Blanca's father and Bernardo join the husband outside his house, where the three men quarrel over Blanca's innocence. The husband, sword in hand, swears he has locked her in a room with a man. Blanca reveals the falsity of his perception by calmly entering and asking: "¿Qué es esto?" ("What is all this?") (204). Two women have fooled all the men, including Félix, who, thinking he was cuckolding Pedro, was having sex with the wrong woman. In a comically judicial mode, Blanca assumes the active role both in distributing "sentences" and in arranging the exchange of women, while the four men passively beg her pardon and accept her judgments (204).

While in this text, *Laura,* and *Cortesía,* the wife is the instrument revealing the rival's guilt, in other plays the rival is finally subordinated to the husband through the instrument of confession. Mortally wounded, the rival of *Celauro* divulges the truth of his deceptions (the false "proof" of the infidelity of husband and wife) and offers his body to the husband's vengeance:

> y así, mi maldad te ruega
> desnudes aquesta espada
> y me atravieses con ella,
> para que muerto a tus manos
> tú mismo vengues tu ofensa.
>
> (132 [63])

The husband refuses, choosing to pardon him instead (132). In his introduction to *The History of Sexuality,* Michel Foucault discusses the central role of confession as truth-producing ritual in Western societies since the Middle Ages (58–59). Confession constitutes the speakers "as subjects in both senses of the word":

> it is also a ritual that unfolds within a power relationship, for one does not confess without the presence . . . of a partner who is not simply the interlocutor but the authority who requires the confession, prescribes and appreciates it, and intervenes in order to judge, punish, forgive, console, and reconcile; a ritual in which . . . the expression alone . . .

> produces intrinsic modifications in the person who articulates it: it exonerates, redeems, and purifies him; it unburdens him of his wrongs, liberates him, and promises him salvation. (60–62)

The wronged husband does not need to overpower the rival through force because his enemy has already assumed the submissive position. In confession, "the agency of domination does not reside in the one who speaks (for it is he who is constrained), but in the one who listens" (Foucault, *History* 62).

In *Rosambuco,* the envious Pedrisco tries to poison the saint, but the vessel breaks into pieces. The alignment of miraculous supernatural power with Rosambuco confers on him the authority that calls forth the confession (391). Rosambuco refuses to have Pedrisco punished and predicts the saintly transformation wrought in him by his confession (391). The rival in *Nacimiento,* stabbed by the son to avenge his mother's dishonor, confesses that he lied to the king about her infidelity. Through his confession, the rival enacts his subjection:

> ¡A ti me entrego,
> ¡Oh Clodoveo! y que me mates pido!
> Confieso ya mi mal, que no lo niego.
> . . . .
> Mas la justicia del inmenso cielo,
> . . . .
> Me derribó de aquesta herida al suelo.
> (518 [64])

Whatever the outcome of the juridical proceedings promised at the end of *Estefanía,* the male subject who thought to dominate another man through the aggressive defense of his private property ends up in a position of total subjection to the figure of authority who listens to his confession, but withholds decisive judgment. In these texts, the rival is as effectively mastered by the one who hears his confession as those who die violent deaths at the hand of the husband in that other truth-producing mechanism, the public execution. Both of these rituals establishing the truth of guilt show the operation of patriarchal power: in one, subjection to the Father is accomplished through physical force bearing down on the body, and in the other, an authoritative male holds the power to judge, punish, and forgive.

The husband who misreads the signs of his dishonor in the texts discussed above at least reacts to an actual rival he knows to be circling his property. Nothing reveals the contradictory demands of masculinity more than those texts in which the rival is clearly non-existent. In such plays, the rival himself is constructed by the hypervigilance of the husband. In *Portugués* and *Mal,* the husband's fearful imagination creates a rival threatening to put the wife back into circulation. That the husbands of these two texts are of very high rank—a duke and a king—suggests that not even the greatest social privilege can deflect the anxieties that attend the performance of the masculine ideal.

By the end of Act I, the Duke of Berganza in *Portugués* has fulfilled his desire in his marriage with Mayor. The second act opens with the mystery of the duke's melancholy, posing the dilemma at the heart of many of Lope's honor plays: if the duke is happily married and adores his wife, "Pues ¿cómo, á quien tiene amor, / Da la posesión disgusto?" ("Then why, to one who loves, does its possession give so much displeasure?") (380). The duke will not reveal the cause of his sadness, even to his most trusted servant (383). He can hardly admit the truth to himself, but finally reveals that he is jealous of Mayor's page.

The duke assumes an adulterous relationship exists between them because he perceives the intimacy of their bond. Since the construction of an autonomous and unified masculine identity depends on distancing the feminine, the duke experiences alienation in the possession of the love object, yearning to return to merged identification with the (m)other. Incapable of emulating the page's relationship with his wife, he imagines a role with which he can feel comfortable. By projecting on the page the role of rival, the duke denies that the page's relationship with Mayor has anything to do with the wife herself. For the duke woman is only the medium of relationships with other men; therefore, the page's relationship with Mayor can only mean a struggle for mastery between the page and himself.[23] Since recognizing the real nature of the threat the page poses to his masculine identity would be too threatening, the duke displaces his resentment onto class differences, expressing his deep shame that his cuckolder is of such lowly social origins (383).

The page escapes the duke's attack and rescues Mayor, who flees to the court. When the king decides in Mayor's favor, the duke still insists on a duel with one of Mayor's brothers. The page breaks the tension by revealing "his" true identity as a woman. The duke asks for forgiveness and attributes his "madness" to jealousy, correcting the title of the play: "Pues llamalda injustos celos, / Y no *Duque de Berganza*" ("Then call it 'unjust jealousy' and not *The Duke of Berganza*") (401).

Actually, the real title of the play is *El más galán portugués* (*The Most Gallant Portuguese*); the words "Duque de Berganza" appear under these on the first page of the play. The multiplication of titles captures the contradictions in the male subject's attempts to act out the amorous ideal associated with Portuguese nationality in the first act and the defense of masculinity associated with the identity of "duke" in the second and third. Up to the achievement of his desire, the hero is characterized in the conventional frame of the Portuguese lover (370, 372, 379). But the subject position of gallant Portuguese lover conflicts with that of husband with private property to worry about. The first part of the title disappears, to be replaced by the subtitle ("Duke of Berganza") and a new title ("unjust jealousy"). Although some seventeenth-century discourses on masculinity present jealousy as mutually exclusive with the social values communicated by the sign "duke," the action of the play implies that *all* male owners are vulnerable to real or imagined predation, regardless of social rank. The vehemence with which jealousy is disavowed in these discourses is an index of the importance the masculine ideal places on the ability to protect sexual possessions from other men. To feel or admit to jealousy is already to admit the possibility of loss of control.

Jealousy bears the blame for the king's predicament in *Mal* as well. The Spaniard Don Juan, illegitimate son of a noble father, has arrived at the court of Naples after avenging an offense to his honor in Spain. Once in Italy, Juan begins courting the king's cousin Casandra, who is promised to the King of Denmark. Casandra convinces the queen to intercede for Juan with the king, who has granted him a low-prestige position at the court because of his social standing. Repeating Casandra's words, the queen praises Juan so much that the king becomes jealous. When a rival for Casandra tries to kill Juan, Casandra convinces the queen to have her husband make peace between the offended parties, which inflames the king's jealousy even more. The king arranges to meet Juan alone, but before he can kill him he learns that the object of the Spaniard's desire is Casandra and not the queen. Compromised by having revealed his jealousy, the king chooses the lesser evil of the title.

Having extracted an oath from Juan never to tell anyone of his jealousy, the king negotiates a series of disreputable maneuvers in order to marry Juan and Casandra, repeating "del mal lo menos" ("the lesser of two evils") as justifying refrain at each step. First, he hides in Casandra's garden for proof of their love, an affront in itself since Casandra is his female relative. Then he pretends that Juan is related to the King of Spain, to warrant naming him admiral (471). When the marquis tells the king he has seen Casandra and Juan together, the king has to shrug off this damaging information, saying that it is time to marry her, and then suffer the marquis's flabbergasted reaction to his choice of Juan: "¿A un hombre Almirante de hoy / y ayer un pobre soldado?" ("To a man, admiral today and yesterday a poor soldier?") (475). The most compromising blow to the king's integrity is having to break his word to the King of Denmark (467).[24] But the King of Naples is not the only sovereign who must choose the lesser evil to avoid losing face. Casandra writes the King of Denmark to ask that he marry her to Juan rather than force her to marry himself against her will. The King of Denmark pretends to concede to a request from the King of Spain to marry Casandra to his "kin," Don Juan. This lets the King of Naples off the hook: "Mas yo pensaba emplealla / en vos, conforme el concierto" ("But I was planning to marry her to you, in accordance with our agreement") (476).

At the beginning, the king defends the power of the sovereign to raise the lowly to a high position for no other reason than the royal will:

> No dan los reyes disculpa,
> que es libre la majestad;
> y hacer hombres de la tierra
> es en lo que imita el rey
> a Dios.
>
> (449 [65])

He exercises this power in elevating Juan ". . . desde el suelo / a las estrellas del cielo" ("from the ground to the stars in heaven") (449), but for reasons that expose the limits to absolute power. If he has "made" Juan from the dirt as God formed Adam, he has done so against his will and in spite of his real opinion of Juan.[25] Unlike heads of state in other texts who lift up a lowborn but worthy man or legitimate the claims of an illegitimate son, for the King of Naples, Juan's good fortune is merely the "lesser of two evils" necessary to maintain his own honor and *hombría* intact. He laments the seemingly unresolvable paradox that subordinates his absolute power as a sovereign to his vulnerability as a man: "¿Qué sirve el cetro en poderosa mano? / Que poderse librar de una sospecha / no cabe en fuerzas del poder humano" ("Of what worth is the scepter in a powerful hand? For it is beyond the force of human power to free oneself from a suspicion") (450). But the fact remains that it is within his power to choose the lesser of two evils precisely because the scepter is in his hand.

The Rival's Trajectory

Not all of Lope's honor plays focus on the husband's recuperation of the dominant position. In a few texts, the rival retains his ascendancy. In *Rústico* and *Cuerdo,* the rivals maintain their control through cognitive mastery, the husbands remaining unaware that they have been cuckolded. As in *Rosambuco,* the secular struggle between two male subjects in *Rústico* is superseded by divine intervention channeled through the figure of a saint. When the wife gives birth during the husband's absence, his sexual neglect is blamed:

> Hombre que tiene heredad,
> Acuda á la sementera;
> No nazcan hierbas de afuera
> Por la mucha sequedad.
>
> (247 [66])

Although the husband recognizes his fault, he locks the wife up to go check her story (that Francisco—the rustic saint of the title—gave her the baby to ease her solitude), swearing to kill her if he fails to corroborate it. After Francisco scolds him for his suspicions, the husband humbly asks his wife's pardon, but his fears are reawakened by the arrival of one of the wife's suitors. Francisco diverts the husband's attention by pretending to remove the child from their care, retracting the threat when the husband gets down on his knees and promises to curb his jealousy. Francisco also takes the wife and her lover to task, impressing the rival to the extent that he becomes a monk. The alliance of saint, wife, and rival accomplishes the moral reform of the adulterers, but it does so through the cognitive control of the husband, underlined by his submissive posture. Since the saint says he told the husband "[e]so que Dios me enseñó" ("[w]hat God showed me") (261), the text positions God at the top of this particular string of dominated and dominating, knowing and unknowing subjects.[26]

In *Ferias,* the abasement of the husband is more severe, since he becomes aware that he is being cuckolded and yet fails to regain his masculinity. Learning of the threat to his honor through a chance encounter with the rival on his street, the husband pretends to be courting at another house to induce the rival to tell his story. Even though he holds the upper hand in terms of awareness, the husband's self-presentation diminishes him: commenting on the amorous associations of the rival's name, Leandro, the husband denigrates his own ability to live up to the connotations of his feigned one, Alejandro ("Mayor que el hombre" ["It is greater than the man"] 602). The rival augments the affront to the husband's honor by asking him to guard the street while he talks to the wife, to which the husband mutters as he complies, "¿No basta ser el cornudo?" ("Is it not enough to be the cuckold?") (604). In his first monologue, the husband recognizes his part of the blame for his dishonor: "¡Yo tengo mi merecido, / que, pues no soy buen marido, / que tenga mala mujer!" ("I have what I deserve, for, since I am not a good husband, I have a bad wife!") (605). At this point, the husband's delay is justifiable, since he plans to murder them both in the act to provide the proof required by law (605).

While other husbands who have recovered their "vision" suffer masochistically as they spy on wife and rival, they sink to the depths in order to rise again to the heights. But these scenes in *Ferias* are too prolonged and numerous, too humiliating to permit a comeback. His is not a temporary slip but a permanent lack of *hombría.* Still pretending to be his friend, the husband reads the wife's love letter to the rival out loud to him and allows him to describe one of their trysts, chiming in when the rival speaks badly of him: "Que digo que es un bellaco / . . . / Mal quiero ese hombre, por Dios. / . . . más vale matalle" ("I say that he is a rogue. . . . I detest that man, by God. . . . Better to kill him") (610, 617). He loses one opportunity after the other to attack the rival, conditioning the audience to expect no final reversal. Even though he speaks with double meaning ("Sin duda que moriréis / cuando en sus brazos estéis" ["Without a doubt you will die when you are in her arms"] 618), the audience now perceives him as utterly incapable of action. Bungling an attempt to catch them together, he rejects direct action for continued pretense:

> ¿Echaré mano a la espada?
> ¿Entraré con alboroto?
> No, que es negocio de honra,
> . . . .
> Quiero entrar disimulado.
>
> (618 [67])

Apprised of their next meeting, he runs to his father-in-law for help, rather than planning their murders alone.

The father-in-law attributes his daughter's misconduct to the husband's neglect of his obligations. When he kneels and begs the husband to kill him, too, the husband's indignant reaction betrays his fear of handling the situation by himself. The father-in-law pretends to go along with the husband, but stabs him instead. Temporarily subordinated to the husband, he protects his own honor and simultaneously eliminates a son-in-law who is lacking in sufficient masculinity:

> Si yo a mi hija mataba
> como adúltera y lasciva,
> dejaba deshonra viva
> que para siempre duraba.
> . . . .
> que yo, sin matar mi hija,
> he defendido mi honor.
>
> (622 [68])

The father-in-law remains free of suspicion, since the husband had a mistress and everyone assumes he was stabbed by a rival.

The husband loses control in both triangles channeling relationships with men through his wife: cuckolded by his rival and murdered by his wife's father. In death he continues to signify lack of *hombría* through a figure capturing the culture's attitudes towards both sodomy and phallic swordplay; observing the death wound, a squire comments: "El era de la esgrima principiante. / Por la nalga le dieron la estocada" ("He was a novice at fencing; they stabbed him through the buttocks") (623).

The successful rival, on the other hand, disassociates himself from the group of young men bonded through heterosexual activity, assuming the complementary subject position in the traffic in women. Promising to marry the widow in a year, he positions himself in a stable, nontriangular relationship (623). Like some husbands in other texts, the rival ends up on top because he can manipulate the entire spectrum of exchange.

Three other plays focus on the rival's trajectory, implying a certain exaltation of his predatory ways whether he is eventually rewarded or punished. *Halcón* and *Porfiar* offer a serious treatment of the rival's persistence. Unlike other representations of the rival that emphasize his masculine attributes and cognitive domination of the husband, these plays depict the rival in terms of masochistic suffering, recasting the feminine gender attribute of "constancy" in pursuit of the love object.

In *Halcón,* the rival's self-sacrifice (living willingly in penury and killing his beloved falcon) is praised as a noble feat by the other characters, recalling *Corona*'s elevation of the wife's self-mutilation: "El hecho ha sido romano / . . . / Que basta para dar gloria / A tu nobleza y memoria" ("The deed is worthy of a Roman . . . and suffices to glorify your nobility and your memory") (477). But even though the killing of the falcon is a masochistic gesture, it is performed on a possession, not his own body. The falcon is his to kill or not kill in a way that the wife's body in *Corona* is not hers to act upon or not.[27] Even though his abnegation involves the death of two people (the husband out of jealousy, and the widow's son out of longing for the falcon), the rival is rewarded at the end with the fulfillment of his desire.

In *Porfiar,* the impulse underlying the rival's desire is fundamentally masochistic, as his pursuit of the love object after her marriage becomes the pursuit of his own death. The text represents the legendary passion of Macías, whose name became a synonym for lover in Spanish literary culture. At the beginning, Macías is repeatedly associated with the masculine ideal. He has decided to abandon the study of letters for arms, and he arrives at Córdoba with letters from the Duke of Alba recommending him to the king. He distinguishes himself by his bravery when he comes to the defense of the Grand Master of the military order of Santiago, another paradigmatic figure of Spanish warlike manliness, and stands out in battle against the Moors as the most valiant soldier. When the king wants to reward him for his service, Macías asks for Clara, but she has already been promised to Tello. Although the sight of the woman was the initial spark igniting his passion, heterosexual desire is but the field for intense bonding and rivalry, not only between Macías and Tello, but also between the king and the Grand Master. The latter are caught in conflicting desires and obligations towards husband and rival. Both are taken with Macías's performance of masculine gender attributes, but they are also great admirers of his poetic gift. Superior to Macías in age, social rank, and prestige, Tello's sense of besieged honor is exacerbated by his rival's perceived superiority in arms and letters. Macías, on the other hand, rather than being dissuaded by Tello's status, is locked into conflict with him because of it.

Macías's passion is inflamed by the very conditions limiting it: "que no hay cosa que más crezca / el amor que un imposible" ("for there is nothing that makes love grow more for a man than impossibility") (700). He increases his suffering by posting himself outside their bedroom, imagining the acts that cause him the most pain and pleasure:

> Dejadme, imaginaciones,
> que de la pintura el arte
> imitáis en mis sentidos,
> pintando figuras tales,
> que me abrasan y me hielan.
>
> (708 [69])

While other rivals use violence to fulfill their desire, Macías's passion hinges on the impossibility of fulfillment, barely masking a desire for death. Clara tells him she would have been his if circumstances had permitted, but warns him that if he exceeds certain boundaries she will not hesitate to tell Tello to kill him. The servant repeats the words that favor Macías, but Macías echoes her threat of physical annihilation (705).

As Gaylyn Studlar points out in her analysis of the masochistic esthetic, Denis de Rougemont's description of Western culture's glorification of passion as a disguised "longing for death" is startlingly similar to a description of masochistic desire (84). A subversive desire that refuses to fear pain or death, masochism attempts to satisfy "the unconscious longing to become part of another being" (84). In its goal of symbiotic nonidentity, masochistic desire emerges as the epitome of transcendent, transfiguring, and tragic passion (84). Studlar suggests that the choice of death creates an "ambiguous, illusionary triumph," representing the "only possible liberation from repetition of desire, a victory over the limitations of reality and socially bound identity" (84).

After Tello threatens Macías's life, the Grand Master rebukes Macías, who ignores both by speaking to Clara. As the bonding with Tello becomes more intense, Macías becomes progressively immobilized, and the exercise of letters replaces that of arms. When the Grand Master intercepts Tello, sword in hand, he orders Macías imprisoned in a tower. Macías accepts this punishment as his due (717). However, since he continues to write poetry about Clara from prison, Tello kills him by throwing a spear through the bars. During the last two scenes, Macías's body, "run through with a lance," remains onstage to signify his domination by Tello, a subjection he augments by confessing his error and asking for forgiveness. While the displayed corpses of murdered wife and rival are made to signify the power of the husband-sovereign to punish transgression, here the emphasis is on the exaltation of the subjected (male) body itself. Instead of approving Tello's exercise of masculinity to protect his honor, the Grand Master, a figure of paternal authority, swears to avenge Macías's death and to place a memorial to his desire on his tomb (719).[28] Macías's masochistic surrender to his desire subverts the symbolic order that his death supposedly restores. As Studlar suggests, the "voluntary submission to death suggests a rebellious, masochistic pleasure that defies rather than confirms" patriarchal law (79).

Caballero presents a comic treatment of the rival's preying on women, in part because it is his means of livelihood. Even though they are more economically than erotically motivated, his exclusive dealings with woman as circulable commodity still feminize him as conceited dandy. His first words are "¿Vengo bien puesto?" ("How do I look?") (145). When his servant replies, "Peregrino talle tienes" ("You have an extraordinary physique"), Luzmán says his question referred only to his clothes,

> que ya yo sé que en mi talle
> puso, el que pudo formalle,
> su poder y gusto junto.
> . . . .
> vestirme es a cuenta mía,
> el talle, a cuenta del Cielo.
>
> (146 [70])

After Luzmán's long disquisition on clothes and cosmetics, his servant Tristán cautions,

> Deja esas vanas quimeras,
> que no es de tu honor decillo,
> . . . .
> Más sabes que una mujer
> y callar será mejor.
>
> (146 [71])

Luzmán is a self-involved narcissist (". . . a Narciso igualas, / como en el talle, en quererte" ["you equal Narcissus, as much in your physique as in loving yourself"] 147), a misogynist who pretends to love women and refers to them as his "tributaries" (147). Besides his physique, Luzmán depends on his verbal ability ("linda labia" ["golden lip"]) to deceive women and dominate other men. The pun of the title refers both to his elaborate deceptions, or "milagros" ("De milagro visto y como" ["I dress and eat from miracles"] 149), and his noble pretensions: he is a gentleman "by miracle" since he was not born one. Tristán sings his praises, as a fellow servant intones the refrain, "Por eso es *Caballero de milagro*" ("That's why he's the miracle gentleman"):

> ¡Qué sagaz, qué fingido, qué doblado!
> . . . .

¡Qué ricamente viste, come y gasta!
. . . .
es hijo de quien quiere, y es tan noble,
que a veces tiene don y a veces título.

(164 [72])

Luzmán juggles three women and as many men, playing them off against each other with his tricks.

The key to the comic treatment of Luzmán's final downfall lies in his aspirations to pass as noble, a rupture of the social order the *comedia* never tolerates. He must be punished, not so much for his exploitation of the traffic in women, but for his refusal to accept his place in the social anatomy. Luzmán believes he must be the product of his mother's affair with a duke or count: "perdóneme mi padre, / . . . / que de esta inclinación autor no fuera / quien oficio mecánico tuviera" ("may my father pardon me, . . . for no manual laborer could have authored a man of my inclination") (165). Deciding to call himself "Don," he chooses not one but five illustrious surnames: "Don Luzmán de Toledo y de Mendoza, / Girón, Enríquez, Lara" (166). He directs his class resentment at those who inherit nobility without merit:

aquél busca el sustento y el vestido,
y éste, porque deciende de los godos,
es adorado y por señor tenido.
    Mas el plazo cumplido
se viene a conocer que el mundo yerra,
pues que juntos los dos se vuelven tierra.

(166 [73])

Luzmán ultimately loses cognitive mastery and control over the narrative. No single male character is capable of gaining power over him, since all of them, including Luzmán, are represented as cowards who pretend to be brave. Luzmán tells his servant, "[s]oy oveja y león me pinto" ("I am a sheep and appear a lion") (149), calls on the commandment prohibiting murder in order to avoid a fight, and claims that to risk marring his beauty would be to insult nature. The others are presented as either "gallinas" ("chickens") or too old or complacent to perform the role of avenger. Luzmán's own greed and narcissistic self-sufficiency precipitate his ruin. When he tricks a woman into giving him the money he needs to set himself up as a gentleman, he dismisses his faithful servant Tristán. Disguising themselves, the resentful Tristán and three others ambush Luzmán and take his clothes. Luzmán turns one by one to the three women for help, and one by one they reject him. Unlike the wives of other texts who are instrumental in unmasking the rival and returning masculinity and narrative control to their husbands, these women are neither innocent nor noble, and they avenge *themselves* more than their men's honor. But their actions are still circumscribed within the phallic economy: they punish Luzmán by withdrawing themselves from circulation to private ownership, returning to their original husband or lover.

The text ends with the spectacle of Luzmán's degraded nudity and a moral: "De milagro al fin subí / y por milagro bajé" ("I rose by a miracle and by miracle I fell") (182). The humorous handling of the rival's defeat seems to position the spectators against him, but the text resists the binary reduction of narrative closure. While the ending attempts to confine the movement of Luzmán's miracles to an "up" that ends disastrously and moralistically in a "down," the audience has heard of Luzmán's *cyclical* fortunes in his servant's praise:

> ¿Hay cosa como verle sin dineros,
> y otras veces desnudo, y en un punto
> jugar, pedir prestado y no volverlo,
> tomar baratos, engañar mujeres,
> . . . .
> y que con todo le aman y le adoran[?]
>
> (164 [74])

Even though the play ends badly for Luzmán, the moral is less than skin deep; he can still use his wits to spring back from misfortune. The possibility of new "miracles" opens up the ending and communicates a certain ambivalence towards Luzmán's ebullient talents. Many spectators must have shared his critique of inherited privilege.

***

The shifting focus in these texts, now on the husband, now on the rival, now on defeat, now on triumph, reveals the remarkable flexibility of the erotic triangle in representing the dynamics of male homosocial rivalry. The lack of consistency in privileging any one position or outcome in the struggle for mastery suggests that the matter of these plays are the very crises precipitated by a predatory construction of masculinity and male fears about living up to this ideal. Whether resolved violently or comically, these texts bare the contradictions in the masculine ideal by exposing the dangers implicit in the subject positions of both husband and rival and in both private and collective ownership. The proliferation of texts in which the husband misreads the signs of his dishonor, either through deceit or misperception, indicates a keen interest in how this construction of masculinity leads to a state of hypervigilance predisposing the male subject to "see" what he most fears. While the danger to woman in all this is clear, these texts divulge the dilemmas and contradictions within the sex-gender system for men and women alike. Even as they affirm the patriarchal social order through death, confession and other punitive forms of domination, these plays betray a certain satisfaction in their insistence that even kings and other high-ranking representatives of the symbolic Father are susceptible to both the power and perils of rivalry.

Chapter Six

Mutuality and Submission

Lope's honor plays represent various kinds of male bonding of mutuality and love: through heterosexual circulation, through the exchange of women in marriage, and through transgressive female desire. The dynamics of domination that characterize bonds of rivalry are tempered in those of mutuality in favor of a more horizontal arrangement, though a hierarchical element is rarely completely absent. In numerous plays, groups of men roam the streets looking for women. In contexts of rivalry, fighting over women is a medium for male contact, replete with competitive admiration for each other's manly appearance.[1] Men may also form mutual as well as hostile bonds through the heterosexual circulation of women, either procuring them for a social superior or sharing them physically or verbally. In these scenarios of shopping for "women on the market," heterosexual desire functions as the field for establishing homosocial bonds between two male partners. For Luce Irigaray,

> the use and traffic in women subtend and uphold the reign of masculine hom(m)o-sexuality [punning with the French *homme*], even while they . . . defer its real practice. Reigning everywhere, although prohibited in practice, hom(m)o-sexuality is played out through the bodies of women, matter, or sign, and heterosexuality has been up to now just an alibi for the smooth workings of man's relations with himself, of relations among men. (172)

In the opening scene of *Venganza,* the duke and his servants indulge in some "comparison shopping" before knocking on Cintia's door. They consider the relative merits of various commodities[2] and take pleasure in verbally dominating the men who stand in their way. One husband is ridiculed for making a profit by keeping his wife on the market: "Pues si muere su mujer, / Ha de gozar la mitad, / Como bienes gananciales" ("For if his wife dies, he enjoys half [of what other men give her] as community property") (238). Another is dismissed as cuckold or impotent.[3]

Teodoro and Leonardo in *Bella* bond through their constant pursuit of anything in skirts: "lo que no quise, no vi; / . . . / En mi vida tuve envidia / sino al Turco" ("what I failed to desire, I didn't see. . . . I've never been jealous of anyone in my life except the Turk") (614). A woman need only be desired by one to be desired by the other (619), and they negotiate exchanges between them: "quizá por no verla al lado, / de balde te la daré" ("perhaps to not see her at my side I will give her to you for nothing") (619); "Truécame aquesta mujer, / pues por ella estás perdido, / por Casandra" ("Trade this woman with me for Casandra, since you have lost your head over her") (621). Their conquests are their "alibi," in Irigarayan terms, for their relationship with each other: Leonardo refers to Teodoro as half of his soul ("media alma" 627) and to them both as forming one soul ("un alma los dos" 613).[4] He prefers to follow Teodoro when his friend goes off with Casandra, even though he has a possible conquest under his nose (617). Just after he decides to give up his mistress and stay at home with his wife, he accompanies Teodoro instead to visit a woman neither has seen:

Leonardo :	Voy, Teodoro, a mi mujer,
	que adoro en ver su traslado.
	Y tú, ¿dónde irás agora?
Teodoro :	¿Ya no conoces mi tacha?
	A ver aquella muchacha,
	que la adoro habrá media hora.
Leonardo :	¿Es hermosa?
Teodoro :	No la he visto;
	pero paréceme a mí
	que es bonita.
Leonardo :	Voy tras ti.

(636 [75])

In *Desposorio,* a similar bond exists between the husband and his single friend, who shadows the husband in courting his mistress. As in *Bella,* the two men are "one soul" who drop everything to see each other:

Feliciano: Con gran prisa me avisaron
              que me llamabas, Lupercio,
              y aunque es verdad que me hallaron
              entre los de mi comercio,
              todas mis cosas cesaron,
              que me ha dado el corazón
              que estás con algún pesar.
Lupercio: Cuando dos un alma son,
              suele esos avisos dar
              la misma imaginación.

(532 [76])

The rival of *Ferias* initially belongs to a group of young men who bond through the use of woman as circulable commodity. The fairs of the title provide the background for the market in women, since during this time it was customary for men to buy women gifts. The *ferias,* or gifts, the men offer the women have a hidden price tag; with them the men hope to purchase sexual favors: "que ha de volver con ferias y obligada" ("for she will return with gifts and obligated") (584);[5] "Tomaré la posesión" ("I will then take possession") (588); "Contento viene el amigo: / debe de haber negociado" ("Our friend looks happy; he must have made a good deal") (589). Always together or looking for each other ("sin vos no hay gusto" ["without you there is no pleasure"] 595), the rival's friends compliment each other on their appearance ("¡Bravo de calzas estáis!" ["You're good in those stockings!"] 608; "¡Galán salís, a fe de caballero!" ["You're looking dashing, on a gentleman's word!"] 619), and discuss which of the latest styles reveal defects and which disguise them. They wander the streets looking at women, referring to their eyes or metonymically to the clothes they wear, as their heavy veils left very little else visible for comment: ". . . pierdo el seso / por unos ojos de una rebozada" ("I'm losing my head over the eyes of a cloaked one") (584); "¡Buena es la ropa que pasa!" ("What good clothes are passing by!") (586).

Although at first the rival tells his friends about the woman he meets during the fair, he becomes increasingly silent as they narrate their exploits.[6] When the rival balks at sharing his story, they decide to gossip instead: "Digamos de Roberto, que está ausente. /. . . Es ruin y de mal talle" ("Let's talk about Robert, since he's not here. . . . He is despicable and has a terrible physique") (599). They demonstrate the same lack of solidarity when they play a practical joke on one of their own to test his masculinity. After they attack him in disguise and he defends himself, he wins their approval: "Es fuerte como un Cid" ("He is strong as a Cid") (596). His bravery contrasts with their own cowardice when an unknown man passing by with a lantern sends them flying (600). Their anxiety concerning the performance of masculinity is further manifested by their humiliation on being deceived or dominated by a woman. While they do not refuse to go to market as commodities, as Irigaray proposes (196), some of the women the men plan to "oblige" with their gifts do manipulate the situation. One buys herself what she wants and ducks out the back door ("Del dinero no me pesa; / mas ¡que me burle mujer!" ["The money doesn't bother me, but that a woman tricked me!"] 590). Another throws water (or worse) on them from a window: "Estoy loco. / ¿Hay una piedra acaso?" ("I'm furious. Where's a stone?") (598). Thinking he is shopping for a woman on the market, one friend learns he has "gifted" or "bought" (*feriado*) his own wife: "Con extremo estoy corrido" ("My shame knows no bounds") (594). The rival's gradual disassociation from his cohorts marks their behavior as immature and unmanly.

The Channeling of Homoeroticism

Bonding through the heterosexual circulation of women, then, seems to be fraught with difficulties for the male subject, entailing a risk of feminization whether the bonding is of mutuality or of rivalry. In Lope's honor plays, bonds of mutuality are most secure when the exchange of women constructs or strengthens ties of kinship or when this bonding transpires through transgressive female desire. These ties appear to be less damaging to the integrity of the subject's masculine identity when a strong hierarchical structure is present as well. Texts like *Bella, Desposorio,* and *Ferias* represent horizontal homosocial bonding of mutuality as dangerously adolescent; *Discreto* and *Carlos* explore a different, but equally difficult, terrain, that of direct bonding between male subjects without the mediation of woman. Both plays foreground the homoerotic dimension of male homosocial desire as threatening to masculine identity when not played out through the bodies of women. As Irigaray points out, since male subjects relate primarily to themselves through woman in the phallic economy, "homosexuality" reigns everywhere, although actual sexual activity between men is taboo.[7] In both texts, the feminizing consequences of male homosocial desire unmediated by woman are put right through the exchange of women in marriage.

In *Carlos,* the duke is so fond of his lowborn but worthy valet that he immediately dismisses his wife's (false) charge that Carlos is trying to cuckold him. His reaction, "¿Carlillos?" ("little Carlos?") (453), contrasts with other husbands' willingness to believe accusations against their wives. This difference rests on the fundamental gender inequality that places more value on a man's word than a woman's, even if false, and disposes a husband to accept the infidelity of the woman he loves but not the infidelity of the man he loves. Because of the greater value attached to relationships among men and male lives in general, the crisis is also more severe when the beloved man's treachery is proven, as in *Venganza.*

The duke of *Carlos* is represented as lacking in masculinity, especially for a head of state. He leans on Count Ludovico to fight his war for him, and when his wife asks him what he is afraid of, he answers, "Mi propio daño, / Fuera de que tengo miedo / De morir en reino extraño" ("My own injury, besides my fear of dying in a foreign kingdom") (450). Even though he couches his reluctance in amorous terms, swearing he would die without her, she is clearly put out by his failure, as warrior nobleman, to put duty before love, since she would like to have the freedom to continue her pursuit of Carlos in his absence.[8] The duke's displacement of his own masculine obligations onto the count parallels his abortive attempt to bond through the exchange of women. He offers his sister as a reward for fighting the war for him, but Leonor disrupts this plan, masquerading as grieving widow while secretly married to Carlos. The ensuing masculinization of the milieu associated with warfare centers on Ludovico, with the duke, embroiled in his attempts to prove Carlos's innocence, very much on the sidelines. He is not even present for the count's departure, a failing underlined in a speech that contrasts the count's military manliness with the duke's inaction and absence:

> Partió bizarro y galán
> En un caballo alazán,

. . . .
> Todos de velle se admiran

. . . .
> Y á toda la Corte pesa
> Que no le fueses á ver,
> Favoreciendo su empresa.

(457 [77])

News of the count's triumphant return only reminds the duke of his inability to keep his promise to give him Leonora (475).

Besides his disadvantageous representation in comparison to the count, the duke is feminized by his hesitance to avenge his honor, as his wife, Casandra, points out: "O yo miento, ó vos queréis / Más á Carlos que la honra" ("Either I am lying, or you love Carlos more than honor") (457). Carlos as well points out the discrepancy between the duke's indecision and the kind of behavior dictated by the masculine ideal: "Otro fuera, que al rigor / Ya hubiera puesto, en efeto, / A la venganza el furor" ("Another man, in such a rigorous extreme, would have already applied his fury to vengeance") (460). The duke's lack of "rigor" allows him to be pulled between Casandra and Carlos, believing first one then the other. Just the sight of Carlos is enough to banish the duke's suspicions and his rage, a fact he attributes alternately to Carlos's charm ("hechizo") and his innocence (459). Casandra also berates the duke for his tepid response to Carlos's secret marriage, reminding him that no other nobleman would tolerate such insubordination (474).[9] The duke not only complacently accepts his exclusion from the exchange of women that makes Carlos his brother-in-law, he declares that Carlos would be a better Duke of Burgundy than he is, since Carlos has proven his virility and he himself has failed to produce offspring (468). The fear of appearing less than a man in the defense of honor drives the duke to take a few half-hearted steps to question Carlos:

> Pero si ésta ha de creer
> Que de ruin sufro mi afrenta,
> Y tengo un paje en más cuenta
> Que el honor de mi mujer.

(473 [78])

In effect, the duke does value a page more than his wife's honor. Cultures like that of seventeenth-century Spain teach men that they are more valuable than women and that they should reserve their deepest love for men, creating the conditions in which they prefer each other to women. For Irigaray, this is the inevitable result of founding culture on the exchange of women; but while male homosociality is the rule, sexual relations among men are forbidden, *because they openly interpret the law according to which society operates*" (192–93). The duke does not err in placing male homosocial relations above heterosocial ones; his error lies in failing to channel his love for Carlos through heterosexual exchange. Without the mediating body of a woman, both Carlos and the duke are feminized, and their homosocial bonding is charged with a homoerotic dimension ascribed negative value by their dominated positions in the text. Casandra consistently uses the verb *adore* to describe the duke's feelings for Carlos, while the fool ventures the most daring formulation of their relationship: "Para mí tengo que el Duque / Os done el cuerno con él" ("In my opinion the duke is cuckolding you with him") (465).

Carlos's manner with the duke is servile, peppered with masochistic imagery stressing his loyalty, dependence, and submission. He rejects Casandra's advances out of a sense of duty to the duke's rights of private sexual ownership ("Que de bueno, leal y fiel criado / Jamás vicié sus cosas . . ." ["For as a good, loyal, and faithful servant, I never contaminated his things"] 452) and because of his debt to the duke: if not even the greatest prince would stain the duke's honor,

> Cuanto más un gusano, un pequeñuelo
> Cual ya me veis, á quien el Duque ha dado
> El ser que tiene desde bien mozuelo,
> Cual yedra entre sus brazos levantado.
>
> (452 [79])

When the duke confronts Carlos with his wife's accusation, Carlos kneels and offers him his head (455). In gratitude for the duke's trust, he prostrates himself as his slave: "Ponme un hierro en esta cara, / Y con tus letras declara / Al mundo mi esclavitud" ("Place a brand on this face, and with your letters declare my enslavement to the world") (460). [10] Carlos's renunciation of the "father's" love object is accompanied by paternal recognition of Carlos's right to his own woman. In this way, male homosocial desire is properly channeled through heterosexual desire, as in the scene in which Carlos hides the duke in the garden where he and Leonora meet, to provide proof of their union. Not only does the duke recognize the marriage publicly, at the end he names Carlos's son his heir and acknowledges Carlos as his own son (487).[11]

In *Discreto* as well, the husband is feminized by his intense bonding with another man without the mediation of woman.[12] As in *Indicios,* the triangulation among three men raises questions of comparative manliness. The opening scene presents an encounter between the husband, Ricardo, and Leonelo, a rival for Hipólita (the object of the husband's extramarital desire). This confrontation strikes a comic note, since they are both lacking in *hombría.* They posture for a while, then Leonelo attacks Ricardo three to one and Felisardo rescues him. Felisardo's performance of the masculine ideal converts him into the object of desire of all, including Ricardo, who makes ample use of the lover's lexicon in his praise of Felisardo to his wife, Casandra, stressing his manliness and his physique:

> ¡Qué talle! ¡Qué gallardía!
> ¡Qué buena presencia de hombre!
> . . . .
> Fuera de ser gentilhombre,
> mucho más lo parecía
> con las galas de camino
> y con la desnuda espada.
>
> (187 [80])

Casandra's borrowings from the same vocabulary underline the amorous tonality of Ricardo's bonding: "¡Por Dios, que venís perdido! / . . . ¡extraña pasión!" ("By God, you're head over heels! Strange passion!") (187–88). At this point, Ricardo is unable to channel his desire through heterosexual exchange, and he laments the lack of a sister to give Felisardo (188). When Casandra questions his frenzy, he gets angry with her and rushes off to look for Felisardo. His servant spoofs the homoerotic dimension of Ricardo's bond in his mention of the "ángel de tu cielo" ("angel of your heaven") (198), referring not to Hipólita, but to Felisardo.

Ricardo rebounds from the feminine position in part by arranging the exchange of Hipólita between her brother and Felisardo, simultaneously hierarchizing his relationship with

Felisardo. Even though Felisardo was ignorant of Casandra's adulterous desire for him, Ricardo indirectly dominates him in the process of punishing his wife, since he has cognitive control of the situation. Disguised as Felisardo, Ricardo has beaten Casandra, setting Felisardo up as object of Casandra's wrath. Ricardo must "correct" his former improper bonding of mutuality, not only by mediating male homosocial desire through the exchange of woman but also by asserting himself in a position of mastery over Felisardo.

In contrast, the homoerotic dimension of the prior's intense bonding with the duke in *Portugués* is immediately channeled through the proper conduit. Having spent the night in the duke's house, the prior is so taken with him that he purposefully leaves a portrait of his sister behind in the bed to arouse the duke's desire for her. The prior's rapturous description details the duke's assets:

> Pero el brío y el despejo,
> Y el gobierno de la casa
> Del Duque, me tiene absorto;
> El donaire, ánimo y gala,
> Enamorado me tiene.
>
> (377 [81])

As in *Discreto,* the woman's desire imitates that of a man for another man, this time, licitly. When she hears her brother's lengthy praise of him, the sister inquires, "¿Tan buen talle el Duque tiene?" ("The duke really has such a fine physique?") (377).

Tenuous Ties

While the prior escapes feminization through timely exchange of women, this text portrays other dangers in male bonding of mutuality. Precisely because the male subjects of the transaction define themselves and their bond in terms of woman as exchangeable property, they leave themselves and their relationships vulnerable. Here and in other texts in which the husband is the direct or indirect cause of the wife's impending dishonor, her male relatives are ready to step in, representing a distinct threat to the husband if she is indeed innocent.[13] When the duke's own anxiety about his ability to guard his private property makes him see rivals where they do not exist, the prior and the wife's other brothers are quite willing to transform bonds of mutuality with the duke into bonds of deadly rivalry, since their own honor and masculinity are at stake (399).

The instability of male bonds of mutuality is patent in other forms of male relationships besides kinship. The rival who dominates the husband cognitively through lies about his wife's chastity in so many texts is supposedly a trusted friend, loyal vassal, or faithful servant. In *Indicios,* the contradictions of male bonding are represented in the complementary figures of the false friend–rival, punished at the end, and the true friend, wrongly suspected of cuckolding the husband, but whose very presence is due to having wounded another husband he was cuckolding in another city. *Veneciano*'s strategic stress on the sacred bonds of friendship strengthens ties of mutuality as an antidote to those of rivalry. After saving the life of his dead rival's son in a fight over Sidonio's daughter, Sidonio decides to make friends with him: "No se iguala bien alguno / Al de procurar amigos" ("There is no higher good than gaining friends") (562). But the text also reveals that the bonds of male friendship are tenuous. Sidonio had thought that his friends would help support his wife financially while he was in exile, declaring them "second fathers" (553). His servant's estimation of them as "second enemies" turns out to be more accurate, as they do not keep Sidonio's family from falling into poverty in his absence. Much less precarious are the bonds of kinship that the text ultimately proposes as the best, though not perfect, solution.

On the other hand, bonds of rivalry may slip into bonds of mutuality.[14] In *Peligros,* the rival Bernardo becomes protective of the husband's honor in his absence when the wife's cousin decides to take the other rival, Félix, for herself. Bernardo is indignant when he sees Félix at the window of the husband's house and swears: "La vida le ha de costar, / que yo tengo de guardar / del Veinticuatro el decoro" ("It will cost him his life, for I must guard the alderman's decorum") (189). Motivated by a dog-in-the-manger mentality ("que lo que no es para mí, / no ha de ser, fuera de ti, / de ningún hombre del mundo" ["for that which is not for me, is not to be, except for you, for any man in the world"] 189), Bernardo accosts Félix in the name of the husband's honor (191). Formerly dedicated to the task of cuck-olding the husband, Bernardo now constructs himself as kin: "porque no somos justicia, / sino deudos a quien toca / la honra del Veinticuatro" ("for we are not representatives of justice, but rather relatives responsible for the alderman's honor") (192). Since kinship is created through the exchange of women in marriage, the defense of those male homosocial bonds positions Bernardo on the side of the husband's male relatives. Félix refers to Bernardo's ambiguous standing: "Salgo a la calle; aquí no sé si arguya / que era galán o deudo, que curioso / la rondaba la calle escura y sola" ("I go out on the street; here I don't know if I should say it was a suitor or a relative, who, curious, pa-trolled the dark and lonely street") (194). On one of his nightly rounds, Bernardo wounds Félix so severely that he believes he has killed him.

Finally, this self-appointed guardian of the husband's honor takes it upon himself to confront the wife with her supposed adultery, repudiating all desire for her. She complains about his actions to her father, who points out his contradictory behavior to Bernardo, reclaiming for himself as male relative the right to protect the husband's honor:

> Yo soy su suegro y soy padre
> de doña Blanca. Entretanto
> que viene, su honor me toca,
> que no al galán, don Bernardo,
> que defender y ofender,
> como tan grandes contrarios,
> son como decir y hacer,
> que no comen en un plato.
>
> (200 [82])

Bernardo insists on taking the father-in-law to the scene to col-lect evidence. Three men converge on the house, in a kind of overkill firepower to cleanse the husband's honor, which, as it turns out, was not stained in the first place.

When the bonds of kinship teeter on the brink of becoming bonds of rivalry, ties between husband and male relatives can be strengthened through the punishment of transgressive female desire. Even though Balduino, the father in *Locura,* suf-fers on losing his beloved daughter, he approves of the husband's action. His only complaint is being unable to kill his daughter himself (309). There is also an element of competition in this strengthening of mutual bonds through the elimination of a woman who threatens the social order. The husband was initially unhappy with his arranged marriage to Balduino's daughter, hoping to make the far more advantageous match with Princess Blanca. The honors heaped on his father-in-law as war hero are an important factor in his acceptance of his marriage, as in the scene in which he juxtaposes Balduino's feats with Blanca's (now unwanted) attentions (296). In addition to his social climbing through another man's *hombría* and status, it is suggested that he did not behave in a manly fashion when the king arranged his marriage to Flordelís: "Porque más nobleza fuera / salirte de Francia . . ." ("For it would have been more noble to leave France") (297). The husband not only recovers his masculinity and honor by eliminating his wife, he also equals his father-in-law in heroism by sparing the rival's life. The husband recalls Balduino's feats, immediately placing his own alongside:

> Más vale, aunque caballero
> soy de tan alto valor,
> que yo viva sin honor
> que Francia sin heredero.
>
> (309 [83])

Balduino recognizes the husband's act as worthy of the world's praise (309), offering himself as the husband's father and protector in his insanity (312). As shown by this example, the bonds cemented by punishing lawless female desire are strongly hierarchical in nature. Even though the husband strives for parity with the authoritative father-in-law, the power is in the hands of the patriarchal figure who bestows approval on the avenging husband. The hierarchical nature of such ties is also apparent in a text like *Carlos,* in which the head of state pronounces Carlos free of all contamination by the banished woman and elevates him in social rank.

Although Carlos's low social position stems from his illegitimacy, and his relationship with the duke can be explained retroactively by his noble blood, bonding between men of radically different social positions through female sexuality and the practice of masculine gender attributes is a constant in Lope's honor plays. It may occur in the context of participation in the flow of women, as in *Venganza,* in which the duke's servants procure women for him. In many texts, the servant of the rival aids him in the pursuit of the wife, often mirroring his master's conquest by cuckolding one of the husband's servants. In some of these cases, the rival's servant shares the same fate at the hand of the husband or his servant.

Another common scenario is bonding of mutuality between offended husband and his servant or slave. For Kaja Silverman, thanks to the male subject's identification with the Father,

> he will find himself "at home" in those discourses and insti-
> tutions which define the current symbolic order . . . and will
> derive validation and support from them on a psychic if not
> at an economic or social level. In other words, he will "rec-
> ognize" himself within the mirror of the reigning ideology,
> even if his race and economic status place him in contradic-
> tion to it. (*Subject* 141)

Conventionally, this vertical bonding takes place when the husband regains cognitive dominance and plans his revenge. He confides his dishonor to his servant or slave, kneeling before him (*Discreto* 200) or offering him his freedom (*Vitoria* 447), and enlists his help. *Comendadores* provides the prototype for these scenes, and it is not ideologically innocent that it is the slave Rodrigo who defines honor as something external to one's being ("Sé que es una cosa / Que no la tiene el hombre" ["I know that it is a thing that a man does not have"] 290) and eggs the husband on to bloody vengeance.[15] His elevation is signaled linguistically by his solemn sonnet on honor (292), in contrast to the earlier comic one of the rival's servant Galindo, who later dies at Rodrigo's hand. Rodrigo, as a slave, occupies the lowest rung of the male hierarchy, but is entitled by his common sharing in honor and *hombría;* the servant in *Discreto* is worthy of his master's confidence because of his origins in the North of Spain, emblem of pure blood and honor (199).[16] In *Locura,* the husband's servant throws the wife's maid off the balcony and kills the rival's servant. Later, in the father-in-law's narration to the king, these murders are ascribed to the husband, revealing that in such cross-class bonding, the servant or slave functions as an extension of the noble husband's arm and his honor/*hombría* is to some degree merely reflective of the nobleman's.

In these cases of solidarity across class, male entitlement camouflages other economic and social relations. As Eve Kosofsky Sedgwick phrases it, "in the presence of a woman who can be seen as pitiable or contemptible, men are able to exchange power and confirm each other's value even in the context of the remaining inequalities in their power" (160). The frequency with which men of disparate rank bond through the performance of masculinity, defending or offending honor, preying on or punishing women, demonstrates the compensatory function of such gender discourses in cloaking hierarchical differences among men.

The Rewards and Perils of Submission

While male homosocial bonding in Lope's honor plays appears to cut across class, joining aristocrat and servant, Old Christian peasant and the highest ranks of Castilian nobility, through the medium of woman, these texts ultimately uphold the unequal distribution of power: the servant remains a servant and the Old Christian peasant acknowledges his "place" in the social structure that exploits him. The collusion of the sex-gender system in the perpetuation of dominant power relations is particularly clear in those plays in which the rival is of higher rank than the husband, either king or heir to the throne.

In his study of the body in seventeenth-century discourse, Francis Barker characterizes the prebourgeois realm as a single, full place (which he designates the "plenum"), a hierarchy sanctioned in practice by force and metaphysically by God (31). The king in the *comedia* is more than head of state; he stands in for Christ on earth, and his body *is* the social body.[17] The insistent representation of the social body as the monarchal or aristocratic body in Lope's honor plays may constitute a response to the growing pressure to problematize the old "imagined community," given the introduction of disparate groups such as the *indio* and the *mestizo* (Mariscal, "*Persiles*" 101). The hierarchical organization of the plenum in these texts is inseparable from the masculine gendering of power: "its paternalism is given in the fact that it assumes the father's role of a real and metaphysical authority which is all-pervasive, backed up by the angry recompense of punishment" (Barker 45–46). While he enjoys power over his wife as king within the family, the husband himself is subjected to the omnipotence of the king as Father within the state, his unconditional loyalty and obedience exacted with the threat of corporal punishment.

Firmeza captures this gendered chain of command simultaneously absorbing and subordinating the family to the state. Fulgencio lectures his son, Count Otavio, on the importance of loyalty to the Father-King:

> El Rey, como a Dios imita,
> dondequiera está presente.
> No se puede murmurar
> del que es supremo en valor,
> que el respeto del señor
> asiste en todo lugar.
> Nunca me vi tan perdido
> que a la suprema cabeza
> se atreviese mi tristeza.
>
> (643 [84])

For Fulgencio, the king's all-pervasive authority issues from his status of representative of God on earth, as does the respect due him (reflected in Fulgencio's understanding of his place in the social anatomy, subordinated to the supreme "head"). Otavio shows that he has learned this paternal lesson well, remaining loyal in spite of the king's repeated attacks on his honor. He articulates the king's dispersion throughout the social plenum in a striking graphic image:

> . . . los reyes,
> de Dios imágenes sacras,
> todos son pecho, señora,
> y que no tienen espaldas;
> y así tienen, aunque ausentes,
> en cualquier lugar la cara.
>
> (652 [85])

In this grotesque and menacing image, both the king's authority and the threat of force implicit in his wakeful omnipresence derive from his identity as "sacred image of God."

The *comedia* in general delights in creating sensationalist situations by placing supposedly omnipotent forces in conflict (Díez-Borque, *Sociología* 74). Where there is no honor conflict, love reigns supreme, while the honor play exploits the clash between all-powerful love and all-powerful honor. The texts under consideration here oppose the nobleman's honor (the equivalent of life itself) and his loyalty to the king. Just as honor wins out over love, loyalty must win out over honor. A man can kill his love object for his honor and still be a man. In fact, he is constituted as male subject by the act of placing honor above love and he is stripped of both masculinity and subject role by placing love above honor, since the loss of honor by definition spells the disintegration of masculine identity as such. The rival-king plays dramatize the debilitating effects of placing one aspect of the nobleman's *social* obligation over another. In two texts, the subordination of the husband's honor to his loyalty to the king culminates in death, the permanent cancellation of the male subject (*Resistencia, Alfreda*).

In most cases, however, the domination of the husband by the king is only temporary, a phase to which the male subject must submit in order to emerge more fully ensconced than before in the symbolic order. These texts enact the phase of "effeminized subordination to the father" in the Oedipal scenario that enables the male subject to adopt his own "proper" heterosexual role (Sedgwick 23). While male characters in other honor plays illustrate what Sedgwick calls the "feminizing potential of desire for a woman," the husbands of the rival-king plays reveal the "masculinizing potential of subordination to a man" (24). With the exception of the two texts mentioned above, the husbands initially dominated by their inability to defend their honor against the rival-king are ultimately rewarded for respecting the inviolability of the social hierarchy. Just as masculine identity may be the reward for temporary subordination to another man, respecting the supremacy of loyalty to one's king over honor may paradoxically augment honor.[18]

As his loyalty is put to the test by the threat to his honor, the husband becomes increasingly immobilized, even bordering on or lapsing into insanity in four of the eight texts.[19] This madness, the result of the inability to protect or avenge honor, is explicitly associated with loss of masculinity: "... no es hombre en rigor, / pues que le falta el sentido" ("he is not a man, strictly speaking, for he has lost his mind") (*Locura* 313). By removing their clothing, signifier of rank and masculinity, the male protagonists distance themselves further from the masculine position. Since clothing is the visual marker of identity, its removal becomes a conventional sign for insanity in Lope's honor plays. In *Locura*, the first thing the husband does when he loses his mind is take off his sword and his clothes (310), and they are the first thing he asks for when he comes to his senses (321). His reappearance before the king, gallantly dressed ("muy galán"), signals the imminent restoration of both honor and masculinity (323).[20] The restoration of the husband to the subject position is accomplished through his own active doing in only one case: in *Príncipe* he kills the rival-king who has raped his wife. But this rupture of the male power hierarchy is only apparent; the action is justified because the rival was actually a usurper and not the legitimate king. The elimination of this rival, who represents both a threat to the husband's masculinity and illegitimate access to the throne, exemplifies the interpenetration of discourses on gender and power in Lope's honor plays.

Locura, instead of testing and celebrating the virtues of both husband and wife, presents a transgressive female. Her early elimination allows the relationship between the husband and the ultimate site of male power to be discerned more clearly. The source of all conflicts in the plot is the marriage between Flordelís, in love with the prince, and Count Floraberto, in love with the princess. The king has arranged this union in order to marry his offspring for reasons of state. The king both refers to the marriage that led to Flordelís's death as an act of folly ("desvarío") and stands on his right to act as he sees fit as "absolute lord": "En ausencia de deudos yo soy padre" ("In the absence of relatives I am father") (294). In effect, he exercises the same power at the end as at the beginning, healing the breaches created in male homosocial relations by the first marriage by arranging two more, this time to the husband's distinct advantage. The alternative title given to the play at the end points to one of its meanings: "el agravio dichoso" ("the fortunate offense") (323). The very affront that forces him through an ordeal of suffering is the instrument through which Floraberto proves himself worthy to be the king's son-in-law.

Although Floraberto is eventually elevated in rank and restored to masculinity, the "feat" of sparing the heir to the throne, his cuckolder, also signifies dishonor. For the moment, the only remedy is madness, communicated verbally as he imagines himself to be Jupiter's eagle and dialogues with the murdered Flordelís, and visually by his antics, his lack of clothing, and his representation of the eagle, wearing feathers on his head (313). Even at the nadir of his fortune, "un cuerpo sin vida" ("a lifeless body") (320), the count knows that loss of sanity can never compensate for the loss of honor (319). His servant tricks him into lucidity by telling him that the prince is dead, but when Floraberto presents himself for punishment at court, his honor is restored through a tight circle of male bonds formed by the exchange of women, who function as rewards for sparing the prince's life (322).[21] The count's sister is raised to the rank of future Queen of France in marriage to the prince, and the count himself is made Great Constable of France and the king's son through marriage to the princess. Floraberto sums up the paradoxical process of gaining masculine authority through temporary submission to a more authoritative male: "Quien queda con tantas honras, / en haber perdido, gana" ("He who is left with so much honor, in having lost, wins") (323).

Príncipe reverses the above scenario, in that the husband's *disloyalty* to supreme male power is directly responsible for his dishonor. His restoration coincides with the recognition of the true king whom he has betrayed. The beginning of the play sets up the opposition between treason and loyalty, incarnated in the two brothers, Martín and Remón. After the death of the king, Remón remains loyal to the succession of the queen's unborn child; Martín and all the other courtiers, motivated by ambition and greed, traitorously support the dead king's brother, Sancho.

Martín's treason is associated with blood betrayal: not only has he disrespected the proper royal blood lines in supporting Sancho, he is also disloyal to his brother. To ease Sancho's fears of Remón's enmity, Martín swears to replace the blood in his veins with loyalty to the new king (140), but his eagerness to repudiate his brother's blood leads to his downfall. When Sancho invents the story that Remón is leading troops against him, Martín rushes off to disprove the rumor that "... la mano / despacio la sangre mueve" ("blood would slow his hand") (141), and Sancho rapes Martín's wife (Blanca) in his absence. In his multiple betrayal, Sancho ignores Martín's major role in placing him on the throne and sets Martín against his own blood (145). The resolution of the initial binary opposition between treason and loyalty defends the primacy of blood over political alliances.[22] Remón's cause is loaded with the weight of divine right from the beginning when he prophesies Martín's ruin (122–23). He takes control of the narrative, suggesting that Martín push Sancho over the cliff, directing his actions, and validating Martín's recovered manhood and their blood tie ("¡Oh, valeroso hermano!" ["Oh, valiant brother!"] 156).

In contrast to Remón's supreme confidence, Sancho appears wavering and fearful. Because he holds power illegitimately, he must constantly reassure himself that it is his to wield. When he finds himself trembling at the thought of speaking to Blanca, he shores up his lack of nerve with the idea of his absolute power (136).[23] The fact that he owes his rule to Martín's power and influence rather than blood right emasculates Sancho. In his obsessive musings, he derives not only his position but his very masculine identity from Martín: "De quitar á un hombre el nombre, / Por quien soy hombre ..." ("To take away from a man the name of man, through whom I am a man") (139). He resolves the conflict between his desire for Blanca and his debt to Martín by interpreting the absolute power of the king as license:

> Si yo soy Rey sin poder,
> ¿De qué me sirve reinar?
> Reinar es ser sobre todo,
> Todo debe al Rey servir.
>
> (139 [86])

After raping Blanca, Sancho regrets betraying Martín and rejects the notion of abusive power that soldered his insecurities in the past (151).

Sancho's illegitimate access to the throne determines his domination, while Martín's loss of the subject position is inseparable from his treason. Remón's loyalty, on the other hand, is masculinizing: he defends the seat of royal power and resolves Martín's honor conflict. By the end, the figure of the loyal vassal, exemplar of steadfastness (139), is doubled as Martín moves from the pole of traitor to reintegration with his faithful brother, and his treason is purged and projected onto Sancho. Swearing his loyalty, Martín kneels to kiss the infant's hand as a sign of fealty (159). Now Martín as well as Remón is an instrument in the divinely contrived course of events. Just as his support of the false king signified both treason and dishonor, his murder of Sancho avenges both personal affront and public offense of usurpation. When the queen exclaims that her dead husband has been avenged, Sancho's response fuses both levels: "Todos lo estamos, señora" ("We all are, Lady") (159).[24]

In *Batalla,* woman is the site of the battle between power and honor, demonstrating the strict limits placed on the vassal vis-à-vis the king, even an authoritative vassal like the admiral, second in command to the king himself. The impact of the text lies partly in the reduction of such a male character to a state of feminized madness by the end of the play. All the admiral's attempts to avoid dishonor are in vain because, as he himself realizes, the king's "invincible power" (599) is a force that cannot be resisted (578). Even though he has warned the king he will kill him to avenge his honor, he knows he cannot: "matarle es cruel maldad, / Dios en su imagen se mira" ("to kill him would be a cruel evil, God sees himself in his image") (598). The continuity between the public and the private spheres, as when the king succeeds in filling the admiral's own house with fleur-de-lis or breaks down a wall to penetrate its innermost recesses, is a dramatic (and highly sexualized, in the latter case) representation of the operation of sovereign power in both spheres. Inasmuch as the social plenum *is* the king's body, male strategies of guarding sexual property as well as feminine virtues such as *vergüenza* are ineffectual.[25]

Since the admiral cannot win, the battle between his honor and the king's absolute power can only be waged on the field of insanity: "Donde no hay igual poder / para resistir violencias, / piérdase el seso" ("Where power is not equal to resist violence, one must go mad") (605).[26] The major development of the title metaphor takes place in an extended narration in which the admiral imagines himself engaging in his battle of honor. His physical antics are later described to the king:

> . . . comenzó a dar voces como loco.
> Desnudóse furioso los vestidos
> y, últimamente, en un estanque, el triste,
> de aquel jardín precipitarse quiso.
>
> (608 [87])

The admiral's madness and attempted suicide convince the king to renounce his claim to the wife. Only complete abjection in feminizing madness and readiness to negate one's physical being as well can bring about the king's abdication. In saving the admiral from dishonor, then, the king also subjects him totally; the admiral is effectively cuckolded by the king without the necessity of sexual or cognitive domination.

This self-renunciation on the part of the figure of maximum authority is merely another aspect of his absolute power, expressing the interplay of male homosocial and heterosexual desire. The king, in the knowledge of his absolute power, freely gives up part of that power in the realm of heterosexual desire in order to tighten his social control in the sphere of male homosocial relations. The contradiction between the king's tyrannical abuse of power and "proper" kingly behavior only appears to be resolved at the end.[27] The text ultimately confirms his power to have it both ways. Rather than focusing on the virtues of the constant wife, the play dramatizes the hierarchizing dynamics of sovereign power among men. At the end, the king's restoration of the admiral's sanity is labeled a "feat," accomplished through the exchange of women (the king's marriage to the admiral's sister).[28]

In *Resistencia,* the contradiction between what the king is and what he should be is not hidden by a voluntary move on the king's part towards a higher position, but by external changes that remove the negative term of the opposition. At the beginning, Prince Enrique is ruled by his passion. His irresponsible pursuit of erotic pleasure conflicts with the affairs of state, namely, the battle against the English for Bayona. In the second act, the king dies, and Enrique becomes the model monarch, leading his troops into combat. When the king and his entourage stop at the palace of the Count of Belflor on their way to battle, Enrique becomes obsessed with the desire to possess the countess. To the newly revived opposition between the war over Bayona and the pursuit of women is added that of the king's desire and the honor of the vassal he is supposed to up-hold. Although he suspects the worst, the count remains loyal to the king. He saves Enrique's life in battle, and even after receiving a letter from his wife confirming his suspicions, he goes back onto the field in the king's service and is killed.

The king's duplicity in the count's death scene creates a dis-quieting effect. Enrique can hardly wait for the count to die so he can acquire the portrait of the wife with which the count comforts himself in his last moments (221). The courtiers' re-actions ("¡Conde! ¡Jesú! / ¡Gesualdo!" "¡Oh, expiró!" ["Count! Jesus! Gesualdo!" "Oh, he is dead!"]) contrast brutally with the king's: "¿Quién tiene el retrato?" ("Who has the portrait?") (222). Minutes later, his aside contradicts his public pose: "¡Qué buen amigo he perdido! / (. . . Todo es fingido, / que a gozar voy la Condesa)" ("What a good friend I have lost! [All is pretense, for I am off to enjoy the countess]") (222). Even Enrique's followers are scandalized at his determination to force the wife, in the presence of her husband's corpse, to marry him (226). The contradictions surrounding the initial opposi-tions associated with the king's desire have dissolved—Bayona has been won and the vassal is dead—but Enrique's image as king is still tainted by the lingering negativity in his portrait.

In *Alfreda* as well, the death of the husband removes the obstacle to the fulfillment of the king's desire. But as in *Prín-cipe,* instead of representing unflagging loyalty to the king the husband exemplifies disloyalty. By marrying Alfreda himself in secret, Godofre not only robs the king of his bride, but also robs the kingdom of heirs, the motivating force behind the royal marriage in the first place. In *Príncipe,* the disloyal vassal's punishment consists of sexual dishonor, and since the rival-king wears the crown illegitimately, he is castigated as well, restoring the husband to loyalty, honor, and masculinity. In *Alfreda,* the problems are of a different nature, entailing a dif-ferent solution. Count Godofre has betrayed the legitimate king, therefore the punishment is his alone. However, he now enjoys the rights of private sexual ownership; therefore, the king cannot claim Alfreda without disrupting bonds of fealty.

Presented with the choice between her husband's honor and the king's desire, Alfreda indignantly chooses the king when she learns she was originally intended to be his wife and not

Godofre's. But since she refuses the king sexual access while she is still married, the king resolves to kill Godofre, an action that would damage the kingly image.[29] Godofre must pay for his prolonged cognitive domination of the king, but this is accomplished without diminishing the representative of Christ on earth. Godofre makes a plea for pity that moves the king to let his vassal keep Alfreda. However, overcome by humiliation, the husband dies. In this way the text engineers an ingenious resolution that allows the king to have it all: voluntary renunciation of the wife that ultimately confirms his absolute power (as in *Batalla*) and possession of the object of his desire following the husband's death (as in *Resistencia*).

In the spectrum of texts dealing with a rival-king, *Corona* occupies the opposite pole from *Príncipe*. Here the male characters are so weak that the relationship of rivalry recedes, foregrounding the wife's task to protect her husband's honor. The wife's brother Iñigo wrestles with the contradictions between the collective use of women and the exchange of women in marriage. Quite willing to pimp for the king when he sends him to approach the beautiful peasant woman he has seen and desired, Iñigo is horrified when he discovers that the woman is his sister in disguise. To avoid a power struggle with the king from which he inevitably must emerge the loser, Iñigo decides to marry Sol off as quickly as possible, shifting the burden from himself to her new husband, Alvaro. Iñigo realizes that the king has awarded Alvaro a position at the court in order to gain access to Sol, but shrugs off the thought with the excuse that she is no longer his responsibility (586). When the king imprisons Alvaro and threatens to execute him, Iñigo feels guilt at betraying male homosocial bonds (596).

In spite of Alvaro's impeccable blood credentials (589, 597), he barely maintains the subject role in the exchange of women. Iñigo cognitively dominates Alvaro, giving him Sol in marriage not because he desires a bond with him, but to avoid being cuckolded by the king. The king ruefully recalls the violence done to the male hierarchy in awarding the noble but insignificant Alvaro his place at court for a woman he has failed to seduce (591). Alvaro's happiness at this honor and his exaggerated servility make him appear foolish, as do his anxious concern with his appearance when he sets out for court and his unmanly admission that his wife's family's services have functioned as a kind of dowry for him (587). This initial characterization of Alvaro establishes his unawareness of the threat to his honor. Even though he saw the king talking to Sol at the beginning, he forgets about it, perhaps blinded by his ambition. At court, each character expresses an appropriate reaction to the situation in asides: Iñigo trembles, Sol is afraid, the queen is on fire with jealousy, and the king with desire; Alvaro's response, in its blissful ignorance, sounds the only discordant note: "Contento estoy" ("I am happy") (590). In this context, the king's gifts and honors only signify his domination of Alvaro (593).

Alvaro learns of the offense to his honor when the king concocts a scheme to execute him for treason. Iñigo, assuming that Alvaro has undertaken this desperate act out of a desire for revenge, unwittingly reveals his dishonor. Alvaro thanks Iñigo for "illuminating" him (595), but the moment of the restoration of his vision coincides with his incarceration, leaving him no opportunity to agonize over the choice between honor and loyalty. Lamenting the fate of men with beautiful wives, he insinuates that it is Sol's responsibility to die in order to save his honor: "Yo muero por ser tú hermosa, / Muere tú por ser yo honrado" ("I will die because you are beautiful, you die so that I can continue to have honor") (596). Even in the case of a husband as thoroughly passive as Alvaro—dominated not only by the rival-king but also by his own brother-in-law—feminization is but a temporary prerequisite to increased masculinity and power at the end. Sol's act of self-mutilation reestablishes Alvaro as subject in male homosocial relations, as the king makes clear: "Que desta fuerte conquista / Ha ganado más honor" ("for from this great conquest he has gained more honor") (602).

The Constant Vassal

In his monograph on Lope's honor plays, Donald Larson does not include the rival-king plays, because "the stress . . . is more on feminine than on masculine values," embodying "the motif of the constant wife" (171). While these plays certainly do celebrate the wife's constancy, loyalty to the king can be seen as the masculine counterpart of feminine faithfulness to the husband. Rather than call them "constant wife" plays, it might be more appropriate to say that the texts embody "the motif of the constant vassal."

In *Cardona* and *Firmeza,* exile attenuates the immediate sexual danger to the husband's honor that in other plays elicits his strong "masculine" reactions only to frustrate them. The combination of manly desire for revenge and frustrating impotence explains the severity of the husband's ultimate feminization in the preceding texts (dishonor, madness, death). The husbands of *Cardona* and *Firmeza* continue to be loyal to their sovereign throughout their trials and tribulations. Even though the male subjects are thoroughly feminized in the process, these plays sport a more celebrative air, exalting the husbands' cultivation of the "feminine" virtues of loyalty and steadfastness ("firmeza"). In the face of the husbands' increasing incapacitation, female characters take a more active role, going beyond the passive resistance of other wives.

Firmeza doubles rival and offended party. Both the king and Ricardo are after Teodora, secretly married to Otavio. Teodora's brother Leonardo receives offense when he learns that the king appointed him head of the armada merely to remove him as obstacle to his possession of Teodora. While Otavio suffers his offense in resignation, Leonardo rises up against the king with his own armada. This doubling allows narrative control to remain in male hands for the greatest part of the play, first through Ricardo's rather inept manipulation of the king in the service of his own desire for Teodora, then, once Ricardo has lost control of the narrative, by the threat posed by Leonardo. The duplication of the figure of the rival allows all the blame for the violence against Otavio's honor to be shifted entirely to Ricardo, leaving the king free of responsibility. The splitting of the male character offended by the king into one who responds aggressively and one who suffers passively underlines the virtue of the "agraviado leal" ("offended yet loyal man"). The text is ultimately a paean to Otavio's seemingly bottomless ability to take punishment and still remain faithful to the king.

Before the couple and Fulgencio, Otavio's father, go into exile, the king demands that either father or son be held prisoner as security until Leonardo can be contained. Otavio's father offers himself, Otavio insists that it be he, and the king decides to hold the children instead. Later, in narrating his misfortune to Flora, the Duchess of Calabria, on her way to marry the king, Otavio foregrounds his suffering while soft-pedaling the king's role in it (653). When Flora joins Leonardo against the king, offering to avenge Otavio and return his children, Otavio renounces any desire for vengeance (657).

The climax of Otavio's submissive suffering occurs when the king, thinking Otavio has betrayed him by joining forces with Leonardo, forces the husband to choose between the execution of his children and that of his father. After anguished deliberation, Otavio tells the king to cut his children's throats, "que hijos podré tener, / pero padre es imposible" ("for I will be able to have children, but a father is impossible") (660). His choice of the father reinforces the deep-seated paternalism of the play and the social hierarchy it performs, based on the internal correspondence between father/king in the family and in the state. Otavio's self-sacrificing subordination to his father mirrors the obeisant attitude with which he absorbs the king's affronts. The passage is also remarkable for the light it throws on the status of woman vis-à-vis paternal authority. Otavio tells his father:

> Id con mis hijos a ser
> su padre y de mi mujer
> marido, que la mejora
> de esposo y padre, a Teodora
> y a ellos dará placer.
>
> (647 [88])

Not only is Teodora the medium and object of exchange between son and father, she supposedly derives pleasure from it. Significant in Otavio's process of feminized subjection to the paternal signifier is his assumption of the role of the daughter transformed into the mother of her own father:

> Si la romana mujer
> los pechos daba a su padre,
> y, por piedad, vino a ser
> de su mismo padre madre,
> dándole preso a comer,

mejor su prisión tomara
y a su padre libertara.

(647 [89])

When Fulgencio reproves his son for preferring father to children, Otavio reminds his father that it was Fulgencio who taught him to place paternal loyalty above all, both in the family and in the state: "y así, sufro; y a mi Rey, / . . . / le sirvo, pues decís vos / que así lo han de hacer los buenos" ("and so, I suffer, and serve my king, for as you say this is the way good men should act") (661). Noteworthy is the semantic chain equating "suffering" and "service" and linking it to a moral judgment ("buenos").

Although Otavio's posture is one of suffering submission, he is not completely emasculated. He is powerless to protect his wife, father, or children from the king's desire, but the scene in which he defends Teodora from a group of soldiers shows that he can still defend his sexual property threatened by other males. He also functions as subject in the exchange of women when he facilitates the union of Flora and his brother-in-law Leonardo. This action contradicts his pose of constant loyalty towards the king, for he disrupts the monarch's own arranged marriage with Flora. Even though Otavio insists that his reason for telling Flora the story of his plight is not to speak badly of the king, he manages to inform her of the king's pursuit of Teodora in the midst of preparing to marry the duchess. At the same time, in persuading her to marry Leonardo, who would live as duke on her land, he insinuates the king's rapacious motives in marrying her: "y ningún Rey con violencia / quiera usurparte a Calabria" ("and not a king who would want to take away Calabria from you") (653). Flora correctly reads Otavio's intention, discarding his transparent cover of protecting the king (653).

Otavio combines a masculine subject position in the defense and exchange of woman with "feminine" strategies of indirect manipulation, reflective of his helplessness vis-à-vis the king. Since he is incapable of breaking the deadlock, Flora acts as an extension of his suppressed masculinity to resolve the narrative conflicts, displaying the same combination of "masculine" and "feminine" roles. First, she appears in men's clothing when she joins forces against the king (657). Then she tricks the king into pardoning Leonardo, Otavio, and Teodora by agreeing to his punishment, "sólo con que no sea en cosa mía" ("with the exception of anything of mine" 663), and only then reveals her marriage to Leonardo. This duplicitous strategy is referred to specifically as feminine: "R: Con industria me engañaste. / F: Soy mujer" ("K: You deceived me with a trick. F: I am a woman") (663). Although Flora dominates the king cognitively, she does so in the service of legitimating heterosexual unions to re-establish bonds among authoritative males.

Teodora also deploys both active and passive strategies. The title virtue of steadfastness is identified with her resistance to the king and her courageous attitude in the face of misfortune (645). Confronted with the king's desire, Otavio can only go pale, tremble, and expose his powerlessness:

> Teodora: ¿Qué piensas hacer?
> Otavio: No sé.
> Teodora: ¡Bien me animas!
>
> (629 [90])

It is she who comes up with the trick of telling the king she is already married to Ricardo (630).[30] Later she tries to lift Otavio's timorous spirits:

> Otavio: Ya me pesa de lo hecho.
> . . . .
> ¿Qué haremos?
> Teodora: Hacer buen pecho,
> y si fuere necesario
> morir.
>
> (631 [91])

Teodora physically resists Ricardo's attempted rape and escapes, hiding out for a while among peasants. In this disguise she goes to the city to search for her children. Her resourcefulness is explicitly defined as feminine: "Una mujer, / en más difíciles casos, / halla camino a su intento" ("A woman, in even more difficult circumstances, finds a way for her intent") (658). When Ricardo tries sexual blackmail, offering not to execute her children, Teodora puts her honor above her children: "toma y córtales los cuellos / con esa daga y tendré / honra viva y hijos muertos" ("take this dagger and cut their throats and I will have my honor alive and my children dead") (662). The male characters' response to her choice urges the audience to admit Teodora to the ranks of Lope's other secular saints who put classical exemplars to shame (662). Both Teodora and Otavio subordinate their love for their children to the paternal signifier (since feminine honor is defined in relation to masculine honor), but the difference between them points to the gendering processes at work in their representations.

Although Otavio is feminized to some degree in his *firmeza,* by the end of the play steadfastness is absorbed into masculinity in opposition to woman's changeability: ". . . la Naturaleza / a la mujer formó de la mudanza / y al hombre trasladó de la firmeza" ("Nature formed woman from change and transferred steadfastness to man") (663). But just as the other elements of the narrative have been doubled, the presence of Teodora in the text belies this attempt to reduce woman to Flora's "mutability" or "deceit" at the end. The dual title that ends the play, ". . . *agraviado leal / y firmeza en la desdicha*" ("the offended but loyal man and steadfastness in misfortune"), captures Otavio's oscillation between feminine and masculine positions. While *firmeza* associates Otavio with Teodora and feminine virtues, the oxymoronic "agraviado leal" joins the oppositions that structure Otavio's narrative. The passivity of "leal" immediately neutralizes the connotations of anger and manly vengeance in "agraviado." Like the others, Otavio reaps the reward for recognizing paternal primacy: augmented status in the world of the fathers.

The title character of *Cardona* follows a similar itinerary, remaining loyal to his sovereign, the King of Aragon, in spite of the most extreme tests. The text insistently drives home his condition of "desdichado leal" ("unhappy but loyal man") (657, 660, 662, 669, 670). Pedro, the heir to the throne of Aragon, has pursued Cardona's wife, Casandra, publicly in his absence. Returning victorious from the war against the King of Sicily, the husband finds no hero's welcome, his wife in mourning to signify his disgrace, and his father in prison for wounding the prince in defense of his son's honor. As opposed to *Firmeza,* in which the father had to instill respect for paternal authority in the son, from the very beginning Cardona places the need to avoid offending one's king above the need to defend one's honor (657). Since "nobility" is synonymous with "loyalty" in the text (662, 663, etc.), Cardona feels that his father's action has reduced him to déclassé status (657).[31] Kneeling between king and prince in a visual sign of his submission, Cardona justifies the execution of his biological father for offending the Father in the state.[32]

The husband's subsequent misfortunes play off loyalties to king, father, and wife. By holding Casandra hostage, the King of Sicily forces Cardona to wage war against the King of Aragon, who in turn threatens to behead Cardona's father if he attacks. Even though the husband recognizes that by divine law he must place wife above father, he refuses to choose, picturing himself as

> ... un fïel
> en medio de dos balanzas
> . . . .
> fïel contigo y con él,
> que el peso de este pesar
> no ha de torcer el fïel.[33]
>
> (671 [92])

He proposes a two-man combat as a way out of this dilemma, but Pedro maliciously sends Cardona's father to fight him. Cardona recognizes Otavio and lays down his arms, pretending to believe his adversary is the prince, which sends his stock as loyal vassal even higher.

Incriminating circumstances make the husband believe that Casandra has been unfaithful with the prince, when in reality she has written Pedro to arrange a marriage between him and the King of Sicily's daughter, Clenarda. With this supposed loss of honor, Cardona believes he has plumbed the depths of his misfortune (679), but there is still more to come. Fearing that her husband will take her life to avenge his honor, Casandra has a servant tell him that she has been murdered by the King of Sicily (680). Repeating the refrain "muerta Casandra, morirá Cardona" ("if Casandra is dead, Cardona will die"), Cardona allows himself to be taken prisoner. Once again on the King of Aragon's side, the husband is torn between his desire to attack the King of Sicily to avenge Casandra's death and the knowledge that if he does, the King of Sicily will kill the prince, who has fallen into the king's hands thanks to Casandra's scheme. This final dilemma results in the total immobilization of the male characters. Acting in her husband's place, Casandra breaks the impasse, and Cardona is restored to favor and heaped with the honors won by his wife's valiant action.

***

Each of these texts puts onstage a vivid signifier of the imbrication of gender in the representation of power relations. Sol's mutilated body in *Corona,* the mourning or shabby clothing of the wives in *Príncipe, Resistencia, Cardona,* and *Batalla,* the corpse of the wife in *Locura,* all signify the negation of the feminine in the power struggle between vassal and king. Male signifiers also partake of the typically feminine condition of negation in the context of power relations, temporarily as in the feminizing madness of the husbands in *Locura, Batalla,* and *Firmeza,* or permanently as in the corpses of the husbands in *Alfreda* and *Resistencia.* In *Resistencia,* the count's dying body pierced with arrows, his appearance to Matilde as a ghost announcing his own death, and finally the exhibition of his armed cadaver throughout the scene in which the king arranges to marry his widow all signify more than the "spectacular body in pain" of which Barker speaks. The dead bodies of the male protagonists in *Alfreda* and *Resistencia* represent the omnipotent authority of the king not so much to punish transgressions of his law as to remove obstacles in the path of his equally omnipotent desire. The corpses are a grim reminder of the potential of sovereign power to subjugate and destroy as well as to empower male subjects. Whereas woman is consistently depicted as vulnerable to a dual subjection, in the state and in the family, these texts present the possibility that the all-powerful male subject in the family may also be feminized and dominated by the king's all-pervasive power in the state, in the realm of male homosocial relations.

Chapter Seven

"Race," Masculinity, and National Identity

In his introduction to *Nation and Narration,* Homi Bhabha speaks of "nation" as "an idea whose cultural compulsion lies in the impossible unity of the nation as symbolic force" (1).[1] The apparently cohesive and homogeneous identity of "Spanishness" depends on the simultaneous exclusion of the Other, not only woman, but Jew and Moor, feudal lord and heretic as well (El Saffar 165).[2] Collapsing the orders of nationality and gender (not Woman), and nationality and ethnicity (not Jew, not Moor), the Spaniard of the early modern state defines himself in terms of what he is not. The construction of the Jewish and Moorish presence as problem or threat makes possible a unified notion of "Spanishness" that clearly demarcates "authentic and inauthentic types of national belonging" (Gilroy 49). This national identity is then naturalized by appealing to the authority of biology to rationalize relations of dominance and subordination (woman is by nature inferior; Jews and Moors lack the pure blood that would grant them social superiority). The imagined unity of the "Spanish" male subject comes at a very high price, the persecution of one part of Spain by another (Poliakov 107). For example, Spanish Jews, according to Américo Castro, at the same time were and were not Spain (*Realidad* 521).

Léon Poliakov cites the Spanish case as the first historical instance of legalized racism. For the first time, religious and cultural differences were construed as genetic or biological differences. Contrasting the development of racism in France and Spain in this period, Jaime Concha remarks that while the French nobility manifested the first two of the three phases of racism (prejudice and theory), in Spain the direct step from prejudice to institutionalization derives from the power of the nobility and their control of the state apparatus (63n74). The practices of the Inquisition and the statutes of pure blood contributed to the institutionalization of racism, in that they created a pool of "statutory suspects": those of Jewish blood "were credited with an irresistible tendency to heresy, *due to their ancestry*" (Poliakov 221, my emphasis). In response to the large numbers of *conversos* in Spanish society, a new theological discourse emerged at the beginning of the fifteenth century, transforming "sectarian hatred" into "racial hatred" (Poliakov 181). Since the efficacy of baptism could not be questioned, it was necessary

> to conclude that the Jews were evil by their very nature and not only because of their beliefs. [For the Franciscan Alfonso de Espina] there were two types of Jews, public Jews and hidden Jews, and . . . both had the same nature. Thus, by means of an implacable dialectic, the ill fame of those who had become Christians in spite of themselves . . . redounded on the Jews, whom earlier Spanish theologians had merely reproached for their erroneous beliefs. . . . (Poliakov 181)

The semantic evolution of the term *converso* itself documents the rise of racist concepts. Originally the term referred to a Jewish or Moorish convert, but over time it came to designate anyone with a Jewish or Moorish ancestor (222). As Poliakov notes, there is "nothing more revealing than this anti-Semitism without Jews" (290), constituting a kind of "ritual attitude" that proved allegiance to Spanish values.[3]

Current theory postulates that race is reducible neither to biological difference nor to economic factors. Race, like gender, functions as a category of relative autonomy; not all forms and histories of subordination are related exclusively to socioeconomic class (Gilroy 18). While race cannot be reduced to the effects of other social relations, it is understood only if not divorced from these other relations (14). In early modern Spain, race enters into the ideology protecting dominant economic interests; in this sense, the subject/object relations of literary representation and political discourse reproduce the subject/object relations in the economic sphere.[4] As representatives of a more dynamic mode of production, *conversos* were systematically persecuted under the guise of religious heresy. The dominant estates used the Inquisition to block the development of economic activity that would have represented a threat to their hegemony:

> Por supuesto, la justificación religiosa hace ver cristianos
> nuevos donde hay, socialmente hablando, plebeyos ligados
> al comercio o a las profesiones liberales. (Concha 54 [93])

At the bottom of the social hierarchy, the peasant classes opposed the social and economic success of *conversos,* perceived as blocking their own upward mobility.

For Henry Louis Gates, Jr., race is not biological difference but a trope "of ultimate, irreducible difference between cultures, linguistic groups, or adherents of specific belief systems which . . . also have fundamentally opposed economic interests" (5). The visible differences of skin, hair, and bone by which we tend to assign people to races are actually minor compared to the overall possibilities of genetic variation (Appiah). While Gilroy does not totally discount biology, he emphasizes the ideological component of race. Rather than having an objective basis, race must be "socially and politically constructed" (38). In recognition of this process, the word often appears in quotation marks. For Gilroy, race is the effect of a number of discourses and practices crucial to the inner workings of a society, particularly in times of national crisis:

> Accepting that skin "colour" . . . has a strictly limited mate-
> rial basis in biology, opens up the possibility of engaging
> with theories of signification which can highlight the elas-
> ticity and emptiness of "racial" signifiers as well as the ideo-
> logical work which has to be done in order to turn them into
> signifiers in the first place. This perspective underscores the
> definition of "race" as an open political category. (39)

An analysis recognizing the limited biological basis of "race" and highlighting its political construction illuminates the representation of the racial other in Lope's honor plays. Black Spaniards might be distinguished visually from Spanish Old Christians by skin color and other morphological characteristics; Spanish Jews could not (Márquez Villanueva 208). Yet both are "empty" signifiers filled with different ideological contents.

The Representation of Blackness

Blacks denote comic inferiority, just as the linguistic and social inferiority of the foolish shepherd (the *pastor-bobo*) is inherent in his or her rusticity.[5] In sixteenth- and seventeenth-century texts, combinations of inferior class, gender, and blackness also communicate a negative closeness to the body and sexuality. In Cervantes's "El celoso extremeño" ("The Jealous Extremaduran"), for example, the male black gatekeeper, the governess, and the female slaves all stand for a kind of moral and sexual debility, providing a contaminating context for the young wife. The black woman as sign gathers together three negative terms of the binary oppositions that define the male subject as not-black, not-woman, and not-slave. While both black men and women are sexualized in Lope's honor plays, the black female slave is the maximum signifier of degraded *female* sexuality.[6]

Not all slaves in seventeenth-century Spanish society were black and not all blacks were slaves.[7] The introduction of Africans into Spain dates from the middle of the fifteenth century, shortly after the inauguration of the Portuguese slave trade. Significant communities of enslaved and free blacks employed as domestic servants and laborers existed in the cities of Portugal and Spain, especially in Andalusia. While free blacks did not enjoy the full range of rights of other Spaniards,[8] they did organize chapters (*cabildos*) and guilds (*cofradías*). The figure of the *bozal* (an African slave speaking broken Spanish) dominated the literary representation of blacks in spite of partial social integration, rapid linguistic assimilation, and considerable racial mixture (Lipski 9). Although some blacks in sixteenth- and seventeenth-century texts speak "normal" Spanish, the need to see Afro-Spaniards as Other determined the preference in the theater for the newly arrived African, singing and dancing and speaking "deformed" Spanish peppered with references to African place names. In his article on black Spanish in these texts, John Lipski concludes that the speech of these characters has little to do with the Spanish actually spoken by recent arrivals from Africa or with the speech of the majority of black Spaniards in sixteenth- and seventeenth-century Spain, who spoke with no distinctive accent. Rather, this literary language responds to a set of ideological projections. Black speech, for Lipski, serves

> as a verbal equivalent of the outlandish costumes and humili-
> ating dances forced upon African actors by the Spanish pub-
> lic, eager to bury its own (Moorish) African roots and laugh
> heartily at Africans culturally and racially at safe remove
> from Golden Age society. (10)

Lope's honor plays draw freely from a reservoir of jokes that attest to the presence of racist attitudes in the culture. These jokes center on skin color or relegate Afro-Spaniards to the level of animals. In *Comendadores,* the altercation between the servant Galindo and the black cook pivots around the use of racial insults. During the murder scene, "Jorgillo, el negro" ("little Jorge, the black") affords the husband the opportunity to pun on his color, exploiting the dual meaning of *blanco* (both "white" and "target"): "Aunque el ser negro le vale, / Jorge es blanco para mí" ("Although being black protects him, Jorge is a target [white] for me") (296–97). Internalizing her culture's devaluation of blackness, the mulatta slave Dorotea in *Vitoria* asks the go-between for a cosmetic to lighten her color (426). The rival's lackey, to whom she is attracted, calls her a "mosca en leche" ("fly in milk") (430) and says that his master wants to give her a chain, "para llevarte a cazar" ("to take you hunt-ing") (431). When Dorotea fears that, like the husband of *Comen-dadores,* her master will not stop at murdering his wife, but will kill the maidservants and even the dogs and cats as well, the lackey replies: "y, si ha de matar los perros, / escóndete" ("if he is to kill the dogs, run and hide") (449).[9]

Isaac Julien and Kobena Mercer characterize the represen-tation of sexuality "as a recurring site upon which categories of race and gender intersect" (8). Their insight is borne out by texts in which the animality of the black slave characters, both male and female, provides a backdrop for the transgressive sexuality of the white, ruling-class wife. The presence of Jorge and other blacks in the husband's household in *Comendadores* stands as an emblem of its general degeneracy. During the husband's blind praise of the pleasures of married life, he em-braces his black dependents as part of his "family" (271), which the audience has already associated with transgressive sexuality and moral weakness.

In *Vitoria,* the wife's slave Dorotea encourages her illicit passion. When the wife recounts how the rival rescued her from a bull, Dorotea asks pointedly if he cut a manly figure ("¿Tenía buen talle?" 418). She incites the wife to disobey the dictum of enclosure by going out to enjoy the festivities for the king's visit to Seville. Although she eventually gives in, the wife's first response is indignant censure; in her outburst of virtuous ire she calls Dorotea "mulatta" and "dog" (419).[10] Since slaves are not always black in the *comedia* and Dorotea speaks "normal" Spanish, she is racially encoded on the linguistic level only when she transgresses proper gender behavior. As giver of bad sexual counsel, the female slave is made to carry part of the blame for the wife's moral fall. While conventional in the female servants of adulterous wives in Lope's honor plays, here this role is overdetermined because it is racialized (419).

Once on the street, Dorotea disappears as if she were the wife's shadowy double, leaving her alone to face the rival. The dancing of *bozales,* men and women, frames and interrupts their conversation. In the *bozales'* song, they praise the imperial ideology that constructs them as Other and celebrate the burning of Lutherans and Jews in the grotesque language that marks their exclusion (421). The rival aligns the wife with the sensuality of the "barbaric" blacks of both genders: "Parece que más atenta / estáis a un baile, en efeto, / de bárbaros que a mis quejas" ("It seems that you are more attentive to the dancing of barbarians than to my protests of love") (422).

Influenced by the rival's gifts, Dorotea leads him to the wife's bedroom.[11] When the wife chastises her, the slave justifies her action with woman's "nature": "¿Qué quieres? Yo vi llorar, / yo desmayar, yo razones; / yo soy mujer" ("What do you expect? I was witness to tears, fainting fits, persuasive arguments; I am a woman") (434). Dorotea had already linked "woman" and transgression in disassociating her mistress from female pleasure for her refusal to go out: "¡Que en nada / sepas jamás ser mujer!" ("You never know how to be a woman in anything!") (419). As the wife abandons her posture of feminine virtue, she and the slave are joined together under the category of womanhood: "Somos mujeres, paciencia" ("We are women; patience") (434). When they next appear, they are one in the anticipation of sexual pleasure, the wife with the rival and Dorotea with his lackey (443).

The representation of the racial other often affirms and denies difference at the same time; some texts disavow absolute otherness through an appeal to an overriding common value or quality (Bhabha, "The Other Question"). In these instances, the Other designated as such on the basis of racial or sexual difference is represented as almost the Same but not quite ("not-quite/not-white," or "not-quite/not-male" in the case of the female Other).[12] Both *Locura* and *Rosambuco* illustrate the tendency of black skin, noted by Bhabha, to split into bestiality or monstrosity and nobility or wisdom. In the latter text the fracture occurs along gender lines. As seen in the texts discussed above, both black men and women may signify a base kind of sensuality, but only male blacks may bear other, more positive meanings. Just as the comically inferior *pastor-bobo* may coexist with the worthy and dignified peasant within the same text, this play presents both the saintly Rosambuco and the comic female *bozal*.

In *Locura* and *Rosambuco,* the racially pure nobleman constructs himself as imperialist subject through the representation of the black as signifier of military conquest. Balduino's entrance in *Locura* with the captive Moorish king Norandino, whom he forces to kiss the king's feet in homage (294), establishes his masculine success in the heroic defense of national territory and the Catholic faith. The lengthy narration of the naval battle and the exaggerated strength and worth of the adversary ("... el gigante / del Africa cruel se opone en vano" ["the African giant opposes you in vain"] 294) heighten the value of the victory. In *Rosambuco,* the heroism of the conquered black is not just verbally represented; the play opens in the midst of battle, ending with Rosambuco's defeat at the hands of Don Pedro Portocarrero. Like Norandino's, Rosambuco's self-abnegation is extreme. If defeat was inevitable, he declares it his good fortune to have been vanquished by Portocarrero, "... un Marte / Que es honra de España" ("a Mars who is Spain's honor") (362).

On the heels of this exchange, in which the formidable martial prowess and masculinity of one is the glory of the other,

Lucrecia enters speaking *bozal* Spanish. As in *Comendadores* and *Vitoria,* the black woman sexualizes the stage in a context of adulterous desire. The rival opportunes the veiled wife to show her face; although she calls on her honor, her speech encourages as much as discourages him. Lucrecia is the target of the rival's racist jokes:

> Por Dios, que de vos me espanto,
> Negra, de ver que os cubráis;
> Que con taparos, tapáis
> Un manto con otro manto.

> (363 [94])

Since the scene hinges on the sexual connotations of veiling, Lucrecia's double cloaking (her color and her veil) strengthens her relationship to transgressive sexuality.[13]

Stripped of his military masculinity, Rosambuco is temporarily categorized with the black woman by the wife because of his color: "Yo le estimo por ser de su Réal mano, / Aunque bastaba en casa aquesta negra / Sin tanta tizne y tinta" ("I value him as a royal gift, although with this *negra* there was already enough soot and ink in this house") (370). But the text soon differentiates them on the basis of his linguistic, social, and moral superiority. He speaks "normal" Spanish, she *bozal* Spanish; she is a slave, he was a captain of African royalty. The contrast between Rosambuco, who speaks standard Spanish even before being enslaved, and Lucrecia, who ostensibly has already lived some time in this household, supports Lipski's thesis that the use of *bozal* Spanish reflects ideological, rather than linguistic, realities. Repulsed by her desire for him, Rosambuco's rejection is at once sexual and *linguistic:* "Que me atormenta / El oirte" ("It torments me to hear you") (370). Rosambuco converts to Catholicism when the statue of Saint Benito miraculously intervenes to prevent the husband's honor murder of his wife. Lucrecia takes advantage of the trancelike state he enters while praying to embrace him; stage machinery and action combine to punish the black woman's aggressive desire: "Haga que le va á besar, y por junto al Santo, hacia la negra, de debajo del tablado salga una cabeza de sierpe con un cohete en la boca echando fuego" ("She goes to kiss him, and near the Saint, towards the *negra*, from under the stage emerges the head of a serpent breathing fire") (376). At the expense of female blackness identified with carnality and slavery, male blackness is salvaged, in this text, first through royal blood and the masculine ideal and then through religiosity. Rosambuco must abandon the markers of his (constructed) racial and cultural difference—transcending carnality through spirituality, rejecting Islam for Catholicism—in order for his "Spanishness" to be guaranteed. But unlike the *negra,* the black male subject *can* be contained and rendered assimilable by the master signifier of national identity (Gilroy 59).

Rosambuco's otherness does not come to an end with this transformation. Pedrisco, Rosambuco's enemy in the monastery, refuses to accept him in spite of his proven saintliness. He verbally abuses Rosambuco with racial insults, kicks him, hires musicians to sing libelous songs about him, tries to drown him, and, in a seventeenth-century version of blackface, doubles as Rosambuco to discredit him with the viceroy. After failing in his attempt to poison Rosambuco, on the saint's deathbed, he repents and reforms. Pedrisco, clearly positioned as Rosambuco's adversary in order to be won over by his miracles, is not the only one who continues to stigmatize him after his conversion. The simultaneous evoking and denying of Rosambuco's difference is embedded in the ideology of the entire play. The underlying (racist) message of the text is that Rosambuco achieves saintliness *in spite of* his blackness; his sainthood itself is a manifestation of God's power and goodness. The stereotyped phrase "aunque neglo gente somo" ("even though we are black, we are people"), conventional in the mouth of the *bozal* in the theater (Lipski 10), provides the structure for this ideological dimension of the play.[14] Every one of Rosambuco's positive traits is articulated within this syntactic construction as having been achieved in spite of his color. Rosambuco introduces it in his initial self-definition as manly warrior: "Aunque negro, temerario" ("Although black, valiant") (362). When Lesbio acquires Rosambuco, he declares his esteem for his slave's valor, ". . . aunque del sol vestido" ("even though he is dressed in black by the sun" 367).

In effect, saintliness and even God are constructed as white by the text. Rosambuco himself is made to voice the split between black bodies and white souls ("Blanca el alma, el cuerpo

negro" ["The soul white, the body black"] 374), while Saint
Francis authorizes this inscription of whiteness and blackness
on the supernatural plane of the action: ". . . he de llevar
conmigo / Un fraile santo, aunque negro" ("I am to take with
me a saintly friar, although black") (374). The celestial song
Rosambuco hears not only constructs God as white, but holds
out the promise that in heaven Rosambuco himself will be
white:

> Un negro rosas envía
> A Dios, que tiene por blanco.
> . . . .
> Que aunque eres negro, habrá día
> Que estés bello, hermoso y blanco.
>
> (375 [95])

The promise that in the next life the black man will be white
recalls a sixteenth-century discussion of women shedding their
biological imperfection in heaven:

> . . . los sanctos doctores ponen que en la Gloria serán los
> bienaventurados sin alguna fealdad personal: y que parescen
> en la mejor figura que se pueda: y como en la especie
> humana la mayor perfection sea la de varón: síguese que las
> mugeres perderán aquella forma . . . restituydas a la mayor
> dignidad y nobleza de la especie humana, que es la de
> varón.[15] [96]

The alignment of the divine with whiteness and maleness reveals a common ground in the construction of racial and sexual
others.

Jewishness as Signifier

In contrast to the representation of blacks, Jewishness in Lope's
honor plays signifies "impure" wealth and cowardice. While
some texts may highlight the black man's bravery to stress the
superior military skill of the white Spaniard who conquers him,
the Jew represents everything the racially pure Spanish male is
not, with special emphasis on lack of *hombría*. The almost complete exclusion of woman in the representation of Jewishness
betrays the importance of this particular racial construction in
discourses of Spanish masculinity.[16]

In *Indicios,* Jewishness and fearfulness are equated in the words of the most manly of the three male characters: "Siempre el miedo fué judío" ("Fear has always been Jewish") (276). In the same text, fear of the Inquisition is used as a metaphor for husbands' hypervigilance. The suspicious husband improvises an explanation to cover his (premature) decision to kill his wife. Overheard saying "aunque muera mi mujer" ("even if my wife dies"), he declares his resolve to make a present of an admired jewel to a friend, "aunque muera mi mujer." The relieved wife tells him to give away all her jewels, and the piece of furniture that holds them as well. The servant Gonzalo maliciously applies the story of a hidalgo (a member of the lowest rank of the nobility) to their situation. Not knowing the Inquisitor had merely sent for some orange blossoms, the hidalgo is terrified by the news of his familiar's visit:

> Pero apenas del recado
> el hidalgo se informó,
> cuando en pie se corrompió,
> sin poder comer bocado.
> Cuanto hizo y cuanto dijo
> en su vida y nacimiento,
> revolvió en su pensamiento
> con un discurso prolijo,
> y llegando averiguar
> después a lo que venía,
> y que por más volvería
> volviéndosele antojar,
> el hidalgo respondió:
> "¡Juro a Dios, no he de tener
> otra vez a qué volver!"
> Y el naranjo le envió.

(288 [97])

The servant directs the story at the wife, whose fear of persecution and relief upon being passed over are analogous to the hidalgo's. But the analogy includes the husband's constant fear of "evidence" of his wife's infidelity, revealing his lack of control over her, and therefore of *hombría.*

When the category of "race" figures explicitly in the erotic triangle involving two noblemen, as in *Galán* and *Pobreza,* the New Christian blood of one determines his "down" position in the conjugal-honor conflict. Upon Celio's return from war in

Galán, he finds his betrothed Ricarda engaged to marry Julio. While Celio is characterized as having honorable parents and wellborn grandparents (122, 132), no information is given concerning Julio's lineage. Tácito's approval of his daughter's marriage indicates that Julio has achieved a level of social acceptance and recognition. After they are married, Julio finds old love letters from Celio[17] and decides to kill Ricarda to safeguard his honor. For Julio the letters are proof of adultery (134), but legally they would not have sufficed to justify wife murder. In addition, Ricarda points out that he would do more damage to his honor by killing her, especially if the rival remained unscathed (133). In spite of Julio's declaration that he will pursue the rival, the wife's comments expose Julio's lack of *hombría* as well as his hypersensitive concern for his honor. After his servant defends Ricarda's virtue, Julio backs down and sends for his wife, only to discover she has escaped her room by climbing down a sheet. Ironically, his overreaction, motivated by anxiety about his ability to guard his wife from other men, has resulted in the total loss of control over his sexual property.

Julio accuses his father-in-law of hiding his daughter and demands that Tácito hand her over to him for punishment. When Tácito asks Julio if he caught Ricarda and Celio together as legal proof of her adultery, Julio interprets this as an attack on his *hombría*: "Si eso fuera, / ¿no los hubiera muerto? ¿Eso preguntas?" ("If that were so, wouldn't I have killed them? How can you even ask?") (137). His rabid defense of his honor at this point masks his sense of inferior masculinity. Tácito calls attention to Julio's attempt to shift the blame for his loss of control from himself to his father-in-law: "¡Bueno es que lo que ha sido tu mal término / de aquesa suerte, Julio, me acumules!" ("What has been your own bad end you attribute to me!") (137). Ricarda has passed from her father's protection to Julio's, but the latter has not been able to uphold his part of the contract. After Tácito dismisses the letters as proof, the conversation degenerates into a shouting match pitting father against husband with respect to the right of ownership and control over woman: "Mira que soy su padre, y que la has muerto"; "Mira que soy su esposo, y que la niegas" ("I am her father, and you have killed her"; "I am her husband, and you withhold her") (138).

In this scene, Julio's lack of *hombría* becomes racially marked as Tácito breaks the stalemate by calling Julio a Jew: "Yo he tenido la culpa en dar mi sangre / a quien la tiene, por ventura, en mezclas" ("The fault is mine for giving my blood to one whose blood is mixed") (138). When Julio defends his *hidalguía,* Tácito accuses him of buying it with his wealth, supplying the reason for the earlier silence surrounding Julio's lineage and Tácito's approval of the marriage:

> Solar. ¿De qué solar? ¿De los que agora
> se labran en Madrid en muladares?
> ¡Qué gallardo que hablas, por ser rico!
> Tendrás quizá las armas en la iglesia.[18]
>
> (138 [98])

Cut to the quick, Julio beats the older man with his cane.[19]

Momentarily defeated by the younger man's superior strength, Tácito pretends to beg his forgiveness, playing on Julio's ingrained respect for paternal authority. When Julio rushes to help him to his feet, Tácito feigns an embrace and stabs his son-in-law to death. Later, Tácito omits the racial conflict when he reports that Julio beat him because he accused his son-in-law of killing Ricarda (142). At the end, Tácito is imprisoned for the murder of Julio, but is soon set free, showing the collusion between the judicial system and the construction of the male subject's *hombría* in the defense of his honor (144). Later, the judges' clemency is explained in terms of their *Christian* nobility ("Son los jueces nobles y cristianos" ["The judges are noble and Christian"] 149). This father-in-law dissolves a less than optimal partnership by murdering his son-in-law, opening the door to a new, more satisfactory exchange. The elimination of the husband responds to a dual threat: the "impure" blood that would taint his lineage as well as the imminent public dishonor of his daughter. Tácito redeems his earlier error of marrying his daughter to a *converso* for his wealth, affirming himself as manly guardian of both woman and Spanish blood purity in the process.[20]

Pobreza depicts a similar conflict between wealth and *limpieza* ("blood purity"). A poor noblewoman whose father has been taken captive by the Moors must choose between a rich *converso* suitor and a poor but pure hidalgo. Dorotea writes to her father for a decision as to which one she should marry, underlining her lack of will in the matter: "De quien él me diere, soy / Cautiva, como él cautivo" ("I am the captive of whomever he may give me, as he is captive") (281). The father chooses the poor but pure Leonido over the *converso* suitor who has purchased his nobility with his wealth.

The different representations of Dorotea's and Leonido's lack of resources highlight the gendered and racialized construction of poverty in this text. Combined with poverty, woman's beauty ensures dishonor. The unmarried daughter, always a dangerous commodity in the phallic economy, becomes much more so in the absence of both father and dowry (270). For woman, poverty and feminine virtue are presented as mutually exclusive (272); the conquest of her virtue by poverty is inevitable.[21] The comic representation of the poor hidalgo in some sixteenth- and seventeenth-century texts (e.g., *Lazarillo* and *El alcalde de Zalamea*) reveals the importance of the frequently unmarked confluence of nobility and wealth. The serious treatment of the same figure, however, shows that for the nobleman it is difficult but possible to maintain honor in poverty. After their marriage, Leonido, Dorotea's noble but poor husband, is forced to leave town and become a soldier, since his honor prevents him from earning a living in any other way (295). His desire to leave before dawn to avoid being seen horseless (295) is not a subject for ironic ridicule, as are the empty pretensions of the hidalgo in *Lazarillo* or of Mendo in *Alcalde,* but an occasion for the exercise of ingenious puns (295).

While poverty equals dishonor for woman, in this text the male subject's poverty actually guarantees his honor, since "poor" and "rich" are presented as synonyms of the corresponding terms *limpio* ("pure") and *mal nacido* ("badly born") characterizing Leonido and Ricardo respectively. The Moorish slave Isabel refers to Leonido as "más limpio que el sol" ("more pure than the sun") (273), and Dorotea writes her father that all four of Leonido's grandparents are Old Christian ("De sus cuatro abuelos limpio" ["He inherits his purity from his four grandparents"] 284). Leonido's (pure) *hidalguía* compensates for his poverty ("Aunque pobre, es buen hidalgo" ["Although poor, he is a good hidalgo"] 273), while the rich *converso* Ricardo's name is linked with wealth:

Heredé tanta riqueza,
Que sólo en decir Ricardo,
En competencia acobardo
A la mayor gentileza.

(274 [99])

Dorotea refers to him as "un rico mal nacido" ("a badly born rich man") (279), and in the letter to her father she expands on these two attributes, using the code words of the times to indicate ancestors punished by the Inquisition for Judaizing: "Cofrade de San Andrés, / Devoto de San Benito" ("Of Saint Andres's guild, a devoté of Saint Benito") (284). The fusion of Ricardo's wealth and his "impure" blood is enshrined as subtitle at the end: "La riqueza mal nacida / Y *la pobreza estimada*" ("Badly born wealth and poverty esteemed") (310).

This twin title captures the shorthand at work in the creation of these semantic constellations: rich but *converso;* poor but esteemed (because "purely" noble). Any one of the attributes on one side can be opposed to any one on the other with the same meaning. For example, when Leonido's friend tells him Ricardo is a *converso,* Leonido's only comment is "¡Oh santa y noble pobreza!" ("Oh holy and noble poverty!") (278). Passages such as these, constructing the interchangeability of the terms of the oppositions, encode as Old Christian the poverty of the "true" hidalgo in opposition to disesteemed *converso* wealth and purchased titles of nobility. The equivalences set up between wealth and Jewishness and poverty and Old Christian nobility reduce the diversity and complexity of social life. Poor hidalgos often lost their titles of "Don," falling into a taxable class (*pecheros*). And while many rich *conversos* acquired both social prestige and tax-free status through the purchase of titles, many plebeian *conversos* lived lives of modest means or penury. By equating Jewishness with (dishonorably gained) wealth, this text fuels the anti-Semitism of those Old Christian classes, including the peasantry, competing with *conversos* for the same positions and economic resources.

This text also illuminates the racialized construction of masculinity. Dorotea prefers Leonido not only for his pure *hidalguía,* but also for his *hombría*. These attributes quickly become inseparable in the text (276, 279), for example, in the description

213

of Leonido as soldier: "Es muy hidalgo soldado, / . . . / Y es muy hombre" ("He is a very gentlemanly soldier. . . . He is a real man") (299). Ricardo's wealthy Jewishness, on the other hand, is conflated with cowardly lack of masculinity. He and his servants attack Leonido and wound him from behind. When Ricardo offers Dorotea a diamond necklace in exchange for the bandage Leonido has given her as a token, Leonido explodes in an anti-Semitic tirade. While triggered by Ricardo's wealth ("Como el vender y comprar / Fué en vuestra casa primero / Que el blasón de caballero" ["Since buying and selling was in your house before the gentleman's coat of arms"] 289), the outburst quickly centers on Ricardo's feminizing cowardice, presented as a factor of his Jewish blood:

> Que entonces, con más recelo
> Que dueña de toca y faldas,
> Me sajaste las espaldas,
> Oficio de vuestro abuelo.
>   Aquella herida, aunque brava,
> No fué herir ni fué blasón,
> Sino hurtar sangre á traición,
> Para honrar la que os faltaba.[22]
>
> (289 [100])

The principles supporting Ricardo's sensible defense may be sound ("Yo soy de mis obras hijo" ["I am the child of my actions"] 289), but the text has assigned him "actions" (stabbing Leonido from behind) that confirm rather than disprove Leonido's judgment.

Dorotea and her slave Isabel complete Ricardo's feminization. When Ricardo, in the company of his servants, enters Dorotea's house with the intention of raping her, the two women force the four men to flee at sword point (304). One of the servants praises their skill at fencing, and Dorotea's words stress how her action emasculates Ricardo: "Es tu espada muy cobarde" ("Your sword is very cowardly") (304). Isabel's use of the word *infamia* ("infamy"), associated with blood impurity, casts Ricardo's emasculation as a function of his Jewishness (304). After they have defeated the men, the two women mirror their pleasure in their active self-defense: "I: ¡Hermosamente acuchillas! / D: Y tú en extremo me agradas" ("I: You

fence beautifully. D: And you please me in the extreme") (304).
But since the text conscripts them in the racial construction of
Jewishness as unmanly cowardice, the women's supposedly
empowering assumption of the masculine role reinscribes their
inferiority to the "real" man: not only is Ricardo dominated by
a more masterful male, he can even be dominated by women.
Inspired by Dorotea's honorable resistance and her saintliness,
Ricardo reforms and joins a monastery (308).[23] The road to
elevation is through further subjection, as Ricardo internalizes
the others' definition of himself:

> Julio, ya estoy muy trocado;
> Su virtud estimo sola;
> Aquí la historia ha cesado
> Desta Lucrecia española
> Y este Tarquino afrentado.
>
> (306 [101])

The text builds certain parallels between Jew and Moor as
racial others of the "pure" Spaniard. The scenes between the
Moor Audalla and Aurelio (Dorotea's father) place the Old
Christian in a position of superiority. Even though the former
is a king and the latter a poor hidalgo, Audalla says he cannot
afford to ransom Aurelio, for the king could not govern even
his own family without Aurelio's advice (283). When the two
discuss Christian and Moorish cultures, Audalla only comments on difference, while the Christian hierarchizes it, listen-
ing politely and revealing his true feelings in asides: "El vuestro
es bárbaro modo" ("Your ways are barbaric") (284). Yet in spite
of his express disdain for the Moor, he asks for advice and
promises to marry his daughter to the man Audalla chooses.[24]

In choosing Leonido, Audalla becomes the mouthpiece of
the ideology of segregation based on blood purity. He natural-
izes the attributes of nobility as inherent in the man of pure
blood ("El mal nacido finge las costumbres; / En el hidalgo
viven naturales" ["The badly born feigns genteel manners; in
the hidalgo they dwell naturally"] 285) and employs the same
word, *barbaric,* assigned to him earlier by Aurelio, to condemn
those who place honor based on virtue above honor based on
blood (pure or noble). In his censure of the Jews for having
killed Christ, Audalla defends a more anti-Semitic position than

Aurelio (285–86), although Aurelio eventually confirms
Audalla's judgment by following his advice and by articulating his decision in explicitly racial terms: "Ansí lo haré sin
duda, / Por no degenerar de mis abuelos" ("I will do as you say
without a doubt, to avoid degenerating my grandparents'
blood") (286). In light of his earlier desire to marry his son
Zulema to Dorotea, Audalla's abhorrence of miscegenation is
contradictory: "Y nunca de dos sangres diferentes / Genízaro
se vió menos que bárbaro" ("Never was the product of two
races anything but barbaric") (285).[25]
The servant Tancredo echoes Audalla in his rejection of
Dorotea's Moorish slave Isabel. When Dorotea and Leonido are
married, Leonido agrees to Isabel's request to marry Tancredo.
But when he consults his servant, Tancredo calls on Audalla's
authority, using the same lexicon of racial segregation wielded
by the Moorish king:

> ¿Qué pleito me han sentenciado,
> Que siendo yo un hombre limpio
> Me quieres mezclar con ellos?
> Si el Rey dijera lo mismo,
> Nunca diera á Dorotea
> A hombre pobre, sino al rico.
>
> (291 [102])

Leonido concurs (291).
Aurelio makes the contradictions in the characterization of
Audalla explicit: "Si puede haber, Leonido, en pecho moro /
Entrañas de cristiano, aquél las tiene" ("If it is possible,
Leonido, for a Christian heart to dwell in a Moorish breast, he
has one") (304). These contradictions are resolved at the end
with the revelation that both Audalla and Zulema have secretly
converted (310). Audalla actually *does* have "a Christian
heart," and his vocal defense of blood purity becomes, retroactively, an attribute of his very Christianity. But the Old Christian servant does not retract his rejection of Isabel in spite of
her own declared conversion to the Christian faith and the dis-
closure that she is Audalla's daughter. As in *Rosambuco,* the
exclusion of woman as racial other remains in force until the
end. The Other constructed on the basis of racial/religious
difference may ultimately be assimilated into the dominant

definition of nationhood by religious conversion; for woman, it is not so simple (El Saffar 168). Black (*Rosambuco*), Jewish and Moorish (*Pobreza*) male subjects can be transfigured through the power of Catholicism because of the split in their construction as Other that simultaneously maintains their difference and denies it. Isabel's continued exclusion is a product of her being at once racial other and woman.

The gendered construction of "race" in these texts as well as the domination of the man racially marked as *converso* by an Old Christian woman in *Pobreza* argue against Melveena McKendrick's thesis that woman in Lope's honor plays stands in for the racial other. In her provocative study, McKendrick suggests that the social obsession with *limpieza* was displaced onto the honor conflict in the theater in an "intuitive translation of obsessional energy from one area of experience to another" ("Honour/Vengeance" 322). One of the mechanisms for accomplishing this transfer was gender, in the honor play's construction of woman as other-than-man; as Other, woman comes to signify all difference, including racial difference.[26] While this hypothesis has much to recommend it, it treads a problematic terrain, for Lope's honor plays actually do represent "layered or multi-faceted difference" (Sullivan 58). In those texts that depict the conflict between Old and New Christians directly, Old Christian women still exercise class and/or "racial" privilege in spite of gender devaluation, while the representation of positive traits disavowing difference in the racial other is limited to men. Rather than see woman as subsuming all difference, it might be more helpful to ask "how it is that Woman becomes the figure for so much displacement" (Modleski 131n6).

The Old Christian Peasant as Spanish Ideal

The use of the racial marker "Jew" to signify a feminized position for the male subject is more problematic in those texts that pit Old Christian peasants against members of the nobility. Since the specification of Jewishness always determines the male subject's domination by a more masterful male, the nobleman's subordination conflicts with his superior social rank. The tensions between opposing hierarchies—Old Christian versus New Christian and noble versus plebeian—become acute in those texts constructing the Old Christian male peasant as Spanish ideal. In *Fuenteovejuna,* the dominating males are lowly shepherds; in *Peribáñez,* the Old Christian husband's wealth compensates partially for his plebeian status. The social distinction between Old Christian and New is attenuated in *Cuerdo:* Mendo is a rich peasant and Leonardo a poor hidalgo, which allows for comic treatment as opposed to the serious modality of the other two texts.

While the sexual rights of feudal lords over peasant women had long been revoked, noblemen's tremendous social advantage permitted a continued abuse of power. In both *Fuenteovejuna* and *Peribáñez,* the conflict between men of opposing social groups over the sexual property of peasant men is racialized. When the commander in *Fuenteovejuna* mocks the peasants' sense of outraged honor, this frequently quoted exchange occurs:

> Comendador: ¿Vosotros honor tenéis?
> ¡Qué freiles de Calatrava!
> Regidor: Alguno acaso se alaba
> De la cruz que le ponéis,
> Que no es de sangre tan limpia.
> Comendador: Y ¿ensúciola yo juntando
> La mía á la vuestra?
> Regidor: Cuando
> Es mal, más tiñe que alimpia.
>
> (542 [103])

In *Peribáñez,* peasants refer to noblemen as Jews and "hidalgos cansados" ("tired hidalgos") (104).[27] In his self-definition, Peribáñez stresses his pure blood as source of value:

> Yo soy un hombre,
> Aunque de villana casta,
> Limpio de sangre, y jamás
> De hebrea ó mora manchada.
>
> (147 [104])

Much has been written about the unusual number of *comedias* that put peasants on the stage, not just as comic *pastor-bobos* but as serious characters concerned with their honor.[28]

Noël Salomon relates the exaltation of rural life in the *comedia* after 1600 to the social and economic crisis of those years, including the deterioration of agriculture and the mass exodus from the countryside into the urban centers. While his argument is too complex to reproduce here, a salient factor in the idealization of rural life, especially of the rich farmer, is a program of reform that saw in the return to farming and the countryside the possibility of economic salvation within the context of hegemonic values condemning all but inherited wealth or wealth obtained from the earth as dishonorable.

Américo Castro and others have studied the representation of the peasant in terms of the obsession with blood purity.[29] Since the nobility was "tainted" by a long process of intermarriage with Jews or *conversos,* the peasant came to incarnate pure blood and a cluster of values and attitudes characterizing the dominant caste of Old Christians. The peasant's claim to honor on the basis of pure blood counters the noble's claim to honor on the basis of noble blood. However, it is important to point out the *ideological* value of the compensatory myth of blood purity in a society which practiced a single system of inclusion (noble blood) and a dual system of exclusion (plebeian and "impure" blood) in relation to the ranks of the privileged.[30]

While Peribáñez's phase of unaware subjection to the noble rival does not last long, the male peasants of *Fuenteovejuna* suffer a prolonged period of feminization, perhaps in part because wealth does not alleviate their plebeian status. Their abjection is all the more severe because they are aware they are being cuckolded by the commander, and still are powerless to avenge themselves. The constraints of the social hierarchy that prevent them from acting against a superior to whom they also "belong" as a village are stronger than their outrage at their sexual dishonor and their feelings of superiority based on pure blood.

The men of Fuenteovejuna have lost male status because they have failed in the performance of masculine gender attributes: to protect their women and avenge their unauthorized sexual use. When the commander kidnaps Laurencia at her wedding, Barrildo queries plaintively, "¿No hay aquí un hombre que hable?" ("Is there no man here to speak out?") (550).

This profound crisis of masculinity requires Laurencia's masculinization to serve as a catalyst for them to become "real men" again. Laurencia's famous speech is a sterling example of the construction of gender ("men" and "women") in terms of the performance of specific roles and behaviors.[31] Laurencia temporarily loses the status of "daughter," since Esteban has not acted as a "father" should: "No me nombres / Tu hija. . . . / Porque dejas que me roben / Tiranos sin que me vengues" ("Don't call me your daughter, . . . since you allow tyrants to take me without avenging me") (551–52). Esteban has reneged on his responsibility in the circulation of women, as Laurencia points out:

> Que en tanto que no me entregan
> Una joya, aunque la compre,
> No han de correr por mi cuenta
> Las guardas ni los ladrones.
>
> (552 [105])

Since the men are no longer men, but sheep, hares, chickens, and, ultimately, "women," the women will have to avenge themselves, ceasing to be "women" in the process and becoming Amazons. Paradoxically, then, if the commander kills all the men in the village, there will be no more "women" left:

> A Frondoso quiere ya,
> Sin sentencia, sin pregones,
> Colgar el Comendador
> De una almena de la torre:
> De todos hará lo mismo;
> Y yo me huelgo, medio hombres,
> Porque quede sin mujeres
> Esta villa honrada, y torne
> Aquel siglo de amazonas,
> Eterno espanto del orbe.
>
> (552 [106])

Laurencia's judgment overlaps masculinity, "race," and nation; in ceasing to be men, they have simultaneously ceased to be Spaniards: "Bárbaros sois, no españoles" ("You are barbarians, not Spaniards") (552). Her strategy is effective, as the men immediately act to become "men" again. The regendering process of recovering *hombría* and honor is so forceful that it affects the whole community, masculinizing both the men and the women of the village. After it is accomplished, the women disappear back into the collective, and those that remain individualized reassume their feminine identity.

The scenes of royal approval which end both *Fuenteovejuna* and *Peribáñez* point to the ideological power of masculinity in conjunction with honor as pure blood to offset power inequalities. The domination of the aristocratic rival as racial other allows Old Christian peasants and monarch to confirm each other's value in terms of racial purity, in spite of the exclusion of "pure" plebeians from power and privilege in seventeenth-century Spanish society.[32] In both plays, "race" creates solidarity between male peasants and the seat of male power, while reaffirming the economic and social structures ultimately benefiting the nobility. The peasants' revolt in *Fuenteovejuna* does not challenge the social hierarchy, but rather records the shift of the locus of power from the powerful and anarchic aristocracy to the absolute but decentralized rule of the early modern state.[33] El Saffar suggests that plays like *Fuenteovejuna* and *Peribáñez* dramatize what the modern state had to offer those who accepted its values: it could guarantee the male subject a kind of personal sovereignty that the feudal state could not, and, in exchange for his loyalty, respect for marriage as opposed to the abusive sexual practices of the aristocracy (177).[34]

Fuenteovejuna and *Peribáñez* are unique among Lope's honor plays in that their resolution of vertical bonds of rivalry inverts the traditional assignment of superiority and subordination on the basis of social rank. Nevertheless, the resulting tensions are not completely resolved. Both texts display uneasiness with the establishment of patriarchal solidarity among men of different estates in flagrant opposition to the hierarchy of power. Critics have commented on the restrained tone of the royal sanction of the peasants' revenge in *Fuenteovejuna* (Donald Larson 109).[35] In *Peribáñez*, although the rich peasant affirms his right to honor and masculinity on the basis of his blood purity, he is also knighted before enacting his bloody vengeance on the "bad" representative of the nobility. The waffling in the text responds to contradictory imperatives: that of incorporating peasants as a social group through bonds of honor, pure blood, and shared masculinity, and that of retaining distance from their "difference" as social and economic inferiors.

This dynamic helps to explain the persistence of comic notes typical of the *pastor-bobo* in the "noble" peasant characters, for example, the childish bedazzlement at the sight of the king typical of the shepherd since the theater of Juan del Encina in the 1490s. Casilda's servants voice the sacralization of the king in the *comedia* as a whole (Díez-Borque, *Sociología* 131):

> Los reyes son á la vista,
> . . . .
> Imágenes de milagros;
> Porque siempre que los vemos,
> De otra color nos parecen.
>
> (121 [107])

The most foolish expression of this belief is placed in Casilda's mouth:

> Casilda: ¡Qué! ¿son
> Los reyes de carne y hueso?
> Costanza: Pues ¿de qué pensabas tú?
> Casilda: De damasco ó terciopelo.
> Costanza: Sí que eres boba en verdad.[36]
>
> (121 [108])

Similarly, although the commander's lackey Luján enters in some editions "enharinado" ("covered in flour") right before Peribáñez stabs him, earlier Peribáñez shares with the audience his own plan to hide in a sack of flour before surprising the commander with his wife (142). Peribáñez's simultaneous representation of the vengeful husband's secret return and a comic gag associated with the social inferiority and unmanly cowardice of the *pastor-bobo* eloquently captures the identification with and distancing of the Old Christian peasant as Spanish ideal. Such contradictions are not unambiguously resolved in texts that struggle to award dominance to subjects lacking one of the three essential grounds for superiority in seventeenth-century Spanish society: masculine gender, "pure" blood, and noble blood.

El cuerdo en su casa

The physiocratic program of strengthening the Castilian economy through a revival of agriculture could only work if the peasants who became rich from farming did not succumb to the temptation to purchase a title in order to enjoy the social prestige and tax-free status their society bestowed on nobility alone. Although rich peasants made up a small fraction of the peasantry (around 5%), they were a key element in proposals of economic reform, and their allegiance to their place in society was crucial. The *comedia* participates in the ideological project of encouraging that allegiance. While fidelity to one's location in the social anatomy is an important component of the Old Christian peasants in *Fuenteovejuna* and *Peribáñez, Cuerdo* is truly remarkable for its deft interweaving of pure blood, masculinity, and class loyalty in the character of Mendo. What is also cloaked by Mendo's steadfast refusal to change class is the intense competition between peasants and *converso* members of the hidalgo class that made their places in the social order far more mutable and interchangeable than this text represents. Instead, through ideological discourses of racialized masculinity, the relationship between peasant and hidalgo, class and caste, is constructed as one of irreducible, hierarchical difference.

Mendo and Leonardo are characterized in opposition to each other in the first scene. The highly class-conscious Mendo is wary of Leonardo's offer of friendship, presenting himself as Leonardo's social inferior: "Vos, letrado; yo, ignorante; / vos, hidalgo; yo, villano" ("You, a lawyer, I, an ignorant man; you, an hidalgo, I, a common peasant") (549). This hierarchy (lettered hidalgo versus ignorant peasant) is inverted by the end of the play through the identification of Mendo with pure blood and loyalty to the social structure and Leonardo with Jewish blood and social climbing.

Leonardo is first classified as a *letrado* ("lawyer"); his identity as hidalgo is subordinated to the beauty of his wife, Elvira: "Es el hidalgo que tiene / aquella hermosa mujer" ("He's the hidalgo who has that beautiful wife") (549). In effect, Leonardo has "married up," barely hanging on to the estate of nobility by his fingernails, while he exerts himself to the utmost to get a leg up. In his first conversation with Mendo, Leonardo discloses that Elvira's father allowed the marriage only because people were talking; his reluctance was related to economic factors (553). Moreover, Leonardo's marriage to a woman textually identified as Jewish (558) associates him with "impure" blood. His membership in the social group of *letrados* fails to protect him against this association, since in spite of the statutes of pure blood exercised by the colleges,

> [p]or un camino u otro, el grupo de letrados continuó compuesto fundamentalmente de nobles verdaderos o contrahechos.[37] (Márquez Villanueva 210 [109])

"Knowledge" itself is assigned to New Christians and "malice" to Old Christian peasants, with connotations of speaking ill of people's lineage.[38] Other cultural connotations encode Leonardo's Jewishness, for example, the contrast between the slow gait of the aristocrat and Leonardo's unseemly haste:

> Convídame esta tarde para el monte
> el señor don Enrique, y, muy despacio,
> al bautismo se viene, y no se acuerda
> que me mandó poner botas y espuelas.
> Por toda la ciudad ando en su busca,
> y está en conversación, tan descuidado
> como si no me hubiera convidado.
>
> (578 [110])

Besides underlining Leonardo's desire to win the higher-placed aristocrat's favor, the passage also gathers together behaviors that communicated caste status for a seventeenth-century Spanish audience: the Old Christian noble was perceived as cultivating an elegant pace as sign of his leisure, in contrast to the quick movements of the "Jew" rushing around in commercial pursuits.

From the beginning, Leonardo announces his intention to help Mendo leave his humble origins behind:

> . . . yo querría
> que ya nuestra amistad fuese
> de provecho, y os hiciese
> hidalgo mi compañía.
>   Vos subís a labrador
> de un padre ya carbonero.
> Aspirad a caballero;
> subid a grado de honor.
>
> (554–55 [111])

He encourages his wife to visit Mendo's wife, Antona, but their encounters are charged with class antagonism. Upon receiving an Elvira "toda cubierta de seda" ("all covered in silk") (558),

Antona excuses her appearance, "mal tocada y peor vestida" ("badly coiffed and worse dressed"), and Elvira untactfully agrees with her: "Cierto; que tanta hermosura / no está bien en ese traje" ("True, for that costume does not suit such beauty") (558). Leonardo urges Mendo to buy his wife an *estrado* (a platform used by the upper classes to receive guests) and criticizes the rustic fare he serves. Since Mendo has the economic means to support a noble lifestyle, Leonardo is incapable of understanding why he would not want to cultivate the external appearances of honor based on nobility (558). Although he presents himself as having Mendo's interest at heart, Leonardo's real motivation in cultivating Mendo's friendship is his own personal gain. To his wife, he stresses Mendo's pure blood and his wealth (555), concluding, "que, aunque es humilde amistad, / es de provecho también" ("for, although it is a humble friendship, it is also profitable") (556).

Mendo, on the other hand, resists all Leonardo's attempts to "help" him change class: "Porque labrador nací, / y labrador moriré" ("Because I was born a peasant, and a peasant I will die") (555). While Leonardo is silent about his own father and paints a picture of tenuous male bonding with his father-in-law, Mendo's autobiographical narration is firmly entrenched in patriarchal authority.[39] His father, the coalseller Sancho, is at once the guarantor of Mendo's pure blood and source of his unshakable fidelity to his social position.[40] When Leonardo advises Mendo to dress his father in finer clothes, Mendo's words show that his attitudes about living and dying a peasant are inherited patrilineally:

> Mi padre quiere morir,
> Leonardo, como nació;
> carbonero me engendró,
> labrador quiero morir.

> (571 [112])

Sancho puts his theory of social segregation into practice, exiting when Leonardo enters, and approving his son's rejection of noblemen's gesture of removing their hats to him: "Hijo, tú eres hombre llano; / la virtud es alto honor. / No tengo que aconsejarte" ("Son, you are a simple man; virtue is honor enough. I need advise you no further") (571). The "virtue" that forms the basis of Mendo's honor is pure blood; in the servants' lying game, Gilote wins the prize for telling the biggest lie: "Mendo es judío" ("Mendo is a Jew") (573).

In addition to aligning pure or impure blood with reward or punishment on the basis of respect or disrespect for existing power relations, the text introduces the exchange of women and the dynamics of cuckoldry into these equations. Two aristocrats, Enrique and Fernando, try to dominate Mendo and Leonardo respectively through their wives. The pure peasant who knows his place dominates all the other male subjects in the play directly or indirectly; the impure hidalgo trying to disrupt the social order is feminized. Leonardo initially argued against Mendo's opposition to their friendship, saying that their mutual regard canceled out social differences (554). The ironic dimension of his words, "Cosas hay en que seremos / muy semejantes los dos" ("There are things in which we two will be very much alike") (550), soon becomes apparent as Enrique and Fernando debate which is more difficult to conquer, the wife of a learned man or that of a peasant. Leonardo invites them to his house to play cards, oblivious to Fernando's attempts to play with his wife's feet under the table. Mendo becomes aware of this, partly because of his general wariness, and partly because at one point Fernando's foot finds his instead of Elvira's. When Mendo arrives home and sees Enrique's feet behind a cloth, he equates his situation and Leonardo's: "Desdichados en pies habemos sido / Leonardo y yo" ("Leonardo and I have had bad luck in feet") (569).

While both run a risk as husbands of beautiful wives, there the similarity ends. Leonardo is so eager to win the favor of the high-ranking aristocrats that he fails to perceive the threat they pose to his honor (571). His rival comments that Leonardo's preoccupation with social climbing gives him easy access to his house (574). It is further insinuated that Leonardo is willing to exploit his wife's beauty as exchange value to get points with Fernando and Enrique. Mendo, on the other hand, stresses Antona's use value—her beauty and her reproductive role—in a context of strictly private ownership. Extremely vigilant, suspicious, and punctilious concerning his sexual property (548–49), he epitomizes the masculine ideal. His wife is afraid of him, hiding the rival behind a cloth when he arrives home unexpectedly even though she is innocent of any wrongdoing, and his rival exaggerates Mendo's manliness in the debate pitting learned man against peasant, trembling when Mendo passes by (571).

The title conceit, "being wise in one's own home," provides a vehicle for the fusion of Old Christian class loyalty and masculine vigilance over one's property. At the end of the first act, Mendo is characterized as "cuerdo" ("wise") because he is faithful to his social position. After rejecting Leonardo's efforts to change his lifestyle, Mendo says: "vos sois en mi casa loco; / que yo soy cuerdo en mi casa" ("in my home you are crazy; for I am wise in it") (560). By the time the title is repeated at the end of the second act, the conceit has been redefined to include a critique, not only of Leonardo's meddling in Mendo's affairs, but also of his incapacity to control his own. All subsequent depictions of Mendo as "cuerdo" include both knowing his place and wily defense of his honor.

The rival continues his siege, offering to be godfather to Mendo's newborn son and sending Antona a costly item of clothing (a *rebociño,* or short cloak) as a baptism present. While Leonardo interprets these things as favors and presses Mendo to accept them, the Old Christian peasant sees them as pretexts for Enrique to have access to Antona. By choosing Gilote as godfather, whose rustic speech and manners contrast grotesquely with those of the nobles present at the baptism, Mendo displays his defeat of the aristocratic rival and his identification with those of his social position.[41] Mendo bonds with Gilote across power differentials—Gilote works for him—but within the same estate. Leonardo's error lies in confusing socially acceptable mobility within one's estate—Mendo's rise from coalseller to rich farmer—with cross-class mobility, which the text condemns.

Mendo's rejection of the *rebociño* culminates a major strain of imagery using clothing to signify social rank. The only time Mendo fails to be "cuerdo" is at the beginning when he allows Antona to wear finery, which Sancho sees as a dangerous deviation from the prescribed norm ("No le tengo por muy cuerdo" ["I don't consider him very wise"] 552). In the course of the play, Mendo redeems himself on this account, rejecting all the aristocratic adornments Leonardo urges him to adopt.[42] The sexual dimension of the theme appears early in the play, when Sancho warns Antona that wearing finery belies her chastity. Antona characterizes commoners by the drab clothing they wear ("que aquí todo es paño pardo" ["for here all is dark cloth"] 568), in sharp contrast to Enrique's sexual positioning of the velvet *rebociño,* trimmed in gold:

> éste le pienso dar, con cierta industria,
> que a doña Elvira persuadí le diese.
> Con esto, la malicia del villano
> no podrá conocer mi pensamiento.
>
> (574 [113])

In refusing the gift, Mendo shows that the *rebociño* signifies both inappropriate class behavior and sexual aggression:

> pero en cuanto a ser mujer
> de un labrador, no es decente:
> que es ocasionar la gente
> a murmurar y ofender.
> . . . .
> porque tales rebociños
> vienen con muchos rebozos.[43]
>
> (575 [114])

Mendo links the *rebociño* with the "feet" leitmotif, signaling his masculine awareness and Leonardo's feminized unawareness: "Y aunque pasamano tiene, / no quiero yo pasamano / que pase del pie a la mano" ("And even though it has a trimming, I don't want a trimming that would extend from the foot to the hand") (576).[44]

Leonardo's overdetermined feminization sets him up as the target of the text's humor. When he returns home unexpectedly, Elvira hides Fernando behind the bed. The suspense mounts as the servants recall the story of the husband's vengeance in *Comendadores,* fearing for their master's and mistress's lives as well as their own. After this build-up, Leonardo's entrance, half-naked, with sword and shield (582), comes as a comic anticlimax. Instead of murdering wife and rival on the spot "like a real man," Leonardo locks them in and goes to Mendo for advice. In Lope's honor plays, a male subject's *hombría* suffers when he does not act alone or with a servant or slave to avenge himself, but rather seeks the aid of an older or more authoritative male (for example, in *Ferias*). Leonardo himself remarks on his unmanly behavior, linking it to "excessive" (*converso*) learning:

> Bien dicen que hay pocos hombres
> valientes con muchas letras,
> porque en habiendo discursos
> no se vengan las ofensas.
>
> (582 [115])

The wife and rival imagine that he has gone to fetch a judicial witness to their adultery on which to found later legal claims for redress, making clear that they consider this the less manly option ("por faltarle el valor de darnos muerte" ["because he lacks the courage to kill us"] 584).

Leonardo's recourse to Mendo culminates his subordination to his Old Christian neighbor, who already shared the aristocrat's cognitive dominance of the hidalgo. The hierarchies introduced at the beginning have been reversed,[45] transforming Mendo's activity as farmer into a kind of writing superior to that of the *letrado*: Leonardo laments his being reduced to asking advice, not from a learned man, "sino a quien las duras piedras / de largos surcos escribe / con la pluma de una reja" ("but rather from one who writes upon the hard rocks of long rows with the pen of the plow") (582). At this moment of maximum humiliation, Leonardo internalizes the play's message and assigns superiority to Mendo within its binary terms:

> Mendo, si lugar me diera
> . . . .
> culpara cuantos presumen
> gobernar en casa ajena;
> . . . .
> que es la ignorancia más cierta.
> Vos, el cuerdo; vos, el sabio,
> y vos, Mendo el que sin letras
> fuistes cuerdo en vuestra casa.
>
> (582–83 [116])

This passage demonstrates the superimposition of power relations and gender enacted throughout the text: Leonardo's attempt to "govern in another's home," pressuring Mendo to change class, has led to his loss of masculinity and sexual honor; Mendo's being "wise in his own home" embraces both his manly success in guarding his sexual property and his respect for the social order.

Mendo's total control of both erotic triangles at the end establishes him as dominant male subject. He advises Leonardo to plan a secret vengeance (583), but rather than bonding with him in the defense of his honor, Mendo continues to dominate him cognitively by replacing Fernando with the aristocrat's servant. Leonardo's raging entrance with drawn sword at this point is ridiculous, given his unmanly delay, as is the speed with which he accepts Mendo's mendacious explanation (the female servant hid the servant there), given his stormy entrance. Although Mendo aligns himself with the now vanished aristocratic rivals in his cognitive domination of Leonardo, he also masters Enrique, whose attempt to cuckold him fails, and humiliates Fernando, who earlier jeered at Enrique for fearing Mendo, by "saving" him.

The elevation of the Old Christian peasant occurs in a context of social segregation. The rigid separation of social groups leads to viewing friendship automatically as a predatory ploy and results in the kind of alienation continually voiced by Mendo, as when he compares Leonardo's foolish trust in his "friends" to his own prized mistrust: "Que quien es cuerdo en su casa, / a solas su vida pasa; / que a solas se pasa bien" ("He who is wise in his own home, spends his life alone, for alone is the best way to spend it") (580). The ideal of social segregation is figured through a construction of masculinity that upholds the private ownership of woman. Each man reigns like a king in his own home, and in this case, the control of woman as use value also protects the "purity" of the gene pool. At the end, the "learning" that has been redefined as knowing one's place and (Old Christian) vigilance over one's sexual property is reduced to the latter, cloaking the text's ideological message in terms of a purely sexual difference:

> Abrid los ojos, guardando
> las ocasiones; haciendo
> Argos el alma, velando;
> a sus cosas asistiendo;

> a las ajenas dejando.
> Nadie se fíe en saber,
> por muy docto y bachiller
> de la República honrosa;
> que es ciencia dificultosa
> esto de guardar mujer.
>
> (586 [117])

The plural imperative extends an invitation to all to internalize this Argos of the soul, hypervigilant and isolated.

El testimonio vengado

In a time of crisis and deepening national anxiety at the slipping of Spanish imperialist hegemony, *Testimonio* (1596–1603) presents a racialized myth of national origins, an imaginative re-creation of a crucial moment in Spain's history. The dates of composition of this text fall squarely within the period designated by George Mariscal as encompassing a transformation of Spain's "imagined community":[46]

> The emergence of "new" groups of people—*indios, indianos, mestizos, criollos,* and others who were made visible through the contact with America—sufficiently problematized the idea of the social body so that the frontiers marking cultural inclusion or exclusion had to be radically realigned. (*"Persiles"* 94)

The forward-looking *Persiles* pushes the limits of "Spanishness" and participates in the "emergent discourse of pluralism" (101) in its use of Antonio, the *mozo bárbaro* ("barbarian youth") or *mestizo* ("mixed-blood") product of an "encounter between Spain and its Others" (97); *Testimonio* retreats into the past to shore up a besieged definition of national identity.

The union of the various "crowns" under Ramiro in the text prefigures the dynastic union of Spain under the Catholic Monarchs. The text produces this narrative of national identity by articulating discourses of nation with those of "race" and masculinity typical of the sexual honor plots discussed above. Set during the early phase of the Reconquest, the play tells how Ramiro, illegitimate son of King Sancho the Great (970–1035), vindicates the innocence of the queen, falsely accused of adultery by her own sons. As a reward, Ramiro becomes heir to Castile, León, and Aragon.

In his analysis of the text's male characters, Renato Rosaldo applies Stephen Gilman's interpretation of Lope's vision of Spanish history as a three-act play. Sancho the Great represents the heroic values of loyalty, honor, and faith of the medieval warrior leader (the "first act"); his legitimate son García, the self-indulgent and anarchic nobles of the fourteenth and fifteenth centuries who abandoned the sacred mission of Reconquest in their internecine struggles for power (the shameful "second act"); and his illegitimate son Ramiro, the faction of nobles who came to power with the Catholic Monarchs. This glorious "third act" saw the renewal of the Reconquest and the reaffirmation of medieval values, redefined as "Spanish." In its fascination with an idealized medieval past on the threshold of the seventeenth century, this narrative of Spain's becoming is profoundly reactionary; in its compaction of three periods of Spanish history into a father/son dynamic, it is profoundly patriarchal. *Testimonio,* as part of what Gayatri Spivak calls the "discursive field of imperialism" (254), positions the subject in two registers: domestic-society-through-sexual-reproduction and civil-society-through-social-mission (244). The two registers are brought together in the figure of the exemplary Ramiro, who reconstitutes the family and Spain as one and the same.

The national mission of battling the infidel provided the ideological glue for unification and, later, justification for imperialist hegemony. Paul Gilroy has commented on the emergence, in times of national crisis and decline, of discourses decrying the "dilution of a once homogeneous and continuous national stock by alien strains" (46). Posing the "impure" as a threat, often in the language of war and invasion, suggests that they have been the cause of the nation's weakness and that their banishment is necessary in order for it to become great again. In this way, racism can be deployed to exclude certain groups from the imagined community of the nation, often by directing attention to national boundaries (Gilroy 45). In Imperial Spain in crisis, texts such as *Testimonio* call for war against the infidel both within and without: the Moor along the shifting border of the Reconquest and the Jew lodged in the very heart of the nation. In its construction of "Spanish" identity, *Testimonio* furnishes an "imperialist narrativization of history" (Spivak 244) that racializes that history as it refigures it: the "true" Spanish values affirmed by Ramiro and carried into the "new" age are marked as Old Christian, in opposition to both Moor and "Jew" (the legitimate but effeminate García).

Ramiro, raised as a peasant far from the court with no knowledge of his true identity, attacks and overpowers García for speaking with the peasant woman Ramiro thinks is his sister. Reprimanded for his attack on a noble, Ramiro formulates his self-worth in terms of "race," assigning purity to himself and the status of racial other to García: "Tan bueno soy como vos. / Bien puedo matar judíos" ("I'm as good as you. I'm certainly capable of killing Jews") (414). On a metaphorical level, this moment activates the popular perception of the nobility as tainted. His keeper's words—"Y aun moros decir podía" ("And he could even say killing Moors") (414)—immediately draw the parallel between Moor without and "Jew" within. A prophetic dream further joins García and the Moors as Spain's/Ramiro's enemies. In the dream, Garci-Ramírez, the first king of the Reconquest, predicts Ramiro's succession to the throne and assigns him the dual task of defending the queen against García, whom he calls "barbarian," and Spain against the Moors, characterized with the same word:

> Quiero ceñirle esta famosa espada,
> Porque se anime á la dichosa empresa;
> Esta, que en sangre bárbara bañada,
> De cortar cuellos bárbaros no cesa.
>
> (416 [118])

The text's insistent anchoring of the term *barbarian* in Spain's traditional Others (Jew and Moor) contrasts with what Mariscal calls the lively "refunctioning" of this category in the face of "previously unimagined peoples and social types" (96).

Ramiro's representation of racially pure "Spanishness" is inseparable from his performance of masculinity, while García's and his brothers' effeminacy and marginalization in the national project of Reconquest[47] equate them metaphorically with Jew and infidel in the textual maneuvers cited above. Although Sancho is the all-powerful father-king and arch-representative of heroic medieval values, his advanced age and failing physical powers make the problem of succession acute. For the order represented by Sancho to continue, his sons must successfully negotiate the Oedipal passage; their coming of age would signal accession to masculinity as well as the expectation of a woman in marriage. As Rosaldo notes, the opposition between Ramiro and García is that of "youth which comes of age and youth which does not" (24). García and his brothers are feminized by their indulgent life at court, their excessive erotic involvement with women, and concomitant rejection of marriage. As challenger, Ramiro relegates his half-brothers to a feminized position: "Flaca y femenil defensa / De sus femeniles cuerpos; / Reto las armas cobardes" ("Weak and effeminate defense of effeminate bodies; I challenge their cowardly arms") (417). Finally, Ramiro defeats García in the combat that proves the queen innocent.

But before Ramiro can come of age as manly defender of both woman and medieval Spanish values, two contradictions must be resolved: his illegitimacy versus his destiny as legitimate heir, and his rusticity versus his royal blood. Ramiro's ignorance of his origins and upbringing as a rustic allow him to portray many of the same values and attitudes that characterize the Old Christian peasants of *Fuenteovejuna, Peribáñez,* and *Cuerdo.* But at the same time, the text deploys the ideology of social determinism to explain the contradiction between Ramiro's rusticity and his heroic action. The spectators' enjoyment of Ramiro as Old Christian peasant is compounded by the knowledge of his noble origins. For example, the count's informed "explanation" of his appearance refutes Ramiro's iconic representation of a peasant cutting and hauling wood:

> Al Rey en su talle miro.
> ¡Qué grave rostro y modesto!
> . . . .
> ¡Buen talle!
> . . . .
> ¡Qué fuerte y bien hecho está!
> Pero de tal tronco vino.
>
> (408 [119])

Even without knowing his origins, Ramiro feels himself superior in some way to other peasants (410). A clear example of the text's having it both ways is Ramiro's sense of honor in attacking García for talking to his "sister." While the audience knows that Ramiro's innate defense of his honor is attributable to his noble blood, by defining his noble adversary as "Jew" he recalls other protagonists whose punctilious defense of their honor rests on another kind of blood.

When Ramiro learns his true identity, the peasant component is evacuated from his representation of *limpieza* and replaced with ancient Gothic ancestry ("De los godos sangre antigua" ["Ancient blood of the Goths"] 414). In addition to embodying purity in seventeenth-century blood mythology, Gothic nobles represented the ideal of medieval, austere virility as celebrated in Quevedo's "Epístola satírica" ("Satiric Epistle") as opposed to "soft" seventeenth-century nobles. The insistent references to Ramiro's upbringing in the wilderness, exposed to winter's frost and summer's heat, present an ideal of nobility tempered by hardship and indifferent to the ease and luxury that characterize García. In this way, Ramiro's rusticity is absorbed as a positive factor of his Old Christian "masculine" nobility, antidote to García's (Jewish) effeminacy.

Three rituals legitimize the illegitimate Ramiro while delegitimizing García: the prophetic dream, the trial of guilt, and the ritual of adoption that closes the play. In the prophetic dream, Ramiro's inheritance of a dynasty reaching back to Garci-Ramírez himself is symbolized by the sword that has been passed down in unbroken succession from father-king to son-king. The dream further links Ramiro's possession of the sword to his defense of the commandment to honor father and mother (416), which he sports on his arms in the hand-to-hand combat (419). The trial of guilt exposes García and his brothers as the "real" bastards, since sonhood is redefined as honoring one's mother instead of biological ties. Ramiro garners definitive legitimacy through the ritual of adoption. Declaring Ramiro her "real" son for honoring her, the queen disinherits the treacherous García. A bizarre, but concrete action symbolizes the transfer publicly:

> Entra debajo el brial,
> Si en las entrañas no puedes,
> Porque legítimo heredes

Lo que pierdes natural;
. . . .
Tu madre soy. Sal, que llega
El parto, aunque sin dolor.

(420 [120])

The ritualized birth cleanses both queen and Ramiro of contamination: the queen of having borne sons whose effeminacy
signals racial otherness, and Ramiro of what Valerie Traub calls
"the filth of maternal associations" ("Prince Hal's" 465).
Through this idealization of the female reproductive body and
birth itself, Ramiro becomes at one and the same time his
father's son and his nation's hero (465). Ramiro's response
("Hoy nací de tus entrañas, / Nuevo hombre y nuevo español"
["Today I am born of your womb, new man and new Spaniard"]) underlines the collapsing of the two ideological registers of the play: what is at stake is not merely sexual reproduction
("new man"), but national mission (the "new" Spaniard).

***

The totalizing aspirations of the early modern Spanish state
produced discourses of cohesive nationhood. In these narratives of cultural identity, ethnic absolutism parallels state absolutism and imperialism. But the project of fixing national
identity in terms of racial purity is a precarious one: the ideological net of nationhood, designed to "screen" national identity from the impure, is made of holes through which many pass
(Gilroy 61). In a time of imperial crisis, these texts offer a
homogenized "Spanishness" for a heterogeneous audience;
what is presented as cultural consensus is actually a struggle
for hegemony. The next and final chapter focuses on some of
the factors that disrupt the desired identification of the spectators with such narratives.

Chapter Eight

The Negotiation of Meaning

What are the implications for sixteenth- and seventeenth-century spectators of the representation of gender, race, and national identity in Lope's honor plays?[1] Recent theories of spectatorship have shifted from textual analyses favoring a rather passive notion of spectatorship to considerations of viewing context. The idea that textual meaning changes in relation to differences in viewing situations allows for a diversity of readings among a diversity of historically and socially constituted spectators. The possibility of conceptualizing varied responses to the same text rests on a fundamental distinction between the textual subject and the social subject (Pribram 4), the former constructed by the text and the latter by the sociohistorical categories of gender, class, race, and sexuality (Gledhill 67).

The move away from textual analysis to reception involves a critique of "classic" feminist film theory. In the psychoanalytic and semiotic model, largely influenced by Laura Mulvey's analyses of mainstream Hollywood cinema, visual pleasure "derives from and reproduces a structure of male looking / female to-be-looked-at-ness (whereby the spectator is invited to identify with a male gaze at an objectified female)" (Gamman and Marshment 5). The female viewer, in this construct, may identify with the active male subject or the passive woman as object, having no active spectatorial position herself. While helpful in accounting for the exclusion of women from dominant cultural forms, this theory is limited by its unitary interest in sexual difference, tending to replicate a phallocentric focus within feminist discourse. The privileging of the Oedipal drama as the transhistorical and transcultural explanation for both subject formation and social division results in a model that is both heterosexist and ethnocentric.

In her critique of the psychoanalytic model, Jane Gaines points out that lesbian feminist critics were the first to expose the hidden heterosexist assumptions underlying the analysis of the male gaze. While recognizing spectatorship as a gendered activity, this psychoanalytic analysis ignored the possibilities that the object of the male gaze may be another man or that female spectators could derive pleasure from looking at other women (15). Even though the "homosexual" as social identity did not emerge until the nineteenth century, juridical documentation provides evidence of same-sex activity in seventeenth-century Spanish society (Perry 125–27), not to mention the homoeroticism that, according to Freud, is available to all psyches. The female characters of Lope's honor plays, especially those disguised as men, as well as the relays of looks among women in such texts as *Portugués,* could have been the source of viewing pleasure for female spectators, just as the male characters may have delighted the male gaze.

The universalizing recourse to the Oedipal narrative makes the psychoanalytic model blind to other kinds of hierarchies as well. The gender binarism and totalizing aspirations of much feminist theorizing produces an understanding of the exclusion of "women" at the expense of the marginalization of non-privileged women. This theory has been particularly color- and class-blind in its failure to understand that women who do not experience oppression solely in opposition to men but also in relation to women of the dominant class and race may feel solidarity with nonprivileged men. Similarly, male spectators in the honor-play audience have grounds for both identification with and distancing from privileged male characters in terms of racial and social differences.

While *Dina* exorcises female looking in general and *Rosambuco* and *Vitoria* that of black females in particular, other texts restrict male access to the gaze through racial prohibitions.[2] In *Rosambuco,* the black slave is positioned with the husband against both lustful female slave and supposedly adulterous wife, but simultaneously excluded from the sadistic voyeuristic position by an attitude of compassion. In every instance of an "impure" *converso* subject's desire, his looking is punished.

For Homi Bhabha, the stereotype, as a mode of representation of otherness, is object of both desire and derision, at once phobia and fetish, involving the simultaneous recognition and disavowal of differences ("The Other Question"). In *Rosambuco,* for example, the saint's blackness is simultaneously recognized and disavowed in his identification with whiteness (saintliness). According to Bhabha, the tension between aggression and narcissism in stereotypical representations mirrors the play between the anxiety of lack and difference and the affirmation of wholeness and similarity. Pedrisco's constant aggression towards Rosambuco is finally absorbed by the latter's saintliness, returning the dominant spectator to a point of total identification. The multiple belief that accompanies the stereotype—Rosambuco is both black (different) and saintly (like us)—involves a shifting of subject positions.

Since "looking," for Bhabha, is the site of subjectification for both colonizer and colonized, a black male viewer of such a text may "turn away from himself, his race, in his total identification with the positivity of whiteness" (28). As Manthia Diawara points out, such texts situate the black characters "primarily for the pleasure of the white spectator (male or female)"; black viewers' pleasure is denied by racial representations that negate the characters' blackness. Black female spectators' identification is even more problematic, as no black female character is allowed to share in the "positivity of whiteness." In the case of the Jew as racial other, the stereotype is verbally rather than visually encoded, with different implications for Spanish Jews, either publicly recognized as *conversos(as)* or "passing" as Old Christians.

While the psychoanalytic model obscures racial and class differences, it has also functioned as a closed system that produces fixed meanings, for example, in its tendency to see patriarchal oppression and ideology as monolithic (Pribram 3). Christine Gledhill suggests that texts do position spectators to receive their meanings, but "the political problem is not positioning as such, but which positions . . . audiences enter into" (66).[3] Diawara develops the notion of the "resisting spectator," including spectators who inhabit the dominant terms of all these hierarchies. While some nonprivileged spectators do identify partially or sporadically with dominant readings, Diawara is interested in exploring the resisting spectator's reluctance to do so. Honor-play viewers would experience what Diawara calls the contradiction between "the rhetorical force of the story"—the dominant reading compelling spectators to identify with the characters as inscribed—and resistance based on their own historical and cultural experiences (68).

Narrativity itself and much narrative theory privilege closure, spelling the exclusion of woman and the negation of difference, but the ending is not always the most important aspect of the experience of narrative for the viewer. It is a topos of *comedia* criticism that the ending upholds the status quo and the dominant ideology, leading Jaime Concha to suggest that critics read, as spectators probably did, "between the lines," in the gestures, silences, and interstices of the texts (55). For Isaac Julien and Kobena Mercer,

> although dominant discourses are characterised by closure,
> they are not themselves closed but constantly negotiated and
> restructured by the conjuncture of discourses in which they
> are produced. (8)

Gledhill denies that "the last word of the text is also the final memory of the audience" (73), rejecting the assumption of both fixed meanings and fixed viewing positions.

To see that "meaning is neither imposed, nor passively imbibed but arises out of a . . . negotiation between competing frames of reference" (Gledhill 68) is to begin to see popular culture, including Lope's honor plays, not as the dispenser of ruling-class ideology, but as a "site of struggle, where meanings are contested and where dominant ideologies can be disturbed" (Gamman and Marshment 1). Processes of negotiation go on simultaneously on institutional, textual, and spectatorial levels (Gledhill). The *comedia,* dependent as it was on the laws of supply and demand, of necessity catered to the desires of its audience, as Lope points out in the *Arte nuevo.* Similarly, the text can enter contested terrain in the attempt to provide what is traditional and familiar and yet satisfy the demand for the new and innovative. In many honor plays, the contradictory negotiation between woman-as-victim and the independent heroine opens up a space for spectators to bend the codes of the representation to alternative readings. As Gledhill points out, it is on the level of reception where the potentially most radical negotiations occur, due to the large range of factors— potentially resistant or contradictory—arising from the different social constitution of the spectators (70).

Beyond the individual's engagement with the text, spectators experienced the *comedia* as part of a group, determined in part by seating arrangements segregated by class and sex. Plebeian women, for example, sat in the *cazuela* ("stewpot"), forming a broad popular base.[4] Their readings were affected by this viewing situation in a way different from that of rich or noble women seated in the boxes with a few select others, both male and female. When displeased with the play, the *cazuela* viewers could stop the show by jangling their heavy keyrings.

Not only may social groupings within the audience produce different meanings of the same text (servants' different from masters', male servants' different from female servants', and so on), individual viewers "may shift subject positions as they interact with the text" (Gledhill 73). Spectatorial positioning was complicated by the contradictory combinations of privilege and oppression likely to be experienced by any one viewer due to what Ruth El Saffar calls the "mix of political, sexual, racial, and educational discriminations" being applied to the populace (175). A shifting position may arise, for example, from a mixed condition of female gender and nobility, of being women, subordinated by patriarchal structures, but privileged in socioeconomic terms. Noble *conversas'* class privilege was also countered by lack of blood purity, further problematizing their relationship to hegemonic representations of national identity. On the other hand, blood purity could function to compensate for gender devaluation, distancing ethnically privileged female spectators from the representation of racial others.[5]

Plebeian Old Christian male spectators may have moved between identification on the basis of gender and pure blood and resistance on the basis of class antagonism. In spite of their social and economic superiority, noble or rich *conversos* may have had a similarly conflictual spectatorial relationship to the representation of male power and the restoration of the social order, their discomfort derived from living both within and outside of the structures of power. The reaction of social groups whose "mirror image is structurally absent" (Julien and Mercer 9)—that is, plebeian *conversos(as)* and, in the vast majority of texts, Afro-Spaniards—would have been different from other groups offered a representation of themselves to identify with or reject.

Applying the negotiation model, the cultural signs deployed by Lope's honor plays—such as woman, racially pure Spaniard, black, Old Christian peasant, or *converso* noble—can be seen as sites of struggle invested with both hegemonic meanings and those drawn from specific sociocultural experiences (76). While Gledhill suggests that these alternative meanings are embedded in the processes of the texts themselves, Jacqueline Bobo locates alternative meanings equally within cultural products and cultural *readings*: "a specific audience creates meaning from a mainstream text and uses the reconstructed meaning to empower themselves and their social group" (93). Spectators as social subjects "can interpret popular forms to their advantage, even without invitation from the text" (Gaines 21).

While the methods of ethnographic analysis are lamentably beyond reach in determining what alternative readings were produced by the spectators of Lope's honor plays, the very heterogeneity of the *comedia* audience argues for the possibility of competing meanings negotiated by "conflicting identities within the 'imagined community' of the nation" (Julien and Mercer 2). The *comedia* critic can recognize the insufficiency of textual analysis alone and combine the psychoanalytic model with considerations of the conditions and possibilities of viewing to restore a sense of active spectatorship for *all* viewers. It is possible to see these plays, not just as monolithic dispensers of the dominant ideology that make "others" of women, plebeians, blacks, and Jews, but as intense cultural negotiations around gender, class, and racial representation. The goal of this kind of analysis is to suggest that the role of "other" is not passively accepted, but negotiated and resisted, and that this is one of the active pleasures of spectatorship (Gledhill 71). Keeping in mind the distinction between the positions the texts invite spectators to occupy and the need to problematize their responses, I would like to explore some of the options of containment and resistance available to the viewers of Lope's honor plays.

Reading the Feminine Ideal

A range of possibilities attends the reception of female characters who embody the feminine ideal, defined by a cluster of gender-specific "virtues," especially (en)closure and submission.

Female spectators could have experienced a self-righteous identification with society's normative description of femininity which afforded them, regardless of or perhaps even due to their lack of various kinds of privilege, a sense of belonging through acquiescence to a sanctioned idealization of womanhood scripted by men. As Mary Elizabeth Perry notes, many Spanish women internalized gender restrictions to the point of creating a kind of "psychic enclosure" around themselves (12). At the same time, these texts address the "double desire" of female spectators (desire to be desired by the other and desire for the other), soliciting a split identification with the active male subject and the passive female character (de Lauretis).

In these scenarios, male spectators could be comforted by the representation of woman subjected and controlled and could identify with the male subject of the action. The assumption of the controlling position by male viewers simultaneously confers that of "Spanishness," given the conflation of race, masculinity, and national identity practiced by Lope's honor plays. The invitation to occupy this position could have seemed very attractive to men lacking in one or more attributes of superiority.

Texts that foreground the ordeal of the falsely accused wife raise more complex questions of spectatorial positioning. How would male and female viewers identify with these characters, who suffer untold indignities, including attempts on their very lives? While the centering of the female character appeals directly to a female audience, *all* spectators ultimately identify with her, regardless of gender (Doane). This identification is an uncomfortable one for male viewers, for it reminds the male spectator of "his *own* passivity and helplessness in relation to the events unfolding before his eyes" (Modleski 82). Feminist film critic Mary Ann Doane has theorized that the female spectator adopts a "transvestite" role in her identification with the active male subject. Tania Modleski points out that in the "woman's film," as in these honor plays featuring a female character, "it is the male spectator who becomes the 'transvestite'" (54). The focus on the extreme suffering of these female characters, their willing embrace of undeserved punishment, and their continued loyalty towards their oppressors, positions both male and female spectators through masochistic identification.

Drawing on recent work on masochism by Kaja Silverman, Gaylyn Studlar, and Leo Bersani, Modleski explores the masochistic dimension of male spectatorship as it relates to male identification and masculine identity, challenging the excessively binary formulation "male-subject-knower-sadist" and "woman-object-known-masochist" in film theory (71). Modleski reminds us that "one of the basic assumptions of feminist film theory" is that "both hero and male spectator derive a great deal of narcissistic gratification from exercising power over the female subject" (69). But not enough attention has been paid to the idea that the "exercise of this power and the witnessing of a 'satisfying representation' of the woman's suffering may be *painful* to the male subject" (70). In texts that represent the actual adulterous desire of the wife, love is quickly subordinated to the duties of honor. But in those texts dwelling on the dilemma of the male subject who erroneously believes his wife to be unfaithful, the struggle between love and honor is prolonged, as is the representation of the husband's pain at losing honor and wife, as well as his guilt at having exiled or supposedly "killed" her.

In the rival-king plays, male spectators are also aligned with the husband, who becomes increasingly paralyzed and humiliated. As the narrative moves to closure, the tension grows with the fear that the male protagonist's masculinity and honor will be suppressed to the point of obliteration. There is a sense in which all Lope's honor plays involve a pleasurable masochistic element, for according to Theodore Reik, suspense plays the leading role in masochistic fantasies. But while Bersani's model neglects gender differences, Modleski points out that

> the inequality of power relations means that the man—hero or spectator—gets to . . . maintain a mastery which enables him to deny his suffering while at the same time safely indulging it. This masochism may be easily repudiated, and it has potentially dire consequences for women when it is. (70)

By the end, male spectators can repudiate identification with suffering wife and husband through the restoration of the husband to the dominant position. Those texts that carry the victimization of the male protagonist to the point of extinction may represent deep-seated fears and anxieties vis-à-vis the Father and the ability to perform the proper heterosexual role in relation to the symbolic order. However, the majority offer a position from which male spectators' masochistic urges are doubly and safely indulged: in the figures of the victimized wife (such as Sol in *Corona*), for whom the reward of masochism is masochism itself, and the victimized vassal readmitted to the world of the fathers.

The shifting between sadistic and masochistic spectator positions has to do with class and ethnic identities as well. Plebeian, *converso,* and Afro-Spanish viewers could take pleasure in identifying with the suffering of the privileged married couples and at the same time distance themselves in enjoyment of the characters' predicaments. The separation of nobility and good sense in the scenes of madness, for example, could have been perceived as tragic by some and as humorous by others.

Female spectators are encouraged to identify with the passive, victimized wife, whose reward for masochistic negation of self (*Corona*) or of love objects (*Firmeza*) is eternal glory and fame as exemplar of feminine virtue. If they split their identification in the texts depicting falsely accused wives, they place themselves in the position of sadistic author of their own suffering and oppression; in the case of the rival-king plays, the male protagonist is also passive and victimized.

On the other hand, while female viewers are invited to internalize a representation of themselves as ideal woman, these women were, as Jean Howard notes, also positioned by the commercial practices of the theater "as consumers, critics, spectators, and spectacles" (40).[6] Although they may enjoy the restoration of the male character to masculinity and the subject role, female spectators are also "already engaged in the active, knowing and rebellious activity of spectatorship" (Modleski 71), and the possibility of other responses besides masochistic identification should not be discounted.

Female spectators may have experienced anger at the unjust punishment of these wives, the double binds in which they are placed by masculine desire, and the representation of woman's supposed powerlessness as her chief virtue. According to Perry, many Spanish women resisted gender restrictions, noting the "gap between gender ideals and their actual conditions" (12). Female viewers also may have had some satisfaction that woman's predicament in seventeenth-century Spanish patriarchal society was represented. The invitation to identify with Sol's self-annihilation may have elicited responses ranging from masochistic pleasure at the glorious realization of the feminine ideal to an awareness that the ideal of the eternal feminine is constructed, quite literally in the case of this text, out of women's bodies.

In plays featuring the falsely accused wife, the representation of woman who paradoxically escapes male control in spite of her perfect submission problematizes the attempt to fix the meaning of the narrative, as well as the identification of male spectators with the supposedly controlling figure of the husband-king. The male construct of ideal womanhood as powerlessness fails to dispel the underlying uneasiness that woman, even as defined by men, cannot be totally brought under patriarchal control. In their depiction of confrontation with phallocentric power, these texts reinforce female spectators' knowledge of the "multiple, slippery significations" of femininity (Hansen 230).

Unlike the violence done to the adulterous wife whose desire clearly threatened patriarchal law and order, the rape or murder of innocent women in *Príncipe, Dina,* or *Estefanía* results simply from being a woman. Is the only position female spectators of these texts can assume that of masochist? As Modleski points out, "rape and violence, it would appear, effectively silence and subdue not only the woman *in* the films . . . but also the women watching the films" (17). For female viewers who also take pleasure in looking at other women in the theater, Dina's punishment for transgressive looking functions as a warning.

Such texts undermine patriarchal law to the extent that they create sympathy for and an identification with the women who are innocent victims of male violence. These plays also show that such violence is not an individual aberration but a systemic outgrowth of the structural view of women as male property. In addition, as subjects engaged in active looking, the female spectators of *Dina* may have resisted the response given by the play to the query, what happens when the woman looks?

In their reading of the passage from Genesis that served as Lope's source material, the editors of *The Tribe of Dina: A*

Jewish Women's Anthology pose a series of questions not answered by the biblical text, specifically concerning Dina's seeking out other women:

> What did she want? What did she want to give? Did she ever reach them before Shechem, the Hivite took her? Did he seduce her? Attract her? Did he rape her? Did *her* soul cleave unto *him*? And when the brothers found out, what did she feel?
>
> No words, no hints. Only what the men felt and thought: *his woman, his wife; their sister defiled, their honor sullied.* Only what the men did and wanted to be done: *taking, force, violence.* (Kaye/Kantrowitz and Klepfisz 3)

Lope's *Dina* answers some of these questions, representing Dina's meeting with the other women, their mutual pleasure in each other, and their promise of friendship. In Lope's text Shechem rapes Dina, and her hatred of him is clear. From this point on in Lope's text, Dina's desire for revenge merges with that of her brothers. Yet what of that other desire figured in *Dina* as the very cause of her rape? Perhaps the women in the audience did not forget the reasons why Dina left her father's house in the first place, and perhaps, like the editors of *The Tribe of Dina,* they left the theater with the following questions unanswered:

> And the women: Did Dina ever speak to the women? Did they gather secretly? Comfort each other? Weep over the blood? Did they tell each other stories? Did they want something for themselves?
>
> And Dina: Did she want something away from the father, away from the brothers? Did she need her mother? Did she long for sisters, for daughters to gather a Tribe of Dina? (3)

Responses to the Female Outlaw

If, as Michel Foucault suggests, sovereign power is strengthened and exalted by its visible exercise on the bodies of its subjects (*Discipline* 57), why do so few of Lope's honor plays represent transgressive female desire and end with the spectacle of punishment? The answer may have to do with the dynamics of spectatorship and the paradox of female desire that grows more elusive in proportion to the extremity of the measures taken to control it.

These texts clearly invite female spectators to internalize woman as loathsome monster. Female viewers may have participated in the celebratory punishment of the murder scenes, or the beating scene in *Discreto,* in order to take vicarious revenge on socially and ethnically privileged women or to distance themselves from female behavior judged criminal by their society. Participatory censure of such a woman aligns them with the majority definition of female virtue. But just as female spectators may not comply with the invitation to identify with the ideal woman, they may also refuse to see themselves in the image of transgression. They may perceive the ways in which woman is not entirely either bad or good or entirely controlled or destroyed by patriarchal power. Female spectators may also be angered by the equation of female desire and criminality and by the force applied to bring active female desire back under control. The considerable violence done to Casandra in *Discreto* to rid her of her desire and coerce her back into the feminine position,[7] is presented comically, including kicks, slaps, and blows with a stick. In effect, it is offered as a joke, a male joke at woman's expense. If a female spectator does identify here with the male subject, this is certainly one of the instances in which she "shifts restlessly in her transvestite clothes."[8]

Mary Ann Doane analyzes a photograph as a parable of the female spectatorship position. This photograph also presents a visual joke at the expense of a woman. In it a man and a woman, in the center of the frame, stand in front of a picture which the person looking at the photograph cannot see. The woman is looking attentively at this picture, but the man on her left is looking towards the right side of the frame at a picture of a naked woman. The woman in the photograph is excluded from the triangular complicity set up among the man, the picture of the naked woman, and the spectator "who gets the joke." For Doane, a woman looking at the photograph must adopt a masochistic position to align herself in the spectator position, assuming the role of Mulvey's transvestite. Modleski critiques Doane's analysis, pointing out the great difference between "getting" a joke and deriving pleasure from it. She cites the example of a person of color who understands a racist joke without adopting the disguise of a white person or assuming the position of a masochist. At times, the one oppressed by the joke understands it best.

Applying Modleski's theory to *Discreto,* it is possible that women in the audience of *Discreto,* objects of a hostile joke, felt anger at the moment of understanding it, even if this anger stayed unconscious or repressed. They did not necessarily experience the unthinking pleasure of those who laughed at Casandra's beating. Though plebeian women might be inclined to share in a joke at their class adversary's expense, the inclusion of Casandra's maid in the punishment may have checked this response.

If the potential anger of female spectators at the spectacle of punishment may have deterred Lope, another possible reason for the scarcity of wife-murder plays is the role of the people in the spectacle of public execution. Foucault comments on the ambiguity of this role:

> drawn to the spectacle intended to terrorize it, [the people] could express its rejection of the punitive power and sometimes revolt.... the great spectacle of punishment ran the risk of being rejected by the very people to whom it was addressed. (*Discipline* 59, 63)

The genre of the "gallows speech," or last words of the condemned, also fostered solidarity with the offender. Any representation of crimes against the law, even in the context of repentance, is equivocal, for the outlaw may be transformed by it into a hero (66–67). Plebeian spectators of both genders may have identified with the female outlaw condemned and punished in these texts. For Foucault, there lies "beneath the apparent morality of the example not to be followed, a whole memory of struggles and confrontations" (67). These honor plays could be considered "two-sided discourses": they exercise some degree of ideological control, but they also provide spectators, especially female viewers, "not only memories but precedents" (68).

The appropriation of the active subject role by a female outlaw and her temporary domination of the male characters have particular implications for male spectatorship. In some honor plays, the offended husband collects evidence of his affront by spying on his wife, allowing the adulterous couple to come together for the purpose of punishing them. The passive spectator position of these male protagonists is one of suffering. For example, in *Venganza,* the duke hides to listen to a conversation between Casandra and Federico (268). But as in those plays featuring the suffering of the ideal wife, the male protagonist does eventually return to a sadistic scenario. The repudiation of the masochistic position coincides with the restoration of the male subject's power through force in the ceremony of punishment.

The male subject of these texts regains control over woman and a secure sense of masculine identity through violence (murder, beating) or banishment. Male spectators are invited to share this secure control with him. But at the same time, the nagging sensation that female desire has not been successfully destroyed or assimilated may have continued to disquiet male spectators, and may help to explain the relative paucity of this scenario in Lope's honor plays.

For plebeian male spectators, identification with the male subject, ultimately strengthened in his power to subject the transgressive wife to his will, may coexist with identification with the female outlaw in her confrontation with the law. For male and female viewers alike, these texts offer a multiplicity of possible spectator positions running the gamut of resistance, affirmation of subjection, or contradictory combinations of the two, depending on gender, racial, and class factors.

Fabia's unique representation of the female outlaw provides spectator positions not offered by Lope's honor plays as a rule. As shown above, the implications of identification with the female outlaw, both feared and desired, are different for male and female viewers. Here the "double desire" of female spectators is conflated in a single female figure. Fabia offers neither masochistic identification with a passive, victimized woman nor identification with the threatening woman who is ultimately brought under masculine domination. Her elusiveness subverts the notion of masculine identity that depends on the control of woman, while providing an occasion to surrender to a fantasy of active female desire.[9]

For female viewers, the availability of Brisena for identification counters the fantasy of the female outlaw with the more familiar role of victim. Unlike Fabia, Brisena is the passive object of male desire and a pawn of male traffic in women: Vitelio uses then discards her for Fabia not once but twice. However, after the second time Brisena articulates her disgust at the nature of heterosexual relationships in male homosocial exchange: "si en su presencia las lloran / en otra parte las venden" ("if in their presence they weep for them, elsewhere they sell them") (109). But Brisena is not the only commodity on the market: Fabia barely survives an assassination planned by her husband and serves as object and sign of exchange in the rivalry between Catulo and Nero, whose desire was sparked by Lelio and Vitelio's desire to possess her in the first place. On some level, Brisena and Fabia are one and the same. When Fabia protests at Nero's profession of desire for her in the presence of Brisena, who has played the part of Fabia's literal double, Nero points to their underlying similarity: "Eres tú" ("It is only you") (108).

While Fabia's shifting between passive object and active subject stimulates anxiety in male spectators, Brisena offers a comforting representation of feminine pliancy. The simultaneous depiction of female complicity and female resistance vis-à-vis the law encourages a complex and contradictory response in female viewers that is not merely complicit or resistant. This response "requires an understanding of woman's placement on the margins of patriarchal culture—at once inside and outside its codes and structures" (Modleski 116). *Fabia,* in its characterization of woman as both outlaw and victim, strengthens the awareness of contradiction involved in women's situation in the social order. Even while identifying with the victimized object of male exchange, female spectators' knowledge of women's predicament is reinforced by Brisena's insight. Such a recognition may trigger a response of anger as well as curiosity: where does Brisena go, how does what she knows change her life, what will she do if Vitelio appears one more time at her door?

A male character such as Catulo further problematizes identification for male viewers because of the way he "oscillates between a passive mode and an active mode, between a hypnotic and masochistic fascination with the woman's desire and a sadistic attempt to gain control over her, to possess her" (Modleski 99). Despite Catulo's efforts to control and possess

Fabia, he cannot acquire the necessary distance from her because of his narcissistic identification with his love object, as
expressed in the words that close the first act: "que ya me muero
por verme / hecho Narciso en sus brazos" ("for I am already
dying to see myself transformed into Narcissus in her arms") (88).

In other texts that acknowledge the masochistic aspect of
man's relation to his love objects, either the male protagonist
eventually returns to a sadistic scenario, as in the case of the
punishing husband, or another male character commands authority, as in the plays in which the sadistic maneuvers of the
king balance the affliction of the offended husband. But Catulo
never satisfactorily repudiates his masochism from the point of
view of male spectators. In the scene in which Lelio awaits an
opportune moment to stab Fabia, Catulo hides and watches,
aligning male viewers with his masochistic voyeur position
(86). When Fabia flees to a tower after the attempt on her life,
the spatial disposition of the actors onstage highlights his submission as he pleads with her helplessly from below. His suicide at the end is an act of self-inflicted suffering.

No dominating male figure compensates for Catulo's subjection, blocking the male spectators' switch from masochistic
to sadistic identification. The young rivals Vitelio and Lelio are
subordinated, first by Fabia, and then by Nero, and the latter is
soon cognitively dominated by Fabia along with the rest. The
last image of a male character in the play is one of masochistic
surrender, as Vitelio, awestruck by Fabia's power, offers her his
hands symbolically bound in marriage: "Dame, señora, tu
mano, / y atadas recibe aquéstas" ("Give me, Lady, your hand,
and accept these tied ones") (110).

Mediating Male Homosocial Relations

The range represented in these texts suggests a tremendous
flexibility in male spectatorial positioning. Caught in the same
contradictory demands of the masculine ideal as the male characters, male viewers can identify with the desire to prey upon
others' sexual property as well as the fear of losing control over
one's own. Within each of these positions, either triumph or
defeat is possible. Male spectators' options include switching
between husband and rival as the balance of power shifts,
guided by the passing of narrative control from hand to hand,

and the use of asides and dramatic irony; indulging in masochistic identification with the cognitively dominated husband, only to return with a vengeance to sadistic control; or surrendering completely to a fantasy of masochistic annihilation. In the more comic pieces, the husband's hypervigilance and blindness could have provided an important release for the tensions of living out a rigid gender role in the everyday world. Male viewers might have found consolation and enjoyment in both serious and comic representations of the predicaments inherent for the male subject in his society's construction of masculinity.

While female spectators may exercise the same options as male viewers within the "masculine" position of their split identification, empathy with the female characters still positions them as object and medium of male homosocial rivalry, even in those texts in which the wife is instrumental in restoring her husband to the dominant position. One wonders whether the gendered experience of spectatorship at these plays produced the diverging readings found in contemporary honor-play criticism. While male critics such as Donald Larson see in texts like *Comendadores* a solemn celebration of recovered honor and masculinity, female critics such as Melveena McKendrick are more likely to "read against the grain" in order to produce a comic interpretation.[10] In general, just as the representation of male homosocial rivalry provides the opportunity for male spectators to feel their experience validated, female viewers may have read between the lines of these texts in order to appreciate the extreme measures necessary to control femininity.

The representation of cross-class bonding among men through the defense of honor and masculinity belongs to what José Antonio Maravall describes as the *comedia*'s program of incorporating the large and potentially unruly class of servants into the social order ("Relaciones"). For Maravall, the *gracioso* functions to garner the identification of his real-life counterpart through humor. Within the classist representation of the master/servant bipolarity, the loyalty of the servant contrasts with the palpably tense relations between real-life masters and servants, based entirely on money paid for services rendered. Such loyalty hearkens back to the feudal bonds between master and *criado* (literally, "raised" in the master's household). In

Comendadores, the slave Rodrigo's preoccupation with his master's honor contrasts with the conduct of the servant "[q]ue se alquila" ("[w]ho is for hire") (279). Rodrigo's honor sonnet is directed at plebeian male spectators who share with noblemen and even kings the same concern for their masculinity and ability to control their sexual property.

For each social level, the approval of the authoritative father figure depends on the ability to distance and control woman. Yet even the bonds founded on kinship and respect for the social hierarchy are capable of slippage beyond the control of the male subject. For all male spectators, the volatility of male bonds of mutuality reinforces a sense of masculine identity that is both rigidly hierarchical and alienated. Male spectators are invited to an identification that, through the corrective coercion of laughter, views horizontal bonding and bonding without the mediation of a woman's body as feminizing.

For female spectators, these texts confirm that, whether nobles or plebeians, Old Christians, blacks, or *conversas,* women are the medium of men's relationships with each other in rivalry as well as in mutuality. Men may be feminized or masculinized through their use of woman, but women are always the commodities, rarely the buyers and sellers. While male servants or slaves share with their masters the general masculine concern for honor, the parallel scenes of female bonding between mistress and maid or slave construct them equally as reflections of male honor: together they resist or together they fall, but neither mistress nor maid/slave constitutes herself as subject in resistance or adultery in the same way the male servant or slave does who carries out masculine vengeance at the side of his master. While these texts do not go further than representing the ways in which women as commodities subvert or manipulate the "market," they may have provoked a confrontation with the limitations of the phallic economy for what Irigaray calls "commodities among themselves."

The Pleasure of Gender Fluidity

The immense popularity of disguises representing multiple social and gender identities in Lope's honor plays contrasts with the rigidity of roles promulgated by official discourses on gender and social status in seventeenth-century Spanish society. In a culture in which both sexual difference and social status were encoded in clothing, audiences were fascinated with such changes in identity and accepted not only the desire to do so but that a "change of costume could affect a remarkable transformation" (Wheelwright 25–26). The fluidity with which identities of all kinds are displaced and transformed must have been a source of compensatory pleasure experienced by male and female spectators alike.

The cross-dressed woman is also a source of erotic pleasure. Although no graphic representations of her appearance on the stage in the seventeenth century exist (Bravo-Villasante 178n15), stage directions and other written descriptions of the time disclose that both spectators' pleasure and moralists' censure were based on the short, close-fitting outfit revealing the shape of the female body. Those who denounced the presence of women onstage in general were particularly incensed by their appearance in men's clothing, which they viewed as more lascivious than their feminine costume. They frequently brandished the passage from Deuteronomy prohibiting cross-dressing for both sexes. Repeated attacks spanning the end of the sixteenth century and the beginning of the seventeenth reveal the inefficacy of all attempts to ban cross-dressing on the stage.[11]

In the action of the plays, the assumption of masculine dress erases the female body and defies codes of enclosure; paradoxically, the same device increases the actor's attractiveness as object of desire of male spectators. The cross-dressed woman's status as sex symbol for male spectators may reflect a masculine need to "eroticize (and thereby possess) the independent woman" (Gubar 483). At the same time, Julie Wheelwright and others suggest that the woman in men's clothing may be a point of male homoerotic tension as well, highlighting "sexuality within male relationships" (59). The affection men feel for each other can be played out in these fantasies where "the attractive young man . . . turned out to be a woman, after all" (59).[12] Besides arousing both heteroerotic and homoerotic pleasure, the cross-dressed woman who excels at arms and exhibits bravery at the front provides a flattering imitation of masculine behavior. The transvestite page in *Portugués,* who boasts of her skill in courting married women and cuckolding husbands, cuts both ways, both affirming male power *and* mocking male behavior through caricature (Wheelwright 55).

This oscillation characterizing the representation of the cross-dressed woman—object of both heteroerotic and homoerotic desire, both flattering and mocking masculinity—can create an ambiguous response in male spectators. The cross-dressed woman, consoling *and* threatening, activates the enigmatic nature of woman in the male imaginary, deriving, according to Freud, from her "bisexuality." The woman in men's clothing is neither/nor, a reminder that with woman, "men never know for sure *with whom* they are dealing" (Modleski 94). The threat posed by the aggressive woman and her otherness is tamed by her representation as man's mirror image. In this way, difference can be simultaneously demanded and erased in a scenario that concedes to woman not equality but *sameness* (Modleski).

In spite of the ambiguities that attended the representation of female cross-dressers, Howard points out that

> the very fact that women went to the theatre to see them attests to the contradictions surrounding this social institution. Women at the public theatre were doing many of the very things that the polemicists who attacked crossdressing railed against. They were gadding about outside the walls of their own houses, spending money on a new consumer pleasure, allowing themselves to become spectacle to the male gaze. (439)

The cross-dressed woman has always exercised a particular appeal for a female audience by her representation of the "potential to cast off the strictures of womanhood" (Wheelwright 114). Like Fabia, the cross-dressed woman provides female spectators the opportunity to surrender to a fantasy of active female desire which goes unpunished. Although her freedom is bought in the service of securing a strong sense of masculine identity for her husband, at the same time her blurring of gender boundaries subverts the very notion of identity. Like Fabia's, the female cross-dresser's oscillation between the positions of object and subject of desire and her simultaneous representation of female complicity and female resistance vis-à-vis patriarchal law solicit a complex and contradictory response.

The representation of the "masculine" woman solicits resistance, because of her "energy of self-direction and the force of [her] assertiveness" (Wolfson 593). On the other hand, she solicits complicity, because such representations appear to "clarify" the hierarchical structure of sexual difference by defining freedom as masculine and human action as male action, reaffirming the belief "that an active, independent life could only be imagined in male terms" (Wheelwright 50). But texts that transfer the attributes of one gender to the other reveal a culture's ambivalence towards gender roles (Wolfson 593). The masculinization of woman and the feminization of man present at one and the same time a challenge to the conventional understanding of gender (these are, after all, women who are acting like men) and a reinforcement of it (they are, after all, exceptions) (Wheelwright 78).

While the binary inversion "feminized man / masculinized woman" seems to perpetuate the conventional codes by presenting "exceptions," the ambivalence at the heart of the representation of the woman dressed as a man manages to "transcend the dualism of sex-role polarities" (Gubar 479). The centuries-old outrage at cross-dressing reveals the uneasiness generated by "perverting the distinctiveness" of the signifiers of sexual difference (Wolfson 594), suggesting that binary inversion may somehow be sidestepped in the creation of a third category. For Wheelwright, cross-dressing can undermine biological concepts of sexual difference and foster an understanding of gender as "something fluid, interchangeable and dynamic" (73). Although gender propriety is re-imposed and woman's "nature" reaffirmed through narrative closure, it is only after a long intermediate period of great flux in gender identity, offering a spectrum of positions for male and female spectators alike.[13]

The different sign systems at work in the performance also function to undermine the binary understanding of sexual difference. While the action ultimately returns woman to the feminine position, this message is at odds with the visual persistence of the woman dressed as a man. In all the texts that feature cross-dressing, the female character retains her masculine attire in the final scene, even as her "true" identity is being revealed. Who is to say which of these messages was the most compelling, and what image remained in the retina of the mind's eye long after the performance was over.

Appendix

English Translations

The following are English translations for the longer Spanish quotations. They are keyed to the text by the number in brackets. All translations are mine unless otherwise indicated. Verse quotations have been translated into English as prose. The aim has been to produce a readable English while remaining as close as possible to the original.

[1]   Of what purpose is so much silence, since there is no greater obstacle in the path to my remedy than shame in speaking?

[2]   Nature has given man more perfection, and, for the same reason, more beauty to woman, and since men come forth from women, they show them that respect.

[3]   King: Is it possible for a king to suffer an offense, who is above the law?
       Don García: Yes, for he is a man, if he is king, and as a man created the opportunity.
       King: I already suspect who it is that offends me, for a man with a woman, even though he is king, can fear any kind of offense.

[4]   I know that he has mirrored me so faithfully in everything that you have taken him for me; for which I promise you, Lady, your just deserts.

[5]   Stop, dear Casandra, your crying and sighing, for you will have more than enough to cry about after I say good bye.

[6]   Ortuño: The nose, with even line, divides the field of snow and coral, joining January and April. She has two fine corals amid gemstone walls of teeth. . . . Of her neck, what shall I tell you? What marble would be sufficient? . . .
       Duke: You are setting me on fire. . . . Doña Mayor will be mine.

[7]   He is certainly quite attractive, if he were not so pretty and vain. Don Pedro, who is more robust, does not seem bad to me. . . . And

259

the contrary should surprise you, for it is not good that a man seem like a woman.

[8] Quickly rinse out four fine sheets. Take out incense from the small desk. Regale your new master. . . . Perfume this whole room. Lay out that Indian bedspread. . . . Perfume a shirt also, and prepare refreshments.

[9] Only one night in one month have I seen him in my arms, and for many months after that he has refused to see me.

[10] Among offenses and vengeance love walks solicitous. . . . Quite mad in my inclination towards wrongdoing, due to so many grievances at the hands of the duke, I imagine that I find vengeance and pleasure in the greatest folly.

[11] I have left the infamous Casandra with feet and hands tied and covered with a cloth, and her mouth gagged to silence her anguished cries.

[12] "[My husband] wore himself out wishing he had a sister to give you in marriage; I offer myself in her place . . ."

[13] The duke must be of the opinion of those who, once taking possession, want to have a woman in their home like a jewel, an adornment, ostentation and finery, a chair, or desk in a room, and this is a condition that I condemn. . . . A woman of honorable demeanor comes to her house to be a woman and not to be a chair, a desk, or a portrait.

[14] I have remained in mourning so that the new wife may remember . . . that there is no man so valiant, who dares to kill another man, seeing the gallows in front of him.

[15] For she is female, in love and jealous, and when she seeks to avenge herself, she will respect neither son, father, nor brother, but will stain sword and hand with blood.

[16] Not by guarding woman can she be kept safely; for he writes on water who becomes aware of worries and jealousies, and even worse things befall him. And so it is reasonable that he who prohibits her her pleasure is deceived by his own efforts; for she is an animal who lives in confidence, and, when you would grasp her tightly, she exceeds the wind. . . . the more they grip her the more she eludes them, for it is like taking a handful of sand that slips between each finger.

[17] The man who seeks an intelligent woman is not wise, but rather insane . . . because he subjects himself to someone who esteems him little. She will understand his weakness and with her learning she will offend him night and day.

[18] Her soul struggles to depart, . . . disfiguring her beautiful body. See her lovely eyes rolled up. . . . See the living scarlet now dead, the snowy color yellow and on each cheek the color of inhuman death. See the ruby tint turn livid, her hand now icy and lax.

[19] I erred in getting married, thinking that a beautiful wife was a life-long delight for the soul; I didn't imagine that envious power and wealth would covet her when they saw her, too.

[20] But I attribute my misfortune to your grace. It is clear that if you were not beautiful, you would not give the commander cause for such irrational love.

[21] And I in Belflor hiding like a timid rabbit? . . . So that they may say that Count Gesualdo, like a coward, reposes in the arms of his loving wife. . . . and does needlepoint with her maids, when the fury of barbaric swords obliges him to be with his king.

[22] And then with these teeth kill the one who is in his arms and send her back in pieces to her infamous relatives.

[23] and if my soul is ashamed of anything, it is only that it has no more than one life to give for honor.

[24] It is just that you kill me, for my husband, if I am alive, cannot marry. Let us give him that pleasure, Claudio.

[25] I have brothers; I know that they will avenge me. . . . Father, I am dishonored: where the sword must cut, there is no need of advice.

[26] But I justly desire to see these ladies, for I believe that Heaven formed in them a natural copy of its divine beauty, besides the artful design of their apparel. In addition, their dances and music are praised. Such grace is seen in their movements and songs.

[27] They please me exceedingly; especially those dancers dressed as gypsies. . . . I find the costumes lovely, lovely figures, lovely faces, lovely movements, Zelfa; for you well know that a woman's grace is in her bearing and the rhythm of her body's gait.

[28] Seeing you has given me great pleasure. How well you dress in Siquen! What lovely costumes you wear! What do you use? What do you bathe with, that you look so charming? . . . I want to be a very good friend to both of you.

[29] A woman who incites me with her beauty, what do I owe to the Heavens who engender her? All the things that God created are for men. . . .

[30] If woman were born without eyes and men without desires, such unseemly things would never happen and a thousand annoyances would be avoided. You went to see, without remembering that they might see you there; as if it could be possible to want to look without being looked at. You are not free of deception, nor excused of treachery, because the one who gives the opportunity is the one who is the cause of the harm. So you should not be surprised at your own [harm] if you went to see the women, without seeing that, if you are one, men might see you.

[31] I am ulcerated with disease . . . for even though you see me elegantly and femininely dressed, I am a red apple whose heart is rotten. Look at these arms, Your Highness, covered with blood and wounds.

[32] Stop! Stop! Do not revolt me further! . . . Take away those bloody cloths, for they turn my stomach. . . . Just look at what I once desired!

[33] Dirty and rusty sword with golden guard! . . . Famous house with excellent facade but deserted within! Oh, black and faded wall covered with a cloth of gold!

[34] Spain deserves no less glory for her women; for there are many feats such as these, worthy of eternal memory. But even if there were none, Doña Sol would suffice to silence Rome and make Athens mute.

[35] Let Roman and Greek women be silent, Porcia, Evadne, and Artemisa; for you alone bear the laurel, palm, and olive branches. Spain remains in debt to your extraordinary virtue. . . . Let you and all your descendants . . . from this day on call yourselves Coroneles.

[36] To think that I imagined he loved Hipólita, and instead it is my own sister! . . . All that one seeks in woman, by God, is alchemy!

[37] Heads fall into the sea, as by the rough hand of the peasant, acorns fall from the oak to the ground.

[38] If she, losing you in life, has ended in such confusion, how shall I, who lose the count in death, be consoled and live on?

[39] It is my fault, really, for once he enjoys a woman a man loses all respect for her.

[40] I never thought I would see you with defensive weapons, for you have always possessed extremely effective offensive arms.

[41] If I had clothes like yours, by God, I would court the most beautiful married woman, without her husband knowing.

[42]   Mayor: Does my coiffure please you?
Lisarda: Adorable, charming. . . . How beautiful! . . .
Mayor: So, I please you?
Lisarda: This ribbon is well-tied; . . . what a lovely prison of love! . . . By God, my Lady, you are like the sun! . . . Has there ever been such grace? Such beauty?

[43]   Enrique: What is this! Why do they call Don Juan "Lady" and "Clavela"?
Isabela: In order that my innocence might be even more clear, if she is a woman.
Clavela: Woman I am.
Enrique: Lofty proof of your innocence, Isabela.

[44] I asked her what they did with those tender creatures they stole from their parents, and she told me—oh, what ferocity!—that they made sacrifices with them to an idol.

[45] If woman is to be governed, woman must have, not one who knows how to obey, but one who knows how to give orders.

[46] Did you see . . . how I organize and control . . . that squadron, and how I pierce the breast of anyone who gets out of line?

[47] even though there is power to spare, *in not seeing a sword at her side,* obeying her offends them! I cannot take a husband, nor cause them to fear me. When the one who is to be feared is afraid, Otavia, government is lost. (My emphasis)

[48] one's own woman should be like a balcony, which, in order not to give offense and to be able to be seen in moderation, should be attached to the house, but always outside.

[49] She is jealous and she is mine, for there is nothing that drives me to distraction more. . . . having woman at mealtime, woman after

eating, woman afterwards in bed, and at all hours woman . . . who would not be dismayed?

[50] there are very few possessions that do not end in contempt. . . . This business of being there at all hours, is less pleasing, because it's too easy. . . . In a year's time a woman is chair, bench, desk, for as long as she causes no trouble, that is what she comes to be.

[51] Everything he touched turned to gold; he ate and drank gold, and even slept on gold. The pleasures of married men must be the same, for, tied to the home, everything they touch is woman.

[52]   Teodoro: From so much seeking pleasure, I have almost come to fear the love of women.
Leonardo: . . . I have come to understand . . . that he who loves woman so much of necessity must be woman.

[53] for since love is weakness, how can he who stumbles being weak be respected? Surely the world is right to think little of a man who is crazy for women.

[54] If you thought that I am a man who guards badly that which was given to me to guard; . . . I am here to show you, my fine fellow, that I am enough of a man for the woman they give me.

[55] Forgive me, my father: you taught me to love what is found in this house, and mine is the lesser transgression; for you sought another's property and I what can be mine, being my wife.

[56] If I see a raging bull coming down the street, am I supposed to wait, or should I flee? . . . Will you say I made the bull up as a pretext to come in here?

[57] that he had killed Indians, crocodiles, and wild beasts on the shores of the newly discovered sea, and that he knew best how to defend me from a little bull.

[58] with this sword half unsheathed, for yesterday I almost drew it, to do what I had thought to do. Once again I calm my sword.

[59] With the generous blood I inherited from my grandparents, and that honor which is purchased in Flanders with a thousand wounds.

[60] Oh, friend of my heart, I kiss your feet a thousand times, pardoning another thousand my ignorance and your annoyance.

[61] Close your door, my dear, as soon as night falls. . . . Cover the coach when you go to Mass and your face with a shawl in church.

[62] let there be reserve in your house . . . and let your doors and lattices show that there are dead people inside who defend living honors.

[63] and so, in my wickedness I beg you to unsheathe this sword and run me through, so that, killed by your hands, you yourself may avenge your offense.

[64] I hand myself over to you, Clodoveo, and beg you to kill me! I confess my wickedness; I do not deny it. . . . But immense Heaven's justice . . . threw me down to the earth with this wound.

[65] Kings give no excuses, for their majesty is free; and it is in making men from the earth that the king imitates God.

[66] A man who owns land should attend to the sowing lest outside weeds spring up due to drought.

[67] Shall I draw my sword? Shall I enter in an uproar? No, for this is an affair of honor. . . . I choose to enter dissembled.

[68] If I killed my daughter as a lascivious adulteress, I would leave my dishonor alive to last forever. . . . without killing my daughter, I have defended my honor.

[69] Leave me, imaginings, for you imitate the art of painting in my senses, painting figures that burn and chill me.

[70] for I already know that he who made my body put his power and taste together in it. . . . dressing runs to my account, my physique, to Heaven's.

[71] Stop talking about those vain ideas, for it does not honor you. . . . You know more than a woman, and it is better to be quiet.

[72] How shrewd, how false, how devious! . . . How richly he dresses, eats, and spends! . . . He is son of whom he pleases, and so noble, that at times he uses "Don" and at times a title.

[73] this man must seek food and clothing, and that one, because he descends from the Goths, is adored and considered a lord. But when the time is up, one learns that the world errs, for they both become dirt.

[74] Is there anything like seeing him penniless and at other times naked, and suddenly gamble, borrow and not return, profit at cards, deceive women, . . . and in spite of everything they love and adore him?

[75] Leonardo: I am going to my wife, Teodoro, whose very portrait I adore. And you, where will you go now?
Teodoro: Are you forgetting my vice? To see that girl, whom I have adored for half an hour.
Leonardo: Is she beautiful?
Teodoro: I haven't seen her; but it seems that she is pretty.
Leonardo: I'm right behind you.

[76] Feliciano: They hurried to tell me that you were at the door, and, although to tell the truth they found me among my business associates, all my affairs ceased, for my heart told me that you bear some sorrow.
Lupercio: When two are one soul, one's very imagination tends to give those warnings.

[77] He departed bravely and gallantly on a chestnut steed. . . . Everyone marveled at seeing him. . . . The whole court regrets that you did not go to see him, favoring his undertaking.

[78] For she will believe that I tolerate my offense like a despicable man, and take a page into more consideration than my wife's honor.

[79] How much more a worm, a little trifling thing such as I, of whom the duke has made me what I am from an early age, like ivy raised in his arms.

[80] What a physique! What gallantry! What a good, manly presence! . . . Besides being good-looking, he appeared much more so with his traveling regalia and his naked sword.

[81] But the duke's energy and alertness, the way he governs his estate, have astonished me; I am enamored of his grace, spirit, and elegance.

[82] I am his father-in-law and father of Doña Blanca. Until he returns, his honor falls to my lot, and not to the suitor's, Don Bernardo, for defending and offending, as such great opposites, are like saying and doing, which do not eat from the same plate.

[83] It is more important, although I am a gentleman of high worth, that I live without honor, than France without an heir.

[84] The king, since he imitates God, is present everywhere. One cannot talk against the one who is supreme in value, for respect towards the Lord is present in every place. I have never been so desperate that I directed my sorrow at the supreme head.

[85] kings, sacred images of God, are all breast, Lady, they have no back; and in this way, even though they are absent, their face is everywhere.

[86] If I am king without power, what good is it to reign? To reign is to be above everything, everything should serve the king.

[87] he began to shout like a madman. He took off his clothes in a fury and finally tried to throw himself into the pool in the garden.

[88] Go with my children to be their father and husband of my wife, for the improvement of spouse and father will give pleasure to them and to Teodora.

[89] If the Roman woman gave her breast to her father, and, out of compassion, came to be mother of her own father, giving him food as a prisoner, it would be better to take his place and free her father.

[90] Teodora: What do you intend to do?
Otavio: I don't know.
Teodora: How encouraging!

[91] Otavio: Now I am sorry for what has been done. . . . What shall we do?
Teodora: Take a stand, and, if necessary, die.

[92] a faithful man between two weights, . . . faithful to you and to him, for the weight of this sorrow must not tip the scales.

[93] Of course, religious justification transforms those plebeians whose social identity was linked to commerce or the liberal professions into "New Christians."

[94] By God, it surprises me, *negra*, to see that you wear a veil; for by covering yourself, you cover one cloak with another.

[95] A black man sends roses to God, whom he knows is white. . . . For although you are black, there will come a day when you will be beautiful and white.

[96] the holy doctors say that in heaven the blessed will be without any personal blemish and that they will appear in the best figure

possible; and since in the human species the greatest perfection is that of the male, it follows that women will lose their form . . . restored to the greatest dignity and nobility of the human species, which is that of the male.

[97] When the hidalgo heard the message, it was as if he had died on the spot. He was unable to eat a bite, turning over and over in his mind every one of his words and actions since the day he was born. When he finally found out what he had come for, and that he would send for more if the fancy took him, the hidalgo answered: "I swear to God, I will not have anything to return for!" And he sent him the whole tree.

[98] Lineage. What lineage? Those that now are manufactured in dungheaps in Madrid? How arrogantly you speak, because you are rich! Your family's coat of arms is probably hanging in the church!

[99] I inherited so much wealth, that I need only mention my name to cow the most genteel competition.

[100] Then, more fearful than a wimpled, skirted duenna, you cut open my back, since cutting was the profession of your grandfather. That wound, though fierce, was neither wound nor glory, but rather a means to treacherously steal the honorable blood you lack.

[101] Julio, I am completely transformed; I esteem only her virtue; here the story has ended of that Spanish Lucrecia and this Tarquino without honor.

[102] What lawsuit has sentenced me, that being a pure man, you want to mix me with them? If the king had said the same thing, he would never have advised giving Dorotea to the poor man, but rather to the rich one.

[103]   Commander: You peasants have honor? What friars of the noble Order of Calatrava!
Town Councilor: Perhaps some think highly of themselves for the cross of the Order they wear, yet do not have blood as pure as ours.
Commander: And I sully it joining my blood with yours?
Town Councilor: When such joining taints more than it cleanses.

[104] I am a pure-blooded man, although of common caste, never stained by Hebrew or Moorish blood.

[105] For until they deliver a jewel into my hands, even though I have bought it, neither guards nor thieves are my responsibility.

[106] The commander intends to hang Frondoso, without trial or public pronouncement, from the battlements of a tower; he will do the same with all of you; and I am glad, half-men, for in this way our honorable town will be left without women, and the time of the Amazons will return, eternal terror of the globe.

[107] Kings are to the eye . . . miraculous images, for every time we see them, they seem to be of another color.

[108] Casilda: What do you say? Kings are flesh and blood?
Costanza: What did you think they were made of?
Casilda: Damask and velvet.
Costanza: You are truly a ninny.

[109] [b]y one path or another, the group of *letrados* continued to be composed fundamentally of nobles, real or counterfeit.

[110] Don Enrique invites me to go hunting in the mountains this afternoon, and, very slowly, he makes his way to the baptism, and doesn't remember that he told me to put on boots and spurs. I have been all over the city looking for him, and find him engaged in leisurely conversation, as if he hadn't invited me.

[111] I would like our friendship to be profitable, and that my company make you a hidalgo. You rose to the level of farmer from a coal-selling father. Aspire to be a gentleman; rise to a level of honor.

[112] My father wants to die, Leonardo, as he was born; coalseller he engendered me, a farmer I shall die.

[113] I plan to give it to her, with Doña Elvira's help, in such a way that in spite of his malice, the peasant will fail to divine my intention.

[114] but it is not decent for the wife of a peasant, and would give people occasion to gossip and offend my honor, . . . because such *rebociños* come with many dissimulations.

[115] It's true what they say, that there are few brave men with a lot of learning, because when speeches abound, offenses are left unavenged.

[116] Mendo, if I had the chance, . . . I would censure those who presume to govern in someone else's home, . . . which is surely the worst kind of ignorance. You are the wise one, you the knowledgeable one, and you, Mendo, the one who, without learning, were wise in your own home.

269

[117] Open your eyes, all of you, defend yourself in all occasions; make your soul an Argos, be vigilant; attend to your own affairs, leave others' alone. Let no one trust knowledge no matter if they are the most learned of the Republic of honorable men; for it is indeed a difficult science, this matter of tending woman.

[118] I will give him this famous sword, to inspire him in his wondrous undertaking; this sword, which, bathed in barbarian blood, never tires of cutting barbarian throats.

[119] I see the king in the figure he cuts. What a solemn and modest demeanor! . . . What a manly figure! . . . How strong and well formed he is! But, after all, he is the offspring of such a man!

[120] Enter underneath my skirt, if you cannot enter my womb, so that you may inherit legitimately what you have lost as the king's natural son. . . . I am your mother. Come out, for the time of labor has arrived, though without pain.

Notes

Introduction

1. The Spanish concept of "honor" had more to do with "reputation" or "opinion" than English notions of "virtue." See Donald Larson for a discussion of the external character of this all-important social value, as well as for bibliography on the topic of honor, particularly the collection *Honour and Shame*, edited by J. G. Peristiany. Of the studies published since Larson's book, see especially Claude Chauchadis's *Honneur, morale et société dans l'Espagne de Philippe II*.

2. Julian Pitt-Rivers remarks on the need to "distinguish between male and female honour, since the carelessness of women relates to their own reputation, while that of men to the steps which they take to cover their vulnerability through women" (67).

3. S. Griswold Morley and Courtney Bruerton suggest that *Toledano* "was probably written by Lope first before 1604, possibly as early as 1596; but how closely the present text approximates it is problematical" (348).

4. Robert Ter Horst characterizes the fundamental dynamic of honor plays as "that between conventional maleness and conventional femaleness, man public in the outer world, and women private in the inner" (1–2).

5. See Anita K. Stoll and Dawn L. Smith, eds., *The Perception of Women in Spanish Theater of the Golden Age* for gender analyses of the *comedia* in general; Esther Beth Sullivan applies Teresa de Lauretis's and Julia Kristeva's narrative theories to Lope's *Venganza* and Calderón's *A secreto agravio, secreta venganza*. Other notable exceptions in the area of Calderonian studies are David Román's articles and Anne J. Cruz's essay on *A secreto agravio* ("Homo Ex Machina?"). See also Melveena McKendrick, *Woman and Society;* Frederick de Armas, *The Invisible Mistress;* and Barbara Matulka, *The Feminist Theme in the Drama of the "Siglo de Oro."*

6. While critiquing both José M. Díez-Borque's and Maravall's interpretation of popular culture as reinforcing the status quo, Walter Cohen stresses the important demystifying function of their work in a Spanish context that represented the "bulwark of dominant reactionary ideology" (*Drama* 30); see also J. H. Elliott's review of Maravall's *Culture of the Baroque*.

7. While recognizing the anachronism in imposing nineteenth-century notions of class on sixteenth- and seventeenth-century social formations, George Mariscal insists on the "radical economic otherness" of non-aristocratic groups and the importance of an "emerging discourse on class" (*Contradictory Subjects* 80). In my study, I use "class" as a kind of shorthand to refer to different social groups' positions in the social hierarchy and the antagonism that springs from opposed economic interests.

8. Mariscal comments that, unlike our contemporary notions of the exercise of power, "in the sixteenth and seventeenth centuries power was the product of blood and its symbolic appropriations. . . . one's position in the social hierarchy, one's inclusion or exclusion from that society, even one's fundamental identity or subjectivity was constituted by the relative value or worthlessness of one's blood" ("*Persiles*" 96).

9. See also Mary Elizabeth Perry, *Gender and Disorder.*

10. In 1982, Charlotte Stern defended a reading of Lope's plays as ambiguous and polysemous ("Lope de Vega, Propagandist?"); in her introduction to *The Perception of Women,* Anita Stoll argues that it is "wrong to suggest dramatists' view of women was monolithic" (21); Matthew Stroud critiques the search for unified meaning in studies of wife-murder plays, aligning himself with "voices that celebrate ambiguity and pluralism" (21). See also Catherine Swietlicki's "Lope's Dialogic Imagination."

11. For an application to theater, see the editors' introduction to the section on psychoanalytic theory in Reinelt and Roach's *Critical Theory and Performance.*

12. This discussion is indebted to Kaja Silverman's feminist reading of Freud and Lacan in *The Subject of Semiotics.*

13. See Valerie Traub ("Desire") for a critique of the conflation of gender and sexuality through the Freudian model of "masculine activity" and "feminine passivity" in contemporary feminist criticism.

14. For Lacan, the lack that defines the subject begins at the moment of birth, at which time the sexual differentiation that occurred within the womb is realized. Besides marking the physical separation of the infant from the mother, this first loss has to do with "the impossibility of being physiologically both male and female. . . . The subject is defined as lacking because it is believed to be a fragment of something larger and more primordial" (Kaja Silverman, *Subject* 152–53). But the *notion* of lack is only learned after entrance into the symbolic order (154).

15. For an overview of the critical reception of Sedgwick's theory of male homosociality, which diffuses homoeroticism throughout all male social bonds, see Traub ("Desire").

16. The term *sex-gender system* is Gayle Rubin's, designating "the set of arrangements by which a society transforms biological sexuality into products of human activity" (159).

Chapter One
The Contradictory Constructs of Gender

1. In the discussion that follows, I refer fundamentally to Castilian women.

2. Milagros Ortega Costa contrasts the low level of formal education for women after 1560 to that advocated by humanists during the preceding decades (98) and relates this attitude to the eradication of heterodox reformation in Spain and the crucial role played by women in this movement.

3. See George Mariscal for a valuable discussion of the meaning of the "individual" in seventeenth-century Spanish society (*Contradictory Subjects,* Ch. 2).

4. The seventeenth-century English text *Patriarcha,* by Robert Filmer, illustrates the use of the language of the family to legitimize absolutist monarchical prerogatives in its phrasing of the law enjoining obedience to kings in terms of "Honour thy Father" (Ferguson et al. xxiv).

5. El Saffar relates the appeal of this autonomous, unified self to that of Lacan's mirror stage: "Against the sense of helplessness and fragmentation . . . the possibility . . . of entering into an order that will give him power and a sense of self-control" (173).

6. El Saffar details the mechanisms that effected the separation of male children from the mother and the home, for example, the growth of urban centers, the establishment of schools and universities, the professionalization of the military, and the discovery and colonization of the "New World" (166, 181).

7. Unless otherwise noted, all references to Perry are taken from *Gender and Disorder.*

8. A constellation of attributes, particularly a set of undesirable traits (deceitfulness, capriciousness, excessive talkativeness, sexual openness, etc.) defining the term *woman* constructs the myth of a natural inferiority that adheres to the biological "fact" of being born a woman. For example, in *Alfreda,* the husband abandoned for the king by his wife decides to go to the court with his son and daughter on each arm; the boy child claims his father's right arm, "que ésta es hembra, en efeto, / y se ha de parecer algo a su madre" ("for my sister is female, in effect, and must resemble her mother") (243).

9. Under the law, both single and married women lacked individual rights (McKendrick, *Woman and Society* 16). Unless otherwise noted, all citations from Melveena McKendrick in this chapter are taken from *Woman and Society.* Although a married woman needed her husband's permission before taking legal action of any sort, McKendrick calls marriage a "passport" to what freedom was permitted respectable women (28).

10. See Richard Vann for a description of such a woman's duties, including supervising and disciplining a small labor force in the richer households. She may also have had supplemental employment in weaving and farm work for which she was paid less than half the amount a man would receive (202–03). George Shipley reminds me that Cervantes's Dorotea prides herself on managing just such a formidable workload:

> la razón y cuenta de lo que se sembraba y cogía pasaba por mi mano; los molinos de aceite, los lagares del vino, el número del

ganado mayor y menor, el de las colmenas. Finalmente, de todo
lo que un rico labrador como mi padre puede tener y tiene, . . .
era mayordoma y señora. . . . Los ratos que del día me quedaban
. . . los entretenía en . . . la aguja y la almohadilla, y la rueca
muchas veces. (*Don Quijote* 279)

(the accounts of the sowing and the harvest passed through my
hands alone, as well as the oil mills, wine presses, herds, flocks,
and hives. I was mistress and stewardess of all that a rich farmer
like my father can and does possess. . . . The hours of the day
that were left . . . I spent with . . . the needle, the sewing-
cushion, and the distaff.)

Vann remarks facetiously that of course the theoretical treatises concerning housewifery (for example, *La perfecta casada* [*The Perfect Wife*] by
Luis de León in Spain) were written by men; women would not have had
the time, given the prodigious amount of work such tracts prescribed for
them (202)!

   11. See Perry (138–41) on the regulation of prostitution, and Perry (Chs. 4
and 5), Electa Arenal ("The Convent as Catalyst"), and Arenal and Schlau
(*Untold Sisters*) on the monitoring of visionary nuns and *beatas*.

   12. Abandonment was one of the major causes of the wandering women
that were seen as such a threat to social order, particularly when the seducer was of a higher class (Perry 58).

   13. See Walter Cohen (*Drama*), José María Díez-Borque (*Sociedad*),
Hugo Rennert, and N. D. Shergold for accounts of the pervasive presence of the *comedia* in seventeenth-century Spanish culture; its influence
was not confined to major urban centers, due to the *compañías de legua*
who toured the countryside until 1646 (McKendrick, *Theatre* 187). According to McKendrick, "no theatre can ever have had a greater and more
sustained impact on the society that produced it" (*Theatre* 196).

   14. See Alison Weber for the justification of silence as a feminine virtue in Saint Paul's dictum against women's speech.

   15. For example, in *Testimonio:*

> Renegad vos del hablar;
> Que por ahí se comienza,
> Y en perdiendo la vergüenza,
> Dios lo puede remediar.
>
> (414)

(Renounce speech, for there it all begins and once shame is lost,
may God help you.)

   16. These feminine virtues are gender specific; *vergüenza* is positive
in women, negative in men, as in *Mal:*

> porque si de no casarte
> resulta a ti y a tu reino

vergüenza, en mal tan forzoso
escoger *del mal lo menos.*

(476)

(for even if not marrying results in shame for you and your kingdom, in such inevitable misfortune one must choose the lesser
evil.)

17. On woman as medium of exchange see Gayle Rubin, and Luce
Irigaray's "Women on the Market" and "Commodities among Themselves" in *This Sex.*

18. This tendency coexists contradictorily with the privileging of *telos,*
as when man is deemed the crown of creation because created last.

19. Other textual examples defining woman within the Aristotelian binary scheme (perfection/imperfection; form/matter; active/passive) are
found in *Pobreza* (296) and *Resistencia* (206).

20. This text demonstrates the plurality of discourses about gender in
sixteenth- and seventeenth-century cultures, combining the single-sex
strain prevalent in medical discourses (privileged by Stephen Greenblatt)
in which women are seen as imperfect men, and other discourses posit-
ing a two-sex gender system, one subordinate to the other. Jean Howard
points out the intensely hierarchical nature of this language of difference,
a necessary underpinning to a hierarchical view of the social order, based
not on biological difference, as in nineteenth-century notions, but rather
on the "lack of masculine perfection" (423).

21. Isabella, who in Milagros Ortega Costa's words "changed the society in which she lived in all respects" (91), belies the passive model of
queens and of women in general as unfit to rule as found in many of
Lope's honor plays.

22. In spite of woman's supposedly prized reproductive function, the
text clearly communicates the devaluation of woman in the culture. When
Teodosia carries off the infant Rosaura after her treacherous sister has
given birth in the wilderness, the bereft mother comforts the king: "mas
puede darte consuelo, / que es mujer" ("but you may be consoled to know
that it was a girl") (430).

23. *Laura* 350; in *Hungría,* her treachery is accomplished through
speech (30). The feminine vice of deceitfulness, inherited from Eve
(*Laura* 371), is deeply rooted in woman's proximity to the body and
sexual pleasure (*Laura* 374).

24. Before falsely accusing Lupercio's wife of adultery, Celauro care-
fully distinguishes good women from bad women (*Celauro* 117). *Resistencia* insinuates that good women are a scarce commodity, since a man
may very well have a million or two in income, "pero la buena mujer /
viene de mano de Dios" ("but a good woman comes from the hand of
God alone") (189).

25. When it is suggested that many married women love men other than
their husbands, the duke replies, "Eso en mujeres bajas, / pero no en

275

nobles mujeres" ("Only lowborn women, but not noble women") (*Laura* 347).

26. Catherine Larson shows how the contradictory signifiers used to fix Angela's identity in Calderón's *La dama duende* ("she is neither an angel, nor a devil, and is, at the same time, both") are subsumed within the sign "woman" by the end of the play ("*La dama duende*" 35).

27. In *Resistencia,* the king's wife-to-be applauds his decision to take care of his cast-off mistress, "que es, en efeto, mujer" ("for she is, after all, a woman") (228).

28. The same collapsing of *woman* and the irrepressible urge to talk is found in *Dina.* When Zelfa refuses to tell Bato the reason for Jacob's strange behavior, he responds: "Que por hacerme pesar / Aun dejas de ser mujer" ("In order to cause me grief, you even leave off being a woman") (227).

29. At times the signified "woman = transgressive sexuality" plays against other meanings, for example, that of "wife," *mujer* in Spanish ("que por ser mujer quisiste / dejar de ser mi mujer" ["for because you are a woman you ceased to be my wife"] *Celauro* 120), or one's supposedly prediscursive and "natural" sex: "Soy una triste mujer, / que por serlo me perdí" ("I am a wretched woman, who for being one, was lost") (*Celauro* 123).

30. See also Anne J. Cruz, "Sexual Enclosure."

31. See David Román ("Spectacular Women") on the disruptive force of sixteenth- and seventeenth-century Spanish actresses as "spectacle."

32. Commenting on the "few mother figures" in the *comedia,* Anita Stoll notes that when the mother does play a dominant role, she is "either idealized or condemned for her overwhelming ambition" (20).

33. Kaja Silverman critiques psychoanalytic theory's exclusion of woman from the symbolic order: "It is preposterous to assume . . . that woman remains outside of signification. . . . If the entry into language is understood as effecting an automatic breach with the real . . . then the female subject's linguistic inauguration must be seen as locating her, too, on the side of meaning rather than being" (*Subject* 189).

34. The term *male bonding* is Lionel Tiger's; see also Joseph Pleck.

35. This same character says that once he has satisfied his desire, man feels a remorse mixed with fear: "Suele, tras haber gozado / . . . / Ver del arrepentimiento / La espada y el rostro airado" ("Once a man has enjoyed himself, he usually sees repentance's sword and angry face") (*Corona* 599). In *Príncipe,* a peasant woman complains, "¡Desdichadas las mujeres, / Que, en faltando á sus placeres, / Somos infamia en los hombres!" ("Wretched are women, for, as soon as we no longer fulfill their pleasures, for men we are infamy!") (127).

36. Given this metonymy, a woman need only strap on a sword to be "read" as a man.

37. When the duke in *Carlos* is loathe to believe his wife's story that Carlos is dishonoring him, she questions his manhood (473), referring to his "flojos aceros" ("flaccid blade") (473).

38. ". . . [S]ois hombre; / Que por sí sólo este nombre / Está de mudanzas lleno" ("You are a man, for in itself alone this name is full of changes") (*Catalán* 404). Compare *Desposorio* (513–14).

39. The duke of *Portugués* is equally outraged that his wife has supposedly betrayed him with her page (383).

40. In *Batalla,* the wife is described as the husband's "hacienda," or property, and the rival-king as "noble thief" (576).

41. In *Cuerdo,* Mendo offers a rustic version of the blazon when he describes his first glimpse of his future wife:

> un brazo rollizo y blanco,
> que, la aljorca en la muñeca,
> parecía que era el mismo
> cirio de dorada cera.
> . . . .
> En la garganta un collar
> de azabaches y de perlas;
> que era nácar la garganta
> y se naciera con ellas.
>
> (553–54)

(a plump white arm, which, with the band on her wrist, looked like a candle of gilded wax. . . . On her throat a necklace of jet and pearls born of her mother-of-pearl throat.)

42. Similar to *Halcón,* which both ironizes and exploits the convention, *Cuerdo* offers two "inventories" of woman: one rustic but serious describing Mendo's wife, quoted above, and the servant's clearly parodic description of a woman he fell in love with, replete with classist overtones:

> ojos zarcos, lindo pico,
> largas cejas, boca grande,
> dientes de marfil bruñido,
> largas manos, alto cuello . . .
> Aunque no sé quién me dijo
> que era la pierna derecha
> más que la izquierda, tantico;
> mas no es cosa que la afea.
>
> (563–64)

(light-blue eyes, pretty lips, long eyelashes, generous mouth, teeth of burnished marble, slender hands, long neck . . . Although I don't know who told me that her right leg was a tiny bit longer than her left, but not enough to spoil her beauty.)

43. Tiger recognizes homoeroticism as a general feature of male bonding; Eve Kosofsky Sedgwick points out that while this is true, most cultures maintain a rigid separation between homosociality and homosexuality (4).

44. *Testimonio*'s Ramiro, another illegitimate son of a head of state, is reborn through his stepmother, after passing through a phase of desire for her. Unlike Federico, Ramiro successfully negotiates the Oedipal rite of passage that allows him to take his place as legitimate heir and patriarch.

45. Lynne Segal comments on the oppressiveness of "masculinities": "For that oppressiveness is precisely men's wretched fear of not being male-enough, which is identical with their fear of 'femininity' " (317).

46. For a discussion of insecurity in patriarchal heroism as artistically figured in biblical love stories, see Mieke Bal.

Chapter Two
Sexual Outlaws

1. I suggest possible explanations for this scarcity in Chapter Eight.

2. Discussing religion's role in the symbolic framework shaping women's self-perception in the sixteenth and seventeenth centuries, Mary Elizabeth Perry traces the shift in the iconography of the Virgin from a pregnant or nursing Mary to the innocent maiden of the Immaculate Conception or the sorrowing Mother. Besides representing an "Other to be venerated and remind[ing] women of their imperfection," these images "denied the sexuality of woman and promoted the belief that it was dangerous and sinful" (41).

3. Bonnie Anderson and Judith Zinsser show that this was trans-European: adultery in both religious and secular law signified only the action of a married woman with no similar popular meaning for the married man; she was submitted to a more difficult test of innocence than her lover, and suffered greater punishment if guilty (341).

4. Unless otherwise noted, the page numbers in the following discussion of adultery refer to McKendrick's *Woman and Society.*

5. Perry cites two instances in which husbands executed adulterous wives and their lovers in public, one in 1565 and another in 1624 (73).

6. A father could kill his daughter and her lover if caught under his roof, though cases of daughters or sisters murdered for this reason are extremely rare, probably since marriage was a possible solution. Widows who committed adultery forfeited half their possessions to the children of their first marriage or to their relations-in-law (McKendrick 16).

7. See McKendrick, "Lope de Vega's *La victoria.*"

8. For Arnold Reichenberger, the *comedia* "follows the pattern from order disturbed to order restored" (307).

9. For Gaylyn Studlar, masquerade is a defensive strategy, a protean evasion permitting women to survive in a society that judges and uses them according to their image. John Berger believes that women are superconscious of their image, what Laura Mulvey calls woman's "to-be-looked-at-ness" ("Visual Pleasure" 11), because it will be the principal source of their sexual and economic power in patriarchal society.

10. Doane also sees it as an alternative to masochistic overidentification. In his analysis of women's fantasies, Theodore Reik suggests that masquerade does not signify the acceptance of femininity but the reverse: it makes visible the position of women in patriarchal society and at the same time expresses contempt for it.

11. Unless otherwise indicated, all citations from Foucault in this chapter are from *Discipline and Punish*.

12. Foucault refers to the "theatrical representation of pain" in public execution, the frequent theatrical reproduction of the crime in the punishment (45), and the carrying out of the execution at the very place the crime was committed (44).

13. The armed justice of the husband is an extension of the sovereign's "right to make war and power of life and death" (Foucault 48). Many honor plays call attention to the husband's dual role as glorious warrior in the battle against the infidel and manly avenger of his honor.

14. For Foucault, the truth/power relation was at the heart of the public execution (55): as truth-producing mechanism, it manifested the juncture between the judgment of men and that of God (46); as political ritual it manifested power (47).

15. For a discussion of "the spectacle of violence, pain, blood, and death" in seventeenth-century Spanish culture, see José Antonio Maravall's *Culture of the Baroque* (162–63).

16. Flordelís in *Locura* considers herself unworthy of being killed by her husband:

> ... No me matéis
> vos, porque sangre tenéis
> que puede ser que se ofenda.
>   Máteme un hombre que ayer
> vuestro caballo guiaba,
> porque una espada tan brava
> no manche tan vil mujer.
>
> (308)

(Do not kill me yourself, for your noble blood may risk offense. Have a man kill me who yesterday led your horse, in order that so vile a woman not stain so brave a sword.)

The wife in *Toledano* does not try to prolong her life, asking only that her husband kill her in such a way that she not feel hatred of him in death (620). Casandra in *Carlos* thanks the duke for banishing her instead of killing her and recognizes her punishment as Heaven-sent (487). *Discreto*'s Casandra also ascribes her punishment to the divine defender of her husband's honor (216).

17. See Marsha Swislocki for the influence of the *romance* "La adúltera" on *Locura*.

18. See Donald Larson for the text's relationship to the *romance* that serves as its source (40–41).

19. The denial of confession in most cases augments physical death with the annihilation of the soul. In *Locura*, the husband says, "¡Del alma sólo me pesa!" ("Only the fate of her soul troubles me!") (308).

20. In the tale by Bandello that probably serves as the source for Lope's play, the incestuous couple is executed publicly; for McKendrick, the duke's decision to kill the pair secretly augments the ambiguity of the text ("Language and Silence" 80).

21. In *Contienda,* the honor conflict is a minor episode contributing to the characterization of Juan de Urbina. Juan stabs his rival at the door of his house with his dagger, "Desde la punta á la cruz" ("From the point to the hilt") (487) and then plots the secret murder of his wife, with overtones that recall the massacre in *Comendadores* (488).

22. "The 'apariencia' was basically something that 'appeared,' being 'discovered' either behind a curtain, or, by extension, on or by means of a machine" (Shergold 234).

23. Of Calderón's *El médico de su honra,* Paul Julian Smith remarks:

> Women, then, serve as objects of exchange, both excluded from and essential to . . . male circulation. . . . Under the aegis of the king, the dead Mencía is replaced by the living Leonor. Each is precisely equal to the other as object of exchange. Order is restored and social practice continues. (164)

24. The association of motherhood and death in this representation of maternal destructiveness suggests the anxieties concerning the contaminating physicality of the female reproductive body repressed by the male subject upon entry into the order of signification.

25. Alix Zuckerman-Ingber draws different conclusions from the fact that Blanca's scheming, deserving of punishment in other female characters, is eventually rewarded (143).

26. The same topos occurs in *Locura* ("¿Encerrar quieres, señor, / el viento en cárcel estrecha?" ["My lord, you wish to lock up the wind in a narrow prison?"] 296) and *Ferias*: "Dadme que la mujer quiera, / que el guardalla es imposible" ("For me, let the woman wish it, for guarding her is impossible") (594).

27. A similar dynamic undermines the containing closure of Shakespeare's *Taming of the Shrew.* As Karen Newman points out, "if one shrew is tamed, two more reveal themselves" (Bianca and the widow): "the seeming resolution of the play's ending is exploded and its heterogeneity rather than its unity is foregrounded" (48–49). Thanks to David Román for this connection.

28. For a longer version of this analysis of *Fabia,* see my "Masquerade, Male Masochism and the Female Outlaw."

29. In *Ferias,* the husband who plots the death of wife and rival is killed by his father-in-law; in *Cuerdo,* the deceived husband is cuckolded physically by his aristocratic rival and cognitively by his Old Christian peasant neighbor, who lies to conceal the infidelity of his wife from him. In

Rústico, the rustic saint's deception of the offended husband establishes God as the ultimate cuckolder in the hierarchy of male dominance.

30. Randel analyzes the complex representation of woman in Calderón's honor plays, in which she is *both* "espejo del honor y el espejo del amor" ("the mirror of honor and the mirror of love") (873).

31.

> éste es Palacio; acá sale
> Nerón, nuestro emperador,
> que lo permite el autor
> que de esta industria se vale;
> porque si acá no saliera,
> fuera aquí la relación
> tan mala y tan sin razón,
> que ninguno la entendiera.
>
> (99)

> (here is the palace, and here, our emperor Nero enters; the author avails himself of this device, because if he didn't enter at this point, the narration would be so wrong and without reason that no one would understand it.)

32. See Chapter Six.

33. See Chapter Three for a discussion of Kristeva's theory of the "nonalternating negation" of narrative.

34. Tania Modleski discusses the dependence of "proper" male identity on his ability to distance woman and make her his "proper-ty" (8).

35. Frederick de Armas points out the conventional combination of great beauty and *burlas* in the Invisible Mistress plot (130).

36.

> Digo que hay muchas muy buenas,
> pero que hay muchas muy malas.
> No siguen el medio igual,
> y claramente se ven:
> la buena, extremo del bien;
> la mala, extremo del mal.
>
> (76)

> (I declare that there are many very good women, but there are many very bad ones. They know no middle ground, it's plain to see: the good woman, extremely good; the bad, extremely bad.)

Chapter Three
Secular Saints

1. In *Peligros* as well, the husband attributes the threat to his honor to his wife's beauty (196).

2. See Tania Modleski's rephrasing of Freud's (in)famous question, "what is it men want?" (50).

3. For a discussion of the double bind produced for male subjects by honor and male bonding in Calderón's *A secreto agravio, secreta venganza,* see Anne J. Cruz, "Homo Ex Machina?"

4. See also *Veneciano* (535).

5. For example, in *Laura* (344). Such wives define themselves in terms of honor identified with the feminine ideal ("soy casada y honrada" ["I am married and honorable"] *Bella* 615 and 619) and at times with high social position ("Yo soy mujer principal" ["I am a noblewoman"] *Indicios* 257).

6. ". . . no te ha querido abrir / de la más alta ventana / el más pequeño resquicio" ("She has not opened to you the tiniest crack of the highest window") (*Indicios* 255). Compare *Bella:* "Amante soy de un diamante, / que estas dos puntas son guarda / de su fuerza inexpugnable" ("I love a diamond, for these two points are the guardian of her impregnable strength") (633).

7. As in *Animal,* the military losses of the king of *Hungría* are perceived as celestial punishment (39, 41), a link he himself recognizes (943). Leonor interprets their chance encounter, in his flight from the siege of Belgrade, as divine vengeance (45). The text of *Pleitos* also places the queen's loyalty to the king above any desire for even divine vengeance (513).

8. See Chapter Four.

9. See Chapter Seven for further discussion of this text.

10. Alix Zuckerman-Ingber points out that even though the husband-kings' actions are ostensibly justified by the honor code, their excessive zealousness concerning their honor leads them into error (130–31).

11. This scene also sheds light on the amorous customs of the time, suggesting that men accosting women on the street had no idea what they actually looked like, but approached them on the basis of what could be glimpsed of their overall figure, their hands, or the status indicated by their clothing. This is precisely the situation the heavily veiled Estefanía exploits in Cervantes's "El casamiento engañoso," hooking Campuzano with "una muy blanca mano, con muy buenas sortijas" ("a very white hand, with very fine rings") (*Novelas ejemplares* 2: 180). When he finally meets with her, recognizing her by her hands, Campuzano finds that "no era hermosa en extremo" ("she was not extremely beautiful") (2: 181).

12. See Michel de Certeau for a discussion of inscriptions of the law on the body (139–41).

13. The pun on the double meaning of *mujer,* both "woman" and "wife," is lost in translation.

14. The phrase is Laura Mulvey's ("Visual Pleasure" 11).

15. See also Teresa de Lauretis, Kaja Silverman, Mary Ann Doane, Jill Dolan, and Lorraine Gamman and Margaret Marshment's anthology *The Female Gaze.*

Chapter Four
Duplicity and Disguise

1. The frequency with which the wife dons the clothing of a peasant woman should be read in the context of the period's fascination with rural life. The pleasure of seeing these costumes harmonized with the demand for picturesque scenes of idealized country life studied by Noël Salomon. See Chapter Seven for further discussion of this phenomenon.

2. Jean Howard's comment on cross-dressing in Middleton and Dekker's *The Roaring Girl* may illuminate Lope's disguised heroines as well: "Another way to read the insistence on chastity is to see it as an interruption of that discourse about women which equates a mannish independence with sexual promiscuity" (437).

3. In *Animal,* there is a similar juxtaposition between a character who questions the falsely accused queen's chastity and the audience's knowledge. When he hears that *two* beastlike creatures now roam the countryside, Lauro thinks the queen has been unchaste (437). Lauro's comment documents the burden of celibacy incumbent on the wives of these texts throughout their lengthy ordeal. Teodora's supposed infraction is deemed even more shameful because of the inferior social status of her imagined lover ("some shepherd").

4. David Román pointed out to me the similarity between this plot and that of Shakespeare's *Winter's Tale.*

5. The pregnant queen of *Príncipe* does not play an active role while she is disguised as an animal. When Sancho usurps the throne, she flees to the mountains, where she gives birth, and later appears "vestida de pieles" ("dressed in furs"). The faithful courtier Remón, also dressed in animal skins, stays with her in the mountains to protect her.

6. Anita Stoll points out that while in the *comedia* in general, women are perceived as "unsettling, even disruptive," they are also "cast in the role of restorative angels, the repository of the enduring values of the hierarchical status quo" (26).

7. The first words of *Desposorio* and the wife's first gesture are ones of "adjusting" the husband: "Aguarda, ¡por vida mía! / que llevas mal puesto el cuello" ("Wait, on my life! Your collar is crooked") (507).

8. De Lauretis's first option describes the wife who resists the rival passively, but does not embark on any active project to help her husband. She functions merely as the space in which the struggle for victory or defeat will occur. The second option describes the female outlaw who colludes with the adulterous desire of the rival. In this scenario, she represents a personified obstacle, "a boundary which the hero alone can cross" in his quest for (self-)knowledge, manhood, honor, and power (139).

9. Melveena McKendrick has examined the absorption of quest by love plot in *comedias* that depict the "mujer varonil" ("virile woman") in *Woman and Society;* see also her "Women against Wedlock" and the essays in *The Perception of Women.*

10. "... for a woman to behave like a man, while unnatural, was at least a step up—into the mannerisms of the higher-caste sex" (Woodbridge 157).

11. Mary Erler and Maryanne Kowaleski distinguish between authority as the socially sanctioned "right" to make decisions binding on others, and power (or informal influence) as the "ability to act effectively, to influence people or decisions, and to achieve goals" (2). Cross-dressed women in Lope's honor plays extend their influence beyond the private into the public sphere.

12. My emphasis. Butler emphasizes cross-dressing's deconstruction of claims to naturalized or essentialist gender identities: "The notion of gender parody defended here does not assume that there is an original which such parodic identities imitate. Indeed, the parody is *of* the very notion of an original" (138).

13. In a tract of 1620, the author criticizing the female transvestites complains that soon *hic mulier* (instead of *haec mulier*) will be good Latin. Another author attacks effeminate men under the rubric *haec vir*.

14. For Mary Elizabeth Perry, Catalina de Erauso's repudiation of her identity as a woman and subsequent celebrity ultimately reinforced male superiority and the values of a patriarchal society (127–36). I return to this aspect of the discussion in Chapter Eight. McKendrick (*Woman and Society* 18, 40) provides more examples and bibliography, including fictionalized accounts of Erauso's and Enríquez de Guzmán's lives. See also Carmen Bravo-Villasante (167 and 196–98).

15. It is difficult to ascertain whether art imitated life in cases of female transvestism or whether life imitated art. As Julie Wheelwright points out in her study of women who passed as men, "fiction drew from myth which drew from fact in a rhythmic cycle"; she cites historical examples such as the sixteenth-century Irish pirate captain Grace O'Malley and the eighteenth-century pirates Mary Read and Anne Bonny (34). On the other hand, Wheelwright affirms the productive force of popular literature; Emma Edmonds, a nineteen-year-old soldier in the American Civil War, was moved, in her own words, to "step into the glorious independence of masculinity" after reading Lieutenant Murray's novel *Fanny Campbell, Or the Female Pirate Captain* (13–14).

16. See also M. Romera Navarro and B. B. Ashcom.

17. See also Lope's *Arte nuevo,* lines 280–83.

18. See Bravo-Villasante for descriptions of Bárbara Coronel and the dramatic conventions governing cross-dressed female actors (205).

19. See Bravo-Villasante for titles; her text is also worthy of study for the mixture of fascination and horror with which she approaches her subject.

20. See Chapter Eight for a discussion of the complexities of *comedia* spectatorship.

21. For Woodbridge, the "transvestite disguise in Shakespeare does not blur the distinction between the sexes but heightens it: case after case demonstrates that not even masculine attire can hide a woman's natural squeamishness and timidity" (154); "woman's essential nature,

Shakespeare insists, shines through any kind of clothes" (155). Paula Berggren states that "while the wearing of pants allows expression of a talent otherwise dampened by convention, it does not, in Shakespeare, lead to a direct challenge of the masculine order," since these characters are "content to reassume their womanly duties" (19). For Clara Claiborne Park, Shakespeare's "perennial appeal" lies in his skill in creating "spunky" cross-dressed heroines, whose assertiveness is mediated "so as to render them nonthreatening" (103).

22. See Bravo-Villasante, in Lope (61n1); in Tirso (116–20); in Calderón (150–51); in Moreto (171). See particularly Lope's *La discreta enamorada* and *El acero de Madrid*.

23. See also Robert Stoller (142–58); Deborah Heller Feinbloom (10–32); Natalie Zemon Davis (124–51).

24. Howard points to the same fusion of sexual perversion with male cross-dressing and sexual incontinence with female cross-dressing in Renaissance England (424).

25. The play's alternate title, "El gallardo catalán" ("The gallant Catalan"), echoes in the description of Clavela in men's clothing: "en una silla de manos Isabela vestida ricamente, y á su lado, muy gallarda, con espada y capotillo y calzas, Clavela" ("on a sedan chair, Isabela, richly dressed, and at her side, very gallant, with sword, short cape, and stockings, Clavela") (420).

26. See Bravo-Villasante for a particularly homophobic account of these texts.

27. The subplot is extremely unclear; the editor states that this *comedia* is one of the worst printed versions of Lope's plays (*Portugués* 376n1).

28. At the end of *Laura,* the jester's true identity is revealed: "Que aquel mancebo gallardo, / señores, era mujer" ("For that gallant youth, gentlemen, was a woman") (375).

29. See also Louis Crompton's "The Myth of Lesbian Impunity."

30. Perry relates the increased repression of sodomy in sixteenth-century Spain to the "authorities' desire to consolidate a newly formed political order" (*Crime and Society* 72), a thesis which harmonizes with El Saffar's theory.

31. Similarly, Perry contrasts the few references to sexual activity between women to the heavyhanded punishments of male same-sex behavior in the sixteenth and seventeenth centuries in Seville (124).

32. The punishment for sex between women was lighter when no instrument was used for penetration, "implying that the serious crime was . . . impersonation of a male" (Perry 125), just as the real crime in male same-sex activity was not in its nonprocreative aspect, but "in requiring a male to play the passive 'female' role and in violating the physical integrity of a male recipient's body" (only women could be receptacles for semen).

33. See Bravo-Villasante for texts which evoke female homoeroticism less equivocally, such as *El genovés liberal* and Cubillo's *Añasco el de Talavera*.

34. I prefer the term *female homoeroticism* to *lesbian sexuality* or *lesbian desire* in this context, for I agree with Valerie Traub that while heterosexuality positioned early modern subjects institutionally, homosexuality as a distinct mode of identity emerged only much later in the eighteenth and nineteenth centuries, largely through sexological discourses. Homoeroticism, on the other hand, which according to Freud's theory of the infant's polymorphous perversity predates the heterosexual organization of desire, was a "position taken in *relation* to desire—a position . . . neither socially mandated nor capable of conferring identity or role" ("Desire" 100). The task facing the critic interested in analyzing early modern representations of sexuality, for Traub, is to identify the historically specific management of the pleasures and anxieties aroused by homoeroticism, as characters "temporarily inhabit a homoerotic position of desire" (104).

35. See also Amy Williamsen's "Sexual Inversion: Carnival and *La mujer varonil.*" Among critics of English Renaissance drama, Clara Claiborne Park favors the recuperative interpretation of cross-dressing, while Juliet Dusinberre, Jonathan Dollimore, Phyllis Rackin, and Catherine Belsey hold that it can allow for the transgressive representation of the plurality and fluidity of gender. Howard echoes Davis's acknowledgment of transvestism's double movement, acknowledging the limits of Shakespeare's cross-dressing comedies, yet recognizing that "this recuperation is never perfectly achieved," as the texts put into question "the naturalness, the inevitability, of dominant constructions of men's and women's natures and positions in the gender hierarchy" (439).

36. Gubar remarks that "clothing plays a crucial symbolic role in the response of women to their confinement within patriarchal structures" (478).

37. Marjorie Garber proposes that the tendency to justify cross-dressing by the plot masks its ultimate potential to destabilize gender categories.

38. Bravo-Villasante provides a breakdown of motivations for the use of the masculine disguise in the *comedia* (223–24), as well as a list of different disguises (225–27). The uneasiness inspired by the woman who takes on masculine dress and behavior out of her own desire is illustrated in Bravo-Villasante's classification of such characters as "pathological viragos" (69). She is much more comfortable with the "femininity" of those who become soldiers out of love (69).

39. See Chapter Six for the dilemma of the husband whose rival is of higher rank.

40. Mary Beth Rose discusses this unusual device in Middleton and Dekker's *The Roaring Girl* ("Women in Men's Clothing").

41. Two of Lope's *comedias* that represent the strength of women are *Las amazonas* and *La vengadora de las mujeres*. On the latter text's ambiguous position on gender, language, and power, see Emilie Bergmann's "(Re)writing History in Lope: Cross-dressing and Feminism in *La vengadora de las mujeres.*"

42. Similarly, Joan Ferrante has pointed out how Brunhild's attempt to take revenge on Hagen for the murder of Siegfried through the legal channel of a public accusation is rebuffed, commenting that it would be "hard to imagine how a man would have been so easily ignored" (215).

43. For example, in the 1705 case of the female soldier Christian Davies, Lord John Hay insisted that she resume marital relations with her husband (Wheelwright 89–90).

44. Paul Julian Smith refers to the "decidedly non-naturalist" staging of the *comedia* (129).

Chapter Five
Rivalry and the Struggle for Dominance

1. See Chapter Six for a discussion of bonds of mutuality.

2. See Sedgwick for a full discussion of cognitive mastery in the context of male homosocial relations.

3. Donald Larson discusses the husband's trajectory from unconsciousness to consciousness as "a process of earthly salvation" and a celebration of the "death and rebirth of a man" in his chapter "Plays of the Middle Period."

4. In *Desposorio,* the husband feels trapped in his marriage of convenience, while his desire is for another woman: ". . . el alma, divertida / en la mujer que adoraba, / vive con la propia esclava" ("my soul, entertained by the woman it loved, lives with its own woman as a slave") (509).

5. See Nancy D'Antuono on Boccaccio in Lope.

6. In *Peribáñez* the husband kills the rival in the act of raping his wife, as well as the lackey and the wife's cousin who have aided the commander; the husband in *Contienda* kills not only wife and rival but the messenger who brings him the news of his dishonor.

7. When Sidonio despairs at seeing suitors parading the street in front of his house, his servant explains: "Como saben que hay aquí / Pobreza con hermosura" ("It's because they know that here there is poverty plus beauty") (561). One of the daughter's suitors has no intention of marrying her, not only because he is the son of the dead rival, but because she is poor (560). Sidonio's son, who, being male, has more mobility and more options, has gone off to be a soldier; in woman, "Escalas suele poner / Al honor y á la vergüenza" ("Poverty lays siege to honor and modesty") (563).

8. The husband is characterized as jealous by the slave Dorotea (418).

9. In the wife's opinion, this is not an isolated incident, but one that is endemic to Valdivia's temperament. McKendrick has pointed out the bellicose tonality of their relationship ("Celebration or Subversion?").

10. Later, he is identified simply as "un indiano" (437). When he visits the father in person he is called "un indiano Capitán" (440).

11. While other husbands craftily absent themselves by pretending to go off to war, hunting, or to the court, Valdivia leaves the rival an opening by feigning concern for his commercial affairs:

Escríbeme mi tío
que cuanto nos ha llegado
tiene Ricardo embargado.

. . . .

Si tengo junto
el crédito y el dinero
de la suerte que sabéis,
¿qué he de hacer?

(428)

(My uncle writes me that Ricardo has laid an embargo on
everything that has arrived. . . . What am I to do if my credit and
money are tied up in this way?)

12. See Chapter One; in Lope's *El caballero de Olmedo,* the fact that
the rival shoots the hero of the title instead of engaging him in a sword
fight is not only proof of his unmanly cowardice, but contrasts with the
idealized masculinity of the fourteenth century.

13. Of Calderón's *El médico de su honra,* Smith remarks:

Women, then, serve as objects of exchange, both excluded from
and essential to the male circulation whose operation they pre-
cede. Under the aegis of the king, the dead Mencía is replaced
by the living Leonor. Each is precisely equal to the other as
object of exchange. Order is restored and social practice continues. (164)

14. See Chapter Two's discussion of *Fabia.*

15. Mieke Bal specifies that patriarchy includes "the social and ideological repression of women in favor of men, as well as the domination
of older over younger men" (6).

16. See Smith's "The Rhetoric of Inscription in the *Comedia*" in *Writing* for a different view on "excess" in the construction of masculine
honor, drawing on the Lacanian concept of desire (164).

17. The praise/vituperation topos appears in other contexts of reversal
as well. In *Pobreza,* the wife praises the loyalty of her servant, who pretends to give her money of his own to help her in her husband's absence.
When she opens the purse and finds a note from the rich rival, she exclaims: ". . . ¡Vil Tancredo, / Vil hombre, criado vil!" ("Vile Tancredo, vile
man, vile servant!") (300). In *Dina,* Jacob praises the peace and harmony
of his life right before Dina's entrance announcing she has been raped.

18. In *Nacimiento, Discordia,* and *Catalán,* the rivals lie to the king
about the queen's virtue because they have been unable to possess her. In
Animal, the character deceiving the king is the queen's sister, who marries the king herself once he has ordered his wife to be killed. In
Testimonio, the eldest son raises false testimony against his mother when
the queen refuses to let him ride the king's horse.

19. The rival derides the husband's blindness in asides. When the husband assures him he will help him win Inés, even though it goes against

his interest, the rival replies, "Esto es lo que yo procuro" ("That is what I intend") (278). Thanking the husband for his support, the rival declares that his love extends further than the husband thinks ("porque se extiende mi amor / a más de lo que pensáis" 278).

20. The duke, intent on his pursuit of a married woman, Laura, is blind to Ricardo's stalking of his own sexual property. Afraid that the object of Ricardo's desire might be the same as his, he presses Ricardo to reveal her identity. Ricardo replies that the duke does not know her, signaling his cognitive dominance through asides ("que quien por otra la deja / no conoce su valor" ["for he who leaves her for another, does not know her value"] 341) and dramatic irony: "que lo que quiero no es cosa / que vos, Duque, la estimáis" ("for what I love is not a thing that you, duke, hold in esteem") (341).

21. The rest of the scene between rival and wife is permeated with references to sight: "verás su loca afición" ("you will see his mad love"); "Verás que lo que se goza / se tiene en poco o fastidia" ("You will see that that which one possesses is thought little of or becomes a nuisance"); "¿Que eso podré ver?" ("I will be able to see that?"); ". . . ¿de qué manera / podré verlo?" ("how will I be able to see it?"); "Todas estas cosas dichas / verás en dando las once" ("All these things I have mentioned you will see when the clock strikes eleven") (99–100).

22. A variation on the same business was used in *Pleitos,* an earlier version of *Hungría.*

23. The fact that the page is really a woman raises questions of female homosocial bonding and homoeroticism (Chapter Four).

24. The lesser evils clothed in fabrications tie in with the relationship between honor and prevarication posed at the beginning of the text. Juan is in Naples because of a "mentís" thrown at him by another noble Spaniard (a challenge to a duel consisting of the words "you lie"). His servant wonders why so many men lie if a "mentís" constitutes an offense against honor, speculating that the damage rests "no que la infamia se haga, / sino en que el otro lo diga" ("not in that the infamy is done, but that the other says it") (441). After a long speech listing people, situations, and things that lie, Juan characterizes the world as rooted in deception: the "mentís" offends "[p]orque anda el mundo fingido / . . . / que todos quieren mentir / y que nadie se lo diga" ("[b]ecause the world is feigned . . . for everyone wants to lie and that no one say they are lying") (442).

25. When the queen tells him he has not honored Juan enough, the king answers, "Señora, engañada estáis, / cuanto él arrogante y loco" ("Lady, you are as deceived as he is arrogant and mad") (449). Although the holds Juan's father in high esteem, he places Juan in the category of "hijos de ganancia" ("bastards") (449). Later he reiterates his true feelings about him: "Poco el español me agrada" ("The Spaniard pleases me but little") (454).

26. Since the category of "race" enters into the alliance between Mendo and the aristocratic rival to cognitively dominate the husband in *Cuerdo,* I will discuss this text in Chapter Seven.

27. Similarly, Sidonio's self-canceling gesture in *Veneciano* seems to parallel that of the wife in *Corona*. But while the sacrifice of woman's body is for the *other,* the male subject gives what is his for himself. As his wife phrases it in her letter to Sidonio, "que si tú puedes guardar tu cabeza, es porque la tienes; que yo no puedo guardar su honra, porque no la tengo" ("if you can guard your head, it is because you have it; for I cannot guard her honor, because I do not have it") (559). Neither woman's honor nor her body is hers to give or take.

28. For Debra Andrist, working within the Girardian model, the Grand Master's words leave the threat to society posed by reciprocal violence open at the end of the play (104).

Chapter Six
Mutuality and Submission

1. It is rare that such situations do not include a reference to the other man's physique, as in *Batalla* (". . . mejor talle tienen, / para poneros temor" ["they have better physiques to inspire fear in you"] 582), *Ferias* ("¡Por Dios, que tiene buen talle! / Ya tengo competidor" ["By God, he has a fine physique! I have competition"] 602), or *Cortesía*: "Celos el novio me ha dado / sólo en verle tan galán. / . . . / Y de buen talle ¡por Dios!" ("Just seeing the gallantry of this suitor has made me jealous. . . . He has a good physique, by God!") (364).

2. "No es mala aquella casada" ("That married woman isn't bad") (238); ". . . dos niñas / Entre majuelos y viñas, / Una perla y otra plata" ("two girls, not quite grown, one a pearl and the other silver") (238); ". . . una dama / Como azúcar de retama" ("a lady like sugar") (238).

3. For A. D. Kossoff, the ox (*buey*) could be a symbol of the cuckold or the male incapable of satisfying the female (235n73).

4. See Cruz for a review of the theme of male friendship in classical literature ("Homo Ex Machina?").

5. The pun is lost in translation: the woman has accepted the *ferias*, or "gifts bought at the fair"; on the other hand, she is obligated because she herself has been "bought at the fair" (*feriar*).

6. The wife describes the rival's exemplary shunning of such male bonding activities:

> no deshonesto le vi
> en corrillos de mancebos,
> sino con un rostro grave
> y una modesta tristeza.
>
> (612)

(I never saw him in indecent cliques of bachelors but always with a grave demeanor and a modest melancholy.)

7. Sedgwick notes that this separation does not always hold trans-historically; in ancient Greece certain kinds of male homoerotic practice were permitted in the spectrum of male homosocial relations (4).

8. The duke parlays his wife's obvious displeasure at his nondeparture ("¿No me parto, y vos lloráis?" ["I am not leaving, and you weep?"] 450) into approval by mentioning the virile count who is taking his place.

9. Compare the king's reaction to a secret marriage in *Firmeza*.

10. Carlos's servility extends beyond his relationship with the duke to other authoritative males, for example, Prudencio, whom the duchess has recruited in her campaign against Carlos. Carlos wins Prudencio over to his side by his strategic humility:

> Prudencio: ¡Que llamándote traidor
> No me respondiste airado!
> Carlos: Hice como amigo honrado
> Resistiendo á tu furor
> Y humillándome contigo.
>
> (470)

(Prudencio: To think that I called you a traitor and you did not respond angrily!
Carlos: I did what an honorable friend would do, resisting your fury and humbling myself to you.)

11. Everybody insults Carlos for being of low birth, including Leonora when she thinks he has betrayed their secret to Casandra. The text is somewhat obscure on this point, but it appears that the duke recognizes Carlos's noble paternity, although he is illegitimate. The fact that he has noble blood makes the duke's willingness to accept Carlos's secret marriage to his sister and to make Carlos's son his legal heir more socially acceptable:

> Nobleza Carlos y virtud esconde
> En la corteza rústica y villana:
> Carlos Baldeo fué su padre, y donde
> Hubo este mozo, fué la más lozana
> Dama que tuvo Italia. . . .
>
> (484)

(Carlos hides nobility and virtue under his rustic and lowly surface: Carlos Baldeo was his father, and he had this boy with the most robust lady in Italy.)

The following lines are less clear, indicating that this man was the duke's uncle, who left Carlos in his father's charge (". . . y él mi tío / Se quedó en este estado al padre mío" 484); a variant reads ". . . Y él murió, / Y hele quedado en lugar de padre yo" ("And he died, and I have remained in place of the father") (484n5).

12. For a discussion of the other factors that jeopardize this character's masculinity, see Chapter Five.

13. Debra Andrist distinguishes between the vengeance-murder of the rival and the scapegoating-murder of the wife, in that the sacrifice of the latter does not carry the risk of reciprocal violence (101–02). Clearly, within the male homosocial dynamics of these texts, the murder of a wife judged innocent by her male relatives could lead to further violence.

14. The former rivals' friendship in *Fabia,* born out of Fabia's criminal desire, is further cemented when they are forced to function as the emperor's go-between with Fabia.

15. As in other texts, Rodrigo is doubly motivated: by loyalty and by his own desire for revenge at being cuckolded.

16. In the Spanish mythology of blood purity, those tracing their lineage back to the northernmost mountainous regions of Spain, strongholds against Moorish invasion, were exempt of suspicion of contamination.

17. Noël Salomon, José Antonio Maravall (*Teatro*), and José María Díez-Borque (*Sociología*) have all analyzed the *comedia*'s depiction of the monarch.

18. Similarly, Carlos's servile submission to the duke in *Carlos* is ultimately masculinizing, a temporary phase in his successful Oedipal passage into the symbolic order.

19. The madness of the impotent husband plays a major role in *Locura* and *Batalla.* Godofre in *Alfreda* loses his mind after the king takes Alfreda away from him (240, 241), but he is still capable of delivering a coherent enough speech at the end to convince the king to give her up. In *Firmeza,* Otavio goes mad at the end of Act I when he learns that his wife has been taken captive; this is a passing phase, however, as he regains lucidity.

20. Similarly, the admiral in *Batalla* strips when he goes mad (608), and asks for clothing as a sign that he has come to his senses (610). The husband in *Alfreda* calls attention to the conventional nature of the device: "Vaya primero el vestido, / que es el indicio primero / de quien no tiene sentido" ("Let the clothing go first, for it is the first indication of one who has lost his mind") (240); when he appears undressed in the king's presence, the guards try to restrain him, thinking he is a beggar (245–46).

21. Lope's honor plays are filled with instances in which women are used to form mutual bonds among men. In *Carlos,* the duke promises to give the count his sister as payment for fighting his war; in *Locura,* the king married Floraberto and Flordelís as a reward for her father's service, and marries Floraberto's sister to his son to repay Floraberto for sparing the heir's life, just as he rewards Floraberto himself for his honorable behavior by marrying him to his own daughter. Threatened by Sancho's usurpation of the throne, the queen attempts to placate him by arranging a marriage between their (as yet unborn) offspring (125). By giving his dead rival's son his daughter in marriage, the husband in *Veneciano* makes amends for killing his father.

22. The queen, separated from her son after childbirth, also displays deference to the force that Cervantes calls "de la sangre" ("of the blood"). Told that the abandoned child she has found is hers, she exclaims: "¡Ay, hijo mío, que un hielo / la secreta sangre abrasa! / No en vano amor os tenía" ("Oh, my son, secret blood is capable of burning ice! Not in vain did I feel love for you") (159).

23. In spite of his momentary insecurity, Sancho tells Blanca not to be upset by his "amorous thoughts" (a euphemism for rape), since he is both ". . . un Rey poderoso / Y un hombre determinado" ("a powerful king and a determined man") (145).

24. Another device joining the political and sexual dimensions is the newborn heir, who functions as the instrument through which Sancho comes to see and desire Blanca. It is the spectacle and noise of the baptismal procession, in which Blanca is present as godmother, that attracts his attention. Later, both Blanca (153) and Martín (156) perceive the child as the cause of their dishonor.

25. The admiral refers to Blanca as a "tower" in the fierce battle between his honor and the king's power (600), but his servant's metaphor indicates that woman's body, equated with sexuality, makes her too vulnerable to function as an effective defense: "que por esa torre Blanca / buscan de tu honor la puerta" ("for through that tower, Blanca, they look for the door of your honor") (605).

26. In her examination of the admiral's linguistic strategies to defend himself from his high-ranking rival, Margaret Hicks interprets his madness as a subterfuge by which he "escapes the ignominy of dishonor and reclaims his place in the social order" (27).

27. As in *Locura,* the text makes use of a conventional justification for the king's abuse of his power, namely, his tender years (574, 578).

28. In the reconciliation scene, two courtiers both ask for the admiral's sister Estela in marriage. When the king says he prefers to give Estela to a third man, they suggest the constable or the Duke of Burgundy before the king reveals he will marry her himself. In the face of this dizzying series of exchanges, in which she has seen herself the potential property of five men in succession, the bewildered Estela can only ask: "¿Es de veras?" ("Is it for real?") (611).

29. After the wife's vehement rejection, the king in *Resistencia* also determines to kill the husband, and is prevented from carrying out this decision only by the count's fatal battle wound.

30. Later, Otavio takes credit for the ploy, another indication that the active roles of the female characters are merely a function of the husband's enforced feminization.

31. When Clenarda, the King of Sicily's daughter, tells Cardona that he is released from his obligation to the King of Aragon because that king has exiled him, Cardona declares that his loyalty, together with his loyal birth, forms a *ser* ("being" or "identity") from which he can never be released (670).

32. Cardona's extraordinary loyalty is further demonstrated by his rejection of the soldiers who urge him to rise up against the king. Cardona's response makes his loyalty a function not only of his nobility but also of his identity as Christian and Spaniard: *because* he is these things, neither self-interest nor desire for vengeance can make him disloyal (663). His refusal to be tempted by the highest seat of power wins him eternal fame (664).

33. Lost in translation are the puns with *fiel*, meaning both "faithful" and "balance," and *pesar*, meaning both "sorrow" and "to weigh."

Chapter Seven
"Race," Masculinity, and National Identity

1. Modern theories such as those proposed by Homi Bhabha, Benedict Anderson, and Paul Gilroy were developed in response to concepts of "nationalism," "nation-ness," and "nationality" that emerged towards the end of the eighteenth century, in an age "in which Enlightenment and Revolution were destroying the legitimacy of the divinely-ordained, hierarchical dynastic realm" (Benedict Anderson 4, 7), the realm that was still operative in sixteenth- and seventeenth-century Spain. Nevertheless, I find the mechanisms of exclusion and homogenization they describe at work in the construction of a national unity, especially as they relate to "race" and gender, remarkably apt for analyzing the dynamics of certain of Lope's honor plays. The use of the word *español* ("Spanish") in texts such as *Cortesía, Fuenteovejuna,* and at the end of *Testimonio* attests to an effort to define a national identity. While other texts, such as *Catalán,* stress regional identifications, I believe that these discourses are not mutually exclusive, but rather constitute coextensive and at times contradictory concerns. I position my use of the term *nation* and its derivatives within a tradition of *comedia* criticism that studies the relation between this "national theater" and sixteenth- and seventeenth-century Spanish society, particularly the ways Spaniards thought of themselves and Spain globally (for example, see Thomas Case's recent essay on Lope's use of history "to inspire nationalism" 212).

2. For an earlier compendium of references to "others" (though not categorized as such) in the *comedia*, see Miguel Herrero García's *Ideas de los españoles*.

3. In *Catalán,* the hero and his servant feign an argument; the worst insult they can think of to justify their violent quarrel is the label of Jew: "¿Es poco haberme llamado / Judío?" ("Is it a small thing to have called me a Jew?") (441).

4. Abdul JanMohamed and Mary Louise Pratt have analyzed this relationship between material and discursive practices in the process of colonization, in which the ruthless exploitation of natural resources is justified by the colonizers' claim to "civilize" the inferior and barbaric native.

5. As Noël Salomon points out, the *pastor-bobo* is only funny in a context that devalues rusticity (26, 47).

6. The woman of color has been a sign of debased sexuality in many different cultures at different times. Sander Gilman has studied the black woman as icon for deviant and unbridled sexuality in nineteenth-century art, literature, and medical writing ("Black Bodies").

7. Antonio Domínguez Ortiz calculates that the c. 50,000 slaves concentrated in Andalusia in the second half of the sixteenth century were distributed almost equally between whites (Berbers, Turks, and Levantines) and blacks (179).

8. As A. C. de C. M. Saunders points out, the limiting of free black Spaniards' rights was more customary than actually spelled out in written law. For example, a letter of manumission written by King João of Portugal dated 1547 documents restrictions on freed slaves' powers of bequest (184).

9. Saunders records that the black Portuguese court jester João de Sá Panasco was the butt of the "fly in milk" joke (185); he himself "alluded to his ornamental gold chain as a dog's leash" (189). The epithet of "dog" applied to blacks, Moors, and Jews alike (Saunders 185). Later in *Vitoria,* the lackey expresses his desire for Dorotea in monetary terms that might refer to her value as a slave, another conventional basis for humor at blacks' expense (189). In *Peligros,* the mulatta Leonor is referred to stereotypically as a "sartén" ("frying pan") (182, 184) and her face compared with the Sierra Morena ("the dark mountains") (184).

10. *Mulato(a)* and *negro(a)* are interchangeable in Lope's honor plays (see *Vitoria* 443 and *Comendadores* 263). In *Peligros,* the mulatta slave Leonor is unworthy of the sexual interest of a nobleman: "¿Hombre de vuestra persona / se prenda de una mulata?" ("A man of your status is taken with a mulatta?") (192). In insisting on her mixed blood, the text assigns whiteness to the man and blackness to the woman: "¡Bien haya cuarenta veces / el buen gusto de aquel blanco / que se pagó de tu madre!" ("Blessed be forty times over the good taste of that white man who took a fancy to your mother!") (171).

11. The mulatta slave Leonor in *Peligros* is easily corruptible through bribery and, like Dorotea, she facilitates the rival's access to the woman he desires.

12. See Gayatri Spivak (244–45) for this adjustment of Bhabha's term, elaborated in "Of Mimicry."

13. Lucrecia is further linked with degraded sexuality in the following scene in which she is caught embracing an aged squire, while Rosambuco acts as the instrument of the husband's punishment of the two. He ties them back to back and they exit, shouting insults at each other. Like other plebeian characters, Lucrecia is closely associated with bodily functions, especially when frightened (373).

14. In *Comendadores,* the husband speaks of his affection for "his" black slaves: "¿Qué hay de Juan? ¿Qué hay de Sicilia? / Todos los he de abrazar, / Que, aunque negros, gente son" ("What about Juan? Where's Sicilia? I must embrace them all, for, even though they are black, they are people, too") (271).

15. Francisco Eximenis, Castilian translation of *Libre de les dones, Carro de las donas,* quoted in Bravo-Villasante 102n26.

16. The one reference to a Jewish woman in Lope's honor plays manifests the same meshing of gender and "race" to connote transgressive female desire present in the representation of black women. In *Cuerdo,* the Old Christian peasant wife rejects the wife of a hidalgo neighbor as a Jew: "¿Qué me quiere la judía?" ("What does that Jew want with me?") (558). Besides portraying the popular fusion of *hidalguía* (nobility) and Jewish blood in Spanish society, the text introduces socially constructed racial categories to shore up the binary opposition between the (Old Christian) ideal wife and the (New Christian) adulterous one. As noted, plebeian New Christian women are simply not represented in Lope's honor plays.

17. Alix Zuckerman-Ingber interprets Julio's sonnet beginning "¡Oh, malditos papeles, cuántos daños / habéis hecho en el mundo" ("Oh, cursed papers, how much harm you have caused in the world!") as a veiled reference to *limpieza* (154), as does Joseph Silverman ("Del otro teatro" 24). Silverman compares the "tragic quality" of the *converso* drama in *Galán* to the rather humoristic treatment in *Indicios* ("Una anécdota").

18. A reference to the penitential garment, or "sanbenito," hung in the church in perpetuity by the Inquisition after the public ceremony of punishment.

19. Julio's violent reaction to being called a Jew contrasts with the commander's aplomb in *Fuenteovejuna.* As Poliakov points out, the anti-Semitism that permeated Spanish society posed no real threat to the high aristocracy, because of their tremendous economic and social power. The commander merely ignores a peasant's comment. Julio's position is more precarious, in part because his membership in the nobility may be fairly recent, in part because the aspersions cast on his blood purity come from a more authoritative male.

20. Joseph Silverman finds evidence that Tácito's violent elimination of Julio to avoid contaminating his lineage may have had parallels in social life ("Del otro teatro" 25).

21. In *Veneciano,* Lucinda writes Sidonio to return to protect his daughter from predation even if it means risking his life, foreseeing the imminent dishonor resulting from their daughter's beauty and poverty (559). In her discussion of poverty as a social problem, Mary Elizabeth Perry notes the distinction in sixteenth- and seventeenth-century culture between immoral women who were willfully promiscuous and those who lost their virtue as a consequence of poverty (49).

22. The profession of tailor was associated with Jews in sixteenth- and seventeenth-century Spanish society.

23. Whether in her masculinization or in her feminine virtue, woman is the medium through which changes are effected in the status of the male subject.

24. Leonido refers to Audalla's participation in the decision as something unheard of: "¡Ved á qué tiempo he venido! / ¡Que pleito de dos cristianos / Pase en tribunal morisco!" ("Upon what times have I fallen! That a lawsuit between two Christians be judged in a Moorish tribunal!") (291).

25. The term *genízaro* appears in the context of the classification mania exemplified in the eighteenth-century oil-painting genre of *pintura de castas* ("depictions of racial mixtures"), representing and labeling the myriad racial combinations of Europeans, Indians, and Africans and their descendants. According to a list reproduced in a recent issue of *Artes de México* alphabetizing 53 such designations, *genízaro* is the final product of a complex genealogy of mixtures of Indian and black blood, whose ancestors include the *barzino, sambaiga, albarasado, india, tente en el aire, mulata, cambujo, chino, lobo,* and *negra* ("La pintura de castas" 79).

26. For Esther Beth Sullivan, narrative is the mechanism that collapses all differences into sexual difference.

27. The reference to the hidalgos is coded as racial through a certain class of Jewish joke popular in sixteenth- and seventeenth-century Spanish society ("tired of waiting for the Messiah"). See Joseph Silverman's "Los 'hidalgos cansados.' "

28. For a discussion of the *pastor-bobo* in the early Spanish theater, see John Brotherton and José María Díez-Borque ("Aspectos").

29. See in particular Castro's preface to *De la edad conflictiva*.

30. For a discussion of the severely limited efficacy of pure blood in social practice, see José Antonio Maravall ("La función del honor").

31. A recent production of the play directed by Tom Wiselcy at the Drama School of the University of Washington, in which all the peasant characters were played by actors of the opposite sex, successfully called attention to the constructed nature of gender in Laurencia's speech and in the scenes following it.

32. In their discussion of the historical event of 1476 upon which Lope based his play, Angus MacKay and Geraldine McKendrick note that the historical referent for "malos cristianos" ("bad Christians"), which the peasants shout in their attack, is the commander's usurpation of tithes and lands belonging to the canons of Córdoba, resulting in his excommunication and the withholding of church services from the inhabitants of Fuenteovejuna (132). In the text, this referent fades, foregrounding *racial* hostility in the people's domination of the commander.

33. Although we easily associate Hapsburg Spain with the negative aspects of absolute monarchy, especially in the areas of the Crown's absolute powers, incessant warfare, and burdensome taxation, it is more difficult to reconcile the concepts of decentralization and absolutism that the Spanish monarchy exemplified (Nader). In the economic interest of replenishing its ever-dwindling coffers, the Hapsburgs practiced a policy of "perpetual decentralization" (208) through the sale of town charters, resulting in the paradox of an "absolutist monarchy inextricably associated with municipal liberty" (2). The resulting fragmentation of administrative authority ultimately benefited the monarchy as much as consolidation and centralization in other European countries: the newly chartered towns (liberated from the control of cities and older towns) were intensely loyal to the Crown (1).

34. The plays discussed in Chapter Six dramatize the potential breakdown of this contract, transferring the sexual abuse of power from the aristocracy to the monarchy.

35. Catherine Larson interprets the "equivocal" nature of the king's ruling (*Language* 123) in a deconstructive context relating issues of truth and justice to speech and writing: "the king's judgment ignores both the literal and moral levels [of truth] . . . in favor of a response that chooses expediency over truthfulness and keeps speech as the privileged member of the violent hierarchy" (*Language* 121).

36. Salomon believes that in the *comedia,* as opposed to the early theater, it is no longer a question of ridiculing the peasant, but simply of calling sympathetic attention to the exemplary simplicity of their existence (47).

37. The problem of blood purity was "obsesivo en todos los niveles del mundo letrado" ("obsessive on all levels of the *letrado* world") (206).

38. While "malicia villana" ("the malice of the peasantry") was often associated with the dishonor caused by "murmuración" ("gossip") about someone's impure blood, this text associates it with Elvira's sexual dishonor (579, 580). Since Elvira has also been called a Jew, the polyvalence of "malicia" and "murmuración" represents one more example of the way the text collapses racial and sexual categories.

39. In *Galán* and *Pobreza* as well, there is a strong bond between Old Christian father and son or son-in-law, while the *converso*'s father (the "biological" cause of *infamia*) is absent and he has a problematic relationship with his father-in-law.

40. While Leonardo is chastised for his attempts to "govern" in someone else's house, Sancho, as Mendo's father, is permitted this function, doubling the patriarchal authority within Mendo's home. Sancho takes it upon himself to lecture Antona about the perils of finery, assuming the protective rights of ownership over Antona in the absence of her own father and her husband (550). The text implicitly upholds his authority in the home through Mendo's rejection of all sartorial markers of *hidalguía*.

41. The exchange between Enrique and Mendo underlines their opposing social positions. When Gilote announces the arrival of the newborn in *sayagués* (the artificial language spoken by stage shepherds), Enrique remarks sarcastically, "¡Buen padrino!" ("What a fine godfather!"); Mendo's reply is both obstinate and pointed: "Muy honrado" ("Very honorable"). Enrique's query implies the relationship of an aristocrat to his servants: "¿Es de casa?" ("Does he belong to your house?"); Mendo's response implies more equality: "En casa está" ("He is in the house") (577).

42. He refers to the undesirable presence of nobles in his house metonymically as "silk visits" ("temí visita de seda" 577).

43. Here Mendo puns on *rebociño,* "a little *rebozo*," and the dual meaning of *rebozo:* "cloak" and "dissimulation."

44. Another untranslatable pun: Mendo plays with the semantic components of "trimming" (*pasamano*), to suggest that it is through this item of clothing that the aristocrat plans to "pass" from "foot" (*pie*) to "hand" (*mano*).

45. Leonardo calls attention to this reversal: "cuánto las cosas se truecan, / pues un villano a un letrado / desta manera aconseja" ("how things become reversed! That a common peasant advise a lawyer in this fashion!") (583).

46. The phrase is Benedict Anderson's.

47. In response to the queen's suggestion that her sons go in his place to battle the Moor, the king's reply disqualifies them as being more suited to a life of leisure than the wizened monarch, or even his queen:

> Bien fuera armar á García,
> A Fernando ó á Gonzalo;
> Pero son de mas regalo
> Que yo y vos, señora mía.
>
> (404)

(It would be good to arm García, Fernando, or Gonzalo; but they are accustomed to more ease and luxury than you or I, my Lady.)

Chapter Eight
The Negotiation of Meaning

1. Herbert Blau points out the "incremental and sometimes radical differences" between such notions as "audience" and "spectator" (18). In the present chapter I am less interested in the "audience" with its "fictions of community" (47) than in the multiple responses of heterogenous and individual "spectators."

2. See Gaines for a discussion of the taboos surrounding the gaze of the black male character (21–22 and 24–25).

3. In his theory of "reading as poaching," Michel de Certeau challenges the understanding of the consumption of cultural products as " 'becoming similar to' what one absorbs" with the notion of "'making something similar' to what one is, making it one's own, appropriating or reappropriating it" (166).

4. Melveena McKendrick notes that when the *corrales* had reached full expansion of 2,000 seats, "there were almost 1,000 public places for men and around 350 public places for women; the rest represents preferential or private accommodation" (*Theatre* 183). For Walter Cohen, "although the plays attracted virtually all urban social strata, the lower classes probably dominated the audience numerically" (*Drama* 19). For further information regarding the *corrales,* see N. D. Shergold and John J. Allen.

5. Mary Elizabeth Perry cites a legal document in which a woman justifies her illicit sexual situation by claiming she chose the lesser of two evils: to be the concubine of a white man is better than to marry a mulatto (121–22).

6. Walter Cohen characterizes the public *corral* as an "institution in which the medium and the message were in contradiction": "however aristocratic the explicit message of a play might be, the conditions of its production introduced alternative effects" ("The Artisan Theatres" 517).

7. The husband states his objective explicitly: "Yo le tengo de quitar / a Casandra ese deseo / sin perder amor" ("I must rid Casandra of that desire without losing love") (200).

8. Mulvey refers to identifying with the male subject as the "masculinisation" of the spectator position:

> . . . as desire is given cultural materiality in a text, for women (from childhood onwards) trans-sex identification is a *habit* that very easily becomes *second Nature.* However, this Nature does not sit easily and shifts restlessly in its borrowed transvestite clothes. ("Afterthoughts" 13)

9. According to Modleski, women have the potential "to identify strongly with and empathize closely with the [female] main character . . . to surrender freely to the fantasies offered" (44).

10. The notion of going "against the grain," employed in the context of feminist re-readings of canonic texts by Judith Fetterley, was used by Walter Benjamin in the phrase "to brush history against the grain" (259).

11. See Bravo-Villasante for the fulminations of moralists and clergy of different periods (212–14).

12. For Susan Wolfson, these "fictions serve . . . in part as an outlet for homoerotic material in disguise" (592–93); Susan Gubar proposes that scarcely beneath the sex-symbol surface of "such seductive cross-dressers" are "only slightly submerged homosexual fantasies" (483), and while agreeing that "characters like Rosalind have always delighted male authors and audiences alike," she suggests that "male actors imitating females obviously had their own reasons for enjoying such roles" (483). Lisa Jardine interprets the relationship between boy actors and male audience in the Elizabethan theater as homoerotic; see Kathleen McLuskie for a critique of this interpretation and Valerie Traub for a consideration of the consequences of conflating gender and sexuality in such analyses ("Desire").

13. An extreme example of the fluidity of gender identities and its multiple erotic possibilities is found in *El Aquiles* by Tirso de Molina.

Aquiles, played by a female actor, disguises herself as a woman, Nereida, and in this disguise "plays" at making love with his/her female cousin. After this frankly homoerotic scene, the aroused "Aquiles" leaves the room and reappears in his male identity, that is, the cross-dressed female actor playing Aquiles. See also *La mujer por fuerza,* attributed to Tirso, for a similar fluidity of gender and sexual definitions through cross-dressing and mistaken identities.

Works Cited

Allen, John J. *The Reconstruction of a Spanish Golden-Age Playhouse: El Corral del Príncipe 1583–1744*. Gainesville: U Presses of Florida, 1983.

Anderson, Benedict. *Imagined Communities: Reflections on the Origin and Spread of Nationalism*. London: Verso, 1983.

Anderson, Bonnie S., and Judith P. Zinsser. *A History of Their Own: Women in Europe from Prehistory to the Present*. Vol. 1. New York: Harper, 1988.

Anderson, Perry. *The Lineages of the Absolutist State*. London: Verso, 1979.

Andrist, Debra D. *Deceit Plus Desire Equals Violence: A Girardian Study of the Spanish "Comedia."* New York: Lang, 1989.

Appiah, Anthony. "The Uncompleted Argument: Du Bois and the Illusion of Race." Gates 21–37.

Arenal, Electa. "The Convent as Catalyst for Autonomy: Two Hispanic Nuns of the Seventeenth Century." *Women in Hispanic Literature: Icons and Fallen Idols*. Ed. Beth Miller. Berkeley: U of California P, 1983. 147–83.

Arenal, Electa, and Stacey Schlau, eds. *Untold Sisters: Hispanic Nuns in Their Own Works*. Trans. Amanda Powell. Albuquerque: U of New Mexico P, 1989.

Arjona, J. Homero. "El disfraz varonil en Lope de Vega." *Bulletin Hispanique* 39 (1937): 120–45.

Ashcom, B. B. "Concerning 'La mujer en hábito de hombre' in the Comedia." *Hispanic Review* 28 (1960): 43–62.

Bal, Mieke. *Lethal Love: Feminist Literary Readings of Biblical Love Stories*. Bloomington: Indiana UP, 1987.

Barker, Francis. *The Tremulous Private Body: Essays on Subjection*. London and New York: Methuen, 1984.

Beauvoir, Simone de. *The Second Sex*. Trans. E. M. Parshley. New York: Vintage, 1973.

Belsey, Catherine. "Disrupting Sexual Difference: Meaning and Gender in the Comedies." *Alternative Shakespeares*. Ed. John Drakakis. London: Methuen, 1985. 166–90.

Benjamin, Walter. *Illuminations*. Ed. Hannah Arendt. Trans. Harry Zohn. New York: Schocken, 1977.

Berger, John. *Ways of Seeing*. London: British Broadcasting Corporation and Penguin, 1972.

Berggren, Paula S. "The Woman's Part: Female Sexuality as Power in Shakespeare's Plays." *The Woman's Part: Feminist Criticism of Shakespeare*. Ed. Carolyn Ruth Swift Lenz et al. Urbana: U of Illinois P, 1980. 17–34.

Bergmann, Emilie. "(Re)writing History in Lope: Cross-dressing and Feminism in *La vengadora de las mujeres*." *"Writing against the Current": Feminism, Gender Criticism, and Women's Writing in Spain*. Ed. Maryellen Bieder. Special issue of *Indiana Journal of Hispanic Literature* 1.2 (forthcoming).

Bergstrom, Janet. "Alternation, Segmentation, Hypnosis: Interview with Raymond Bellour." *Camera Obscura* 3–4 (1979): 92–93.

Bersani, Leo. *The Freudian Body: Psychoanalysis and Art*. New York: Columbia UP, 1986.

Bhabha, Homi. "Of Mimicry and Man: The Ambiguity of Colonial Discourse." *October* 28 (Spring 1984): 125–33.

————. "The Other Question." *Screen* 24.6 (Nov.-Dec. 1983): 18–36.

————, ed. *Nation and Narration*. London: Routledge, 1990.

Blau, Herbert. *The Audience*. Baltimore and London: Johns Hopkins UP, 1990.

Bobo, Jacqueline. "*The Color Purple:* Black Women as Cultural Readers." Pribram 90–109.

Bravo-Villasante, Carmen. *La mujer vestida de hombre en el teatro español (siglos XVI–XVII)*. Madrid: Revista de Occidente, 1955.

Bridenthal, Renate, and Claudia Koonz, eds. *Becoming Visible: Women in European History*. Boston: Houghton, 1977.

Brotherton, John. *Pastor-Bobo in the Spanish Theatre before Lope de Vega*. London: Tamesis, 1975.

Brown, Judith C. *Immodest Acts: The Life of a Lesbian Nun in Renaissance Italy*. New York and Oxford: Oxford UP, 1986.

Butler, Judith. *Gender Trouble: Feminism and the Subversion of Identity*. London and New York: Routledge, 1990.

Case, Thomas. "A Time for Heroines in Lope." Stoll and Smith 202–19.

Castle, Terry. "The Carnivalization of Eighteenth-Century English Narrative." *PMLA* 99 (1984): 903–16.

————. "Eros and Liberty at the English Masquerade, 1710–90." *Eighteenth-Century Studies* 17.2 (1983–84): 156–76.

Castro, Américo. *De la edad conflictiva*. Madrid: Taurus, 1972.

————. *La realidad histórica de España*. Mexico: Porrúa, 1954.

Castro, Américo, and Hugo Rennert. *Vida de Lope de Vega*. Salamanca: Anaya, 1968.

Cervantes, Miguel de. *Don Quijote de la Mancha*. Ed. Martín de Riquer. Barcelona: Juventud, 1969.

⸻. *Novelas ejemplares*. Ed. Francisco Rodríguez Marín. Vol. 2. Madrid: Espasa-Calpe, 1969.

Chauchadis, Claude. *Honneur, morale et société dans l'Espagne de Philippe II*. Paris: CNRS, 1984.

Cohen, Walter. "The Artisan Theatres of Renaissance England and Spain." *Theatre Journal* 35.4 (Dec. 1983): 499–518.

⸻. *Drama of a Nation: Public Theater in Renaissance England and Spain*. Ithaca and London: Cornell UP, 1985.

Concha, Jaime. "Introducción al teatro de Ruiz de Alarcón." *I & L* 11.9 (1979): 34–64.

Cowie, Elizabeth. "Woman as Sign." *The Woman in Question: M/f*. Ed. Parveen Adams and E. Cowie. Cambridge, MA: MIT P, 1990. 117–33.

Crompton, Louis. "The Myth of Lesbian Impunity: Capital Laws from 1270 to 1791." *Historical Perspectives on Homosexuality*. Ed. Salvatore J. Licata and Robert P. Petersen. New York: Haworth; Stein and Day, 1981.

Cruz, Anne J. "Homo Ex Machina? Male Bonding in Calderón's *A secreto agravio, secreta venganza*." *Forum for Modern Language Studies* 25 (1989): 154–66.

⸻. "Sexual Enclosure, Textual Escape: The Pícara as Prostitute in the Spanish Picaresque Novel." *Seeking the Woman in Late Medieval and Renaissance Writing: Essays in Feminist Contextual Criticism*. Ed. Sheila Fisher and Janet E. Halley. Knoxville: U of Tennessee P, 1989. 135–59.

D'Antuono, Nancy. *Boccaccio's "Novelle" in the Theater of Lope de Vega*. Madrid: Porrúa Turanzas; Potomac, MD: Studia Humanitatis, 1983.

Davis, Natalie Zemon. *Society and Culture in Early Modern France*. Stanford: Stanford UP, 1975.

de Armas, Frederick. *The Invisible Mistress: Aspects of Feminism and Fantasy in the Golden Age*. Charlottesville, VA: Biblioteca Siglo de Oro, 1976.

de Certeau, Michel. *The Practice of Everyday Life*. Trans. Steven Rendall. Berkeley: U of California P, 1984.

de Lauretis, Teresa. *Alice Doesn't: Feminism, Semiotics, Cinema*. Bloomington: Indiana UP, 1984.

Works Cited

Diawara, Manthia. "Black Spectators: Problems of Identification and Resistance." *Screen* 29.4 (Autumn 1988): 66–76.

Díez-Borque, José María. *Aspectos de la oposición "caballero-pastor" en el primer teatro castellano.* Bordeaux: Institut d'Etudes Ibériques et Ibéro-Américaines de l'Université de Bordeaux, 1970.

——. *Sociología de la comedia española del siglo XVII.* Madrid: Cátedra, 1976.

——. *Sociedad y teatro en la España de Lope de Vega.* Barcelona: Bosch, 1978.

Dillard, Heath. *Daughters of the Reconquest: Women in Castilian Town Society, 1100–1300.* Cambridge: Cambridge UP, 1984.

——. "Medieval Women in Castilian Town Communities." *Women's Studies* 11 (1984): 115–38.

Doane, Mary Ann. "Film and the Masquerade: Theorising the Female Spectator." *Screen* 23.3 and 4 (Sept.-Oct. 1982): 74–87.

Dolan, Jill. *The Feminist Spectator as Critic.* Ann Arbor: UMI Research P, 1988.

Dollimore, Jonathan. "Subjectivity, Sexuality, and Transgression: The Jacobean Connection." *Renaissance Drama* 17 (1987): 53–81.

Domínguez Ortiz, Antonio. *El antiguo régimen: los Reyes Católicos y los Austrias.* Madrid: Alianza, 1973.

DuPlessis, Rachel Blau. *Writing beyond the Ending: Narrative Strategies of Twentieth-Century Women Writers.* Bloomington: Indiana UP, 1985.

Durán, María Angeles. "Lectura económica de fray Luis de León." *Nuevas perspectivas sobre la mujer.* Vol. 2. Ed. María Angeles Durán. Madrid: Universidad Autónoma, 1982. 257–73.

Dusinberre, Juliet. *Shakespeare and the Nature of Women.* London: Macmillan, 1975.

Elliott, J. H. Rev. of *Culture of the Baroque,* by José Antonio Maravall. *New York Review of Books* 9 Apr. 1987.

El Saffar, Ruth. "The Evolution of Psyche under Empire: Literary Reflections of Spain in the Sixteenth Century." *Cultural and Historical Grounding for Hispanic and Luso-Brazilian Feminist Literary Criticism.* Ed. Hernán Vidal. Literature and Human Rights 4. Minneapolis: Institute for the Study of Ideologies & Literature, 1989. 165–91.

Erler, Mary, and Maryanne Kowaleski, eds. *Women and Power in the Middle Ages.* Athens and London: U of Georgia P, 1988.

Evans, Peter W. "Golden Age Dramatic Criticism Now." *The Seventeenth Century* 2 (1987): 49–53.

Feinbloom, Deborah Heller. *Transvestites and Transsexuals*. New York: Delta, 1976.

Ferguson, Margaret, Maureen Quilligan, and Nancy Vickers, eds. *Rewriting the Renaissance: The Discourses of Sexual Difference in Early Modern Europe*. Chicago: U of Chicago P, 1986.

Ferrante, Joan. "Public Postures and Private Maneuvers: Roles Medieval Women Play." Erler and Kowaleski 213–29.

Foucault, Michel. *The History of Sexuality*. Trans. Robert Hurley. Vol. 1. New York: Vintage, 1980.

———. *Discipline and Punish: The Birth of the Prison*. Trans. Alan Sheridan. New York: Random, 1979.

Freeman, Michelle. "The Power of Sisterhood: Marie de France's 'Le Fresne.' " Erler and Kowaleski 250–64.

Gaines, Jane. "White Privilege and Looking Relations: Race and Gender in Feminist Film Theory." *Screen* 29.4 (Autumn 1988): 12–27.

Gamman, Lorraine, and Margaret Marshment, eds. *The Female Gaze: Women as Viewers of Popular Culture*. Seattle: Real Comet, 1989.

Garber, Marjorie, ed. *Cannibals, Witches, and Divorce: Estranging the Renaissance*. Baltimore: Johns Hopkins UP, 1987.

———. *Vested Interests: Cross-dressing and Cultural Anxiety*. New York: Routledge, 1992.

Gates, Henry Louis, Jr., ed. *"Race," Writing and Difference*. Chicago and London: U of Chicago P, 1986.

Gilman, Sander L. "AIDS and Syphilis: The Iconography of Disease." *Aids: Cultural Analysis, Cultural Activism*. Ed. Douglas Crimp. Cambridge, MA: MIT P, 1989. 87–107.

———. "Black Bodies, White Bodies: Toward an Iconography of Female Sexuality in Late Nineteenth-Century Art, Medicine and Literature." Gates 204–42.

Gilroy, Paul. *"There Ain't No Black in the Union Jack": The Cultural Politics of Race and Nation*. London: Hutchinson, 1987.

Gledhill, Christine. "Pleasurable Negotiations." Pribram 64–89.

Gordon, Linda. "On Difference." *Genders* 10 (Spring 1991): 91–111.

Greenblatt, Stephen. *Shakespearean Negotiations*. Berkeley: U of California P, 1988.

Gubar, Susan. "Blessings in Disguise: Cross-dressing for Female Modernists." *Massachusetts Review* 22.4 (Autumn 1981): 477–508.

Hall, Stuart. "Notes on Deconstructing 'The Popular.'" *People's History and Socialist Theory*. Ed. Raphael Samuel. London and Boston: Routledge, 1981. 227–40.

Hansen, Elaine Tuttle. "The Powers of Silence: The Case of the Clerk's Griselda." Erler and Kowaleski 220–49.

Heilbrun, Carolyn G. *Writing a Woman's Life*. New York and London: Norton, 1988.

Herrero García, Miguel. *Ideas de los españoles del siglo XVII*. Madrid: Gredos, 1966.

Hicks, Margaret R. "Strategies of Ambiguity: The Honor Conflict in *La batalla del honor*." *Things Done with Words: Speech Acts in Hispanic Drama*. Ed. Elias Rivers. Newark, DE: Juan de la Cuesta, 1986. 15–27.

Howard, Jean E. "Crossdressing, the Theatre, and Gender Struggle in Early Modern England." *Shakespeare Quarterly* 39.4 (Winter 1988): 418–40.

Irigaray, Luce. *This Sex Which Is Not One*. Trans. Catherine Porter. Ithaca, NY: Cornell UP, 1985.

JanMohamed, Abdul R. "The Economy of Manichean Allegory: The Function of Racial Difference in Colonialist Literature." Gates 59–87.

Jardine, Lisa. *Still Harping on Daughters: Women and Drama in the Age of Shakespeare*. Totowa, NJ: Barnes, 1983.

Julien, Isaac, and Kobena Mercer. "Introduction: De Margin and De Centre." *Screen* 29.4 (Autumn 1988): 2–10.

Kaplan, E. Ann. "Is the Gaze Male?" *Women and Film: Both Sides of the Camera*. London and New York: Methuen, 1983. 23–35.

Kaye/Kantrowitz, Melanie, and Irena Klepfisz, eds. *The Tribe of Dina: A Jewish Women's Anthology*. Boston: Beacon, 1989.

Kelly-Gadol, Joan. "Did Women Have a Renaissance?" Bridenthal and Koonz 137–64.

Kofman, Sarah. *The Enigma of Woman*. Trans. Catherine Porter. Ithaca: Cornell UP, 1985.

Kossoff, A. David, ed. *El perro del hortelano. El castigo sin venganza*. By Lope de Vega. Madrid: Castalia, 1970.

Kristeva, Julia. *Desire in Language: A Semiotic Approach to Literature and Art*. New York: Columbia UP, 1977.

Kuhn, Annette. *The Power of the Image: Essays on Representation and Sexuality*. London: Routledge, 1985.

Lacan, Jacques. *Ecrits: A Selection*. Trans. Alan Sheridan. New York: Norton, 1977.

Larson, Catherine. "*La dama duende* and the Shifting Characterization of Calderón's Diabolical Angel." Stoll and Smith 33–50.

————. *Language and the "Comedia": Theory and Practice*. Lewisburg, PA: Bucknell UP, 1991.

Larson, Donald. *The Honor Plays of Lope de Vega*. Cambridge, MA: Harvard UP, 1977.

Lipski, John M. "Golden Age 'Black Spanish': Existence and Coexistence." *Afro-Hispanic Review* 5.1–3 (Jan., May, and Sept. 1986): 7–12.

MacKay, Angus, and Geraldine McKendrick. "The Crowd in Theater and the Crowd in History: *Fuenteovejuna*." *Renaissance Drama* 17 (1988): 125–47.

Maravall, José Antonio. *Culture of the Baroque: Analysis of a Historical Structure*. Trans. Terry Cochran. 1975. Minneapolis: U of Minnesota P, 1986.

————. *Estado moderno y mentalidad social*. Madrid: Alianza, 1972.

————. "La función del honor en la sociedad tradicional." *I & L* 2.7 (1978): 9–27.

————. "Relaciones de dependencia e integración social: criados, graciosos y pícaros." *I & L* 1.4 (1977): 3–32.

————. *Teatro y literatura en la sociedad barroca*. Barcelona: Crítica, c1990.

Mariscal, George. *Contradictory Subjects: Quevedo, Cervantes, and Seventeenth Century Spanish Culture*. Ithaca, NY: Cornell UP, 1991.

————. "History and the Subject of the Spanish Golden Age." *The Seventeenth Century* 4 (1989): 19–32.

————. "*Persiles* and the Remaking of Spanish Culture." *Cervantes* 10.1 (1990): 93–102.

Márquez Villanueva, Francisco. "Letrados, consejeros y justicias." *Hispanic Review* 53.2 (Spring 1985): 201–27.

Matulka, Barbara. *The Feminist Theme in the Drama of the "Siglo de Oro."* New York: Columbia U Institute of French Studies, 1935.

McKendrick, Melveena. "Celebration or Subversion?: Lope's 'Los Comendadores de Córdoba' Reconsidered." *Bulletin of Hispanic Studies* 61.3 (1984): 352–60.

McKendrick, Melveena. "Honour/Vengeance in the Spanish 'Comedia': A Case of Mimetic Transference?" *Modern Language Review* 79 (1984): 313–35.

———. "Language and Silence in *El castigo sin venganza.*" *Bulletin of the Comediantes* 35.1 (Summer 1983): 79–95.

———. "Lope de Vega's *La victoria de la honra* and *La locura por la honra*: Towards a Reassessment of His Treatment of Conjugal Honour." *Bulletin of Hispanic Studies* 64.1 (1987): 1–14.

———. *Theatre in Spain 1490–1700.* Cambridge: Cambridge UP, 1989.

———. *Woman and Society in the Spanish Drama of the Golden Age: A Study of the "Mujer Varonil."* London: Cambridge UP, 1974.

———. "Women against Wedlock: The Reluctant Brides of Golden Age Drama." *Women in Hispanic Literature: Icons and Fallen Idols.* Ed. Beth Miller. Berkeley: U of California P, 1983. 115–46.

McLuskie, Kathleen. "The Act, the Role, and the Actor: Boy Actresses on the Elizabethan Stage." *New Theatre Quarterly* 3 (1987): 120–30.

Modleski, Tania. *The Women Who Knew Too Much: Hitchcock and Feminist Theory.* New York and London: Methuen, 1988.

Morley, S. Griswold, and Courtney Bruerton. *Cronología de las comedias de Lope de Vega.* Trans. María Rosa Cartes. Madrid: Gredos, 1963.

Mulvey, Laura. "Afterthoughts on 'Visual Pleasure and Narrative Cinema' Inspired by 'Duel in the Sun'(King Vidor, 1946)." *Framework* 15/16/17 (1981): 12–15.

———. "Visual Pleasure and Narrative Cinema." *Screen* 16 (1975): 6–18.

Nader, Helen. *Liberty in Absolutist Spain: The Hapsburg Sale of Towns, 1516–1700.* Baltimore and London: Johns Hopkins UP, 1990.

Newman, Karen. *Fashioning Femininity.* Chicago and London: U of Chicago P, 1991.

Nyquist, Mary. "Gynesis, Genesis, Exegesis, and the Formation of Milton's Eve." Garber 147–208.

Ortega Costa, Milagros. "Spanish Women in the Reformation." *Women in Reformation and Counter-Reformation Europe: Public and Private Worlds.* Ed. Sherrin Marshall. Bloomington: Indiana UP, 1989. 89–119.

Park, Clara Claiborne. "As We Like It: How a Girl Can Be Smart and Still Popular." *The Woman's Part: Feminist Criticism of Shakespeare.*

Ed. Carolyn Ruth Swift Lenz et al. Urbana: U of Illinois P, 1980. 100–16.

Parker, Patricia. *Literary Fat Ladies: Rhetoric, Gender, Property*. London: Methuen, 1987.

Perry, Mary Elizabeth. *Crime and Society in Early Modern Seville*. Hanover and London: UP of New England, 1980.

—————. *Gender and Disorder in Early Modern Seville*. Princeton: Princeton UP, 1990.

Peristiany, J. G. *Honour and Shame: The Values of Mediterranean Society*. Chicago: U of Chicago P, 1966.

"La pintura de castas." Special issue of *Artes de México* ns 8 (Summer 1990).

Pitt-Rivers, Julian. "Honour and Social Status." Peristiany 19–77.

Pleck, Joseph H. *The Myth of Masculinity*. Cambridge, MA: MIT P, 1981.

Poliakov, Léon. *From Mohammed to the Marranos*. Trans. Natalie Gerardi. Vol. 2 of *The History of Anti-Semitism*. New York: Vanguard, 1973.

Pratt, Mary Louise. "Scratches on the Face of the Country; or, What Mr. Barrow Saw in the Land of the Bushmen." Gates 119–43.

Pribram, Deirdre, ed. *Female Spectators: Looking at Film and Television*. London and New York: Verso, 1988.

Rackin, Phyllis. "Androgyny, Mimesis, and the Marriage of the Boy Heroine on the English Renaissance Stage." *PMLA* 102 (1987): 29–41.

Randel, Mary Gaylord. "Amor y honra a través del espejo." *Calderón: Actas del "Congreso Internacional sobre Calderón y el teatro español del Siglo de Oro."* Ed. Luciano García Lorenzo. Madrid: Consejo Superior de Investigaciones Científicas, 1983.

Reichenberger, Arnold. "The Uniqueness of the *Comedia*." *Hispanic Review* 27 (1959): 303–16.

Reik, Theodor. *Masochism in Modern Man*. Trans. Margaret H. Kurth. New York: Farrar and Rinehart, 1941.

Reinelt, Janelle, and Joseph Roach, eds. *Critical Theory and Performance*. Ann Arbor: U of Michigan P, 1992.

Rennert, Hugo A. *The Spanish Stage in the Time of Lope de Vega*. 2nd ed. New York: Dover, 1963.

Riviere, Joan. "Womanliness as a Masquerade." *International Journal of Psychoanalysis* 10 (1929): 303–13.

Román, David. "Calderón's Open Secret: Power, Policy, and Play in *El secreto a voces* and the Court of Philip IV." *New Historicism and Comedia Studies*. Ed. José Antonio Madrigal. Boulder: U of Colorado P, forthcoming.

——. "Spectacular Women: Sites of Gender Strife and Negotiation in Calderón's *No hay burlas con el amor* and on the Early Modern Spanish Stage." *Theatre Journal* 43.4 (Dec. 1991): 445–56.

Romera-Navarro, Miguel. "Las disfrazadas de varón en la comedia." *Hispanic Review* 2.4 (1934): 269–86.

Rosaldo, Renato. "Lope as a Poet of History: History and Ritual in *El testimonio vengado*." *Ensayos sobre la comedia del Siglo de Oro español, de distintos autores*. Vol. 2 of *Perspectivas de la Comedia*. Ed. Alva Vernon Ebersole. Valencia: Ediciones Albatross Hispanófila, 1979. 9–32.

Rose, Mary Beth. "Gender, Genre, and History: Seventeenth-Century English Women and the Art of Autobiography." *Women in the Middle Ages and the Renaissance: Literary and Historical Perspectives*. Ed. Mary Beth Rose. Syracuse: Syracuse UP, 1986.

——. "Women in Men's Clothing: Apparel and Social Stability in *The Roaring Girl*." *English Literary Renaissance* 14 (1984): 367–91.

Rothe, Arnold. "Padre y familia en el Siglo de Oro." *Iberoromania* 7 (1978): 120–67.

Rubin, Gayle. "The Traffic in Women: Notes on the 'Political Economy' of Sex." *Toward an Anthropology of Women*. Ed. Rayna Reiter. New York: Monthly Review, 1978. 157–210.

Salomon, Noël. *Recherches sur le thème paysan dans la "comedia" au temps de Lope de Vega*. Bordeaux: Féret et Fils, 1965.

Sartre, Jean-Paul. *Being and Nothingness*. Trans. Hazel Barnes. New York: Washington Square, 1966.

Saunders, A. C. de C. M. "The Life and Humour of João de Sá Panasco, o Negro, Former Slave, Court Jester and Gentleman of the Portuguese Royal Household (fl. 1524–1567)." *Mediaeval and Renaissance Studies on Spain and Portugal in Honour of P. E. Russell*. Ed. F. W. Hodcroft et al. Oxford: The Society for the Study of Medieval Languages and Literature, 1981. 180–91.

Sedgwick, Eve Kosofsky. *Between Men: English Literature and Male Homosocial Desire*. New York: Columbia UP, 1985.

Segal, Lynne. *Slow Motion: Changing Masculinities, Changing Men*. New Brunswick, NJ: Rutgers UP, 1990.

Shergold, N. D. *A History of the Spanish Stage from Medieval Times until the End of the Seventeenth Century*. Oxford: Clarendon, 1967.

Silverman, Kaja. "*Histoire d' O:* The Story of a Disciplined and Punished Body." *Enclitic* 7.2 (1983): 63–81.

—. *The Subject of Semiotics.* New York: Oxford UP, 1983.

Silverman, Joseph H. "Del otro teatro nacional de Lope de Vega: el caso insólito de *El galán escarmentado.*" *Hispania* 67.1 (1984): 23–27.

—. "Los 'hidalgos cansados' de Lope de Vega." *Homenaje a William L. Fichter.* Madrid: Castalia, 1971. 693–711.

—. "Una anécdota en Lope de Vega y Juan de Luna: 'Mirad a quien alabáis,' 'En los indicios la culpa' y la 'Segunda parte de la vida de Lazarillo de Tormes.'" *Estudios sobre el Siglo de Oro en homenaje a Raymond R. MacCurdy.* Ed. Angel González et al. Madrid: Cátedra, 1983. 103–08.

Smith, Paul Julian. *Writing in the Margin: Spanish Literature of the Golden Age.* Oxford and New York: Oxford UP, 1988.

Spitzer, Leo. "Soy quien soy." *Nueva Revista de Filología Hispánica* 1 (1947): 113–27.

Spivak, Gayatri. "Three Women's Texts and a Critique of Imperialism." Gates 262–80.

Stallybrass, Peter. "Patriarchal Territories: The Body Enclosed." Ferguson, Quilligan, and Vickers 123–42.

Stern, Charlotte. "Lope de Vega, Propagandist?" *Bulletin of the Comediantes* 34 (1982): 1–36.

Stoll, Anita K., and Dawn L. Smith, eds. *The Perception of Women in Spanish Theater of the Golden Age.* Lewisburg, PA: Bucknell UP, 1991.

Stoller, Robert. *Sex and Gender.* New York: Aronson, 1975.

Stone, Lawrence. *The Family, Sex and Marriage in England 1500–1800.* New York: Harper, 1977.

Stroud, Matthew D. *Fatal Union: A Pluralistic Approach to the Spanish Wife-Murder Comedias.* Lewisburg, PA: Bucknell UP, 1990.

Studlar, Gaylyn. *In the Realm of Pleasure: Von Sternberg, Dietrich, and the Masochistic Aesthetic.* Urbana and Chicago: U of Illinois P, 1988.

Sullivan, Esther Beth. "A Feminist Analysis of Narrative in Spanish Golden Age Honor Plays." *Literature in Performance* 8.1 (Nov. 1988): 53–62.

Swietlicki, Catherine. "Lope's Dialogic Imagination: Writing Other Voices of 'Monolithic' Spain." *Bulletin of the Comediantes* 40.2 (Winter 1988): 205–26.

Swislocki, Marsha. "On the *Romancero* in *Peribáñez: La esposa fiel* and *La adúltera.*" *Revista de Estudios Hispánicos* 9 (1982): 233–40.

Ter Horst, Robert. *Calderón: The Secular Plays*. Lexington: UP of Kentucky, 1982.

Tiger, Lionel. *Men in Groups*. London: Nelson, 1969.

Traub, Valerie. "Desire and the Difference It Makes." *The Matter of Difference: Materialist Feminist Criticism of Shakespeare*. Ed. Valerie Wayne. New York: Harvester Wheatsheaf, 1991. 81–114.

————. "Prince Hal's Falstaff: Positioning Psychoanalysis and the Female Reproductive Body." *Shakespeare Quarterly* 40.4 (Winter 1989): 456–74.

Vann, Richard T. "Toward a New Lifestyle: Women in Preindustrial Capitalism." Bridenthal and Koonz 192–216.

Vega y Carpio, Lope de. *El arte nuevo de hacer comedias en este tiempo*. Ed. Juana de José Prades. Madrid: Consejo Superior de Investigaciones Científicas, 1971.

————. *Obras*. Ed. Marcelino Menéndez y Pelayo. Madrid: Real Academia Española, 1890–1913.

————. *Obras* (nueva edición). Ed. Emilio Cotarelo y Mori et al. Madrid: Real Academia Española, 1916–30.

Vickers, Nancy. " 'The Blazon of Sweet Beauty's Best': Shakespeare's *Lucrece.*" *Shakespeare and the Question of Theory*. Ed. Patricia Parker and Geoffrey Hartman. New York and London: 1985. 95–115.

Weber, Alison. *Teresa de Avila and the Rhetoric of Femininity*. Princeton: Princeton UP, 1990.

Wheelwright, Julie. *Amazons and Military Maids: Women Who Dressed as Men in the Pursuit of Life, Liberty and Happiness*. London: Pandora, 1989.

Williamsen, Amy R. "Sexual Inversion: Carnival and *La mujer varonil* in *La fénix de Salamanca* and *La tercera de sí misma.*" Stoll and Smith 259–71.

Wolfson, Susan J. "Their She Condition: Cross-dressing and the Politics of Gender in Don Juan." *ELH* 54.3 (1987): 585–617.

Woodbridge, Linda. *Women and the English Renaissance: Literature and the Nature of Womankind, 1540–1620*. Urbana and Chicago: U of Illinois P, 1984.

Yarbro-Bejarano, Yvonne. "Masquerade, Male Masochism and the Female Outlaw: A Feminist Analysis of Lope's *Embustes de Fabia.*" *Revista de Estudios Hispánicos* 24.3 (1990): 11–29.

Zuckerman-Ingber, Alix. *El bien más alto: A Reconsideration of Lope de Vega's Honor Plays*. Gainesville: U Presses of Florida, 1984.

Index

Works by Lope de Vega are listed by title. All others will be found under their authors' names.

Index

Sedgwick, Eve Kosofsky, 7, 125,
126–27, 130, 180, 182
Sex-gender system, 106, 148,
165, 180, 272n16
Sexuality, 5, 27, 113, 286n34
equated with woman, 21,
275n23, 276n29, 293n25
female, 15, 17, 19, 41, 52,
65–66, 178
and race, 202–05, 206–07,
295nn6 and 13, 298n38
Shakespeare, 106, 280n27, 283n4
Shipley, George, 273n10
Siete partidas, 113
Silence, 16–17, 77, 274n14
Silverman, Joseph H., 296nn17
and 20
Silverman, Kaja, 6, 7, 84, 179,
244, 276n33
Smith, Paul Julian, 139
Sodomy, 159, 285n30
Spanishness, 10, 94–95, 231, 232,
243
and gender, 8, 26, 233
and the Other, 25, 199
and race, 207, 236
Spectators, 7, 24, 105, 164, 236,
299n1
Spitzer, Leo, 39
Spivak, Gayatri, 232
Studlar, Gaylyn, 161, 244, 278n9
Subject, 4, 6, 78, 182, 237. *See
also* Female subject; Male
subject; Psychoanalytic theory
in psychoanalytic theory,
5–7, 88–92, 272n14

Telos, 275n18
Testimonio vengado, El, 10, 30,
36, 37, 81, 114, 231–36,
274n15, 278n44, 288n18,
294n1, 299n47

Toledano vengado, El, 1, 23, 31,
32, 34, 41, 44–45, 51, 57–58,
59, 79, 132, 133, 271n3, 279n16
Traffic in women. *See* Male
traffic in women
Traub, Valerie, 4, 25, 130, 236,
272n13, 286n34

Valeroso catalán, El, 107–09,
111, 112–13, 116, 123,
277n38, 285n25, 288n18,
294nn1 and 3
Vann, Richard, 273n10
Vega y Carpio, Lope de, 1, 70,
286n41
Vengeance, 30, 65, 78, 292n13
Vergüenza (shame), 2, 58, 75,
186, 274n16
as antidote to feminine
speech, 17
in relation to male honor, 29
Vitoria de la honra, La, 23, 37,
41, 45–46, 47, 53, 56–57, 59,
65, 79, 132, 136–39, 179, 203,
204, 238, 287nn8–11, 295nn9
and 10

Weber, Alison, 75–76
Wheelwright, Julie, 116–17, 120,
255, 284n15
Wife murder, 42, 53, 210, 249
Wolfson, Susan J., 113
Woman, 16, 17–20, 24, 73–74,
273n8. *See also* Gender
doubling of, 23–24, 60–62
difficulties in controlling,
145, 246
Woodbridge, Linda, 102, 104,
105

Zuckerman-Ingber, Alix, 1, 2,
280n25, 282n10, 296n17

324